Working Papers

for

Fundamental Financial Accounting Concepts

Eighth Edition

Thomas P. Edmonds
University of Alabama–Birmingham

Frances M. McNair
Mississippi State University

Philip R. Olds
Virginia Commonwealth University

Prepared by
Frances M. McNair
Mississippi State University

McGraw-Hill
Irwin

McGraw-Hill
Irwin

Working Papers for
FUNDAMENTAL FINANCIAL ACCOUNTING CONCEPTS
Thomas P. Edmonds, Frances M. McNair, and Philip R. Olds

Published by McGraw-Hill/Irwin, an imprint of The McGraw-Hill Companies, Inc., 1221 Avenue of the Americas, New York, NY 10020. Copyright © 2013, 2011, 2008, 2006, 2003, 2000, 1998 by The McGraw-Hill Companies, Inc. All rights reserved. Printed in the United States of America.

Printed in the United States of America
4 5 6 7 8 9 0 QVS/QVS 18 17 16 15

ISBN: 978-0-07-743388-8
MHID: 0-07-743388-2

www.mhhe.com

Table of Contents

SOLUTIONS TO EXERCISES - SERIES A - CHAPTER 1

EXERCISE 1-1A or 1-1B

EXERCISE 1-2A or 1-2B

a.

b.

EXERCISE 1-3A or 1-3B

Entities	Distribution/Effect of/on Cash

EXERCISE 1-4A or 1-4B

a.

b.

	Accounting Equation					
Event	Assets	=	Liabilities	+	Stockholders' Equity	
					Common Stock	Retained Earnings
		=		+		

c.

	Accounting Equation					
Event	Assets	=	Liabilities	+	Stockholders' Equity	
					Common Stock	Retained Earnings
		=		+		

d.

	Accounting Equation					
Event	Assets	=	Liabilities	+	Stockholders' Equity	
					Common Stock	Retained Earnings
		=		+		

EXERCISE 1-5A or 1-5B

a.

b.

c.

EXERCISE 1-6A or 1-6B

a.

	Cash	+	Land	=	Creditors	+	Stockholders' Equity
Bal.		+		=		+	

b.

Creditor's Claim	÷	Total Assets	=	Percent of Total

c.

Investor's Claim	÷	Total Assets	=	Percent of Total

d.

	Cash	+	Land	=	Creditors	+	Stockholders' Equity
Bal.		+		=		+	

EXERCISE 1-7A

a.

b.

c.

d.

e.

EXERCISE 1-7B

a.

b.

Company	Assets	=	Liabilities	+	Stockholders' Equity		
					Common Stock	+	Retained Earnings
Abbot							
Wayne							

c.

d.

EXERCISE 1-8A or 1-8B

| | | | | | Stockholders' Equity | | |
| | | | | | Common | | Retained |
Company	Assets	=	Liabilities	+	Stock	+	Earnings
A							
B							
C							
D							

EXERCISE 1-9A or 1-9B

a.

Assets	=	Liabilities	+	Stockholders' Equity		
Cash	=	Note Payable	+	Common Stock	+	Retained Earnings
	=		+		+	

Retained Earnings =

EXERCISE 1-9A or 1-9B (cont.)

b. & c.

	Effect of 2014 Transactions on the Accounting Equation							
	Assets	=	Liabilities	+	Stockholders' Equity			
Event	Cash	=	Notes Payable	+	Common Stock	+	Retained Earnings
Beginning Balances							
1. Earned Revenue							
2. Paid expenses							
3. Paid dividend							
Ending Balance		=		+		+	

d.

Cash	=	Note Payable	+	Common Stock	+	Retained Earnings
	=		+		+	

Liabilities + Stockholders' Equity = _____

Assets   = Liabilities + Stockholders' Equity

e.

EXERCISE 1-10A or 1-10B

				Stockholders' Equity	
Event Number	Assets	= Liabilities	+	Common Stock	Retained Earnings
1.					
2.					
3.					
4.					
5.					
6.					

Accounting Equation

EXERCISE 1-11A or 1-11B

a.

	Accounting Equation for 2013						
	Assets		= Liabilities +		Stockholders' Equity		
Event	Cash	+ Land	= Notes Payable	+ Com. Stock	+ Retained Earnings	Acct. Title/RE
Bal. 1/1/13						
1.						
2.						
3..						
4.						
5.						
6.						
7. Land Value						
Totals						

b.

Assets	=	Liabilities	+	Stockholders' Equity

c.

EXERCISE 1-12A or 1-12B

a.

	Assets	=	Liabilities	+	Stockholders' Equity

b.

EXERCISE 1-13A or 1-13B

Event	Classification
1.	
2.	
3.	
4.	
5.	
6.	
7.	
8.	
9.	
10.	
11.	

EXERCISE 1-14A or 1-14B

EXERCISE 1-15A or 1-15B

a.

	Accounting Equation for 2013							
	Assets	=	Liabilities	+	Stockholders' Equity			
Event	Cash	=		+	Common Stock	+	Retained Earnings
1.							
2.							
3.							
Ending Balance		=		+		+	

b.

Income Statement For the Year Ended December 31, 2013	
Revenue	$
Expense	
Net Income	$

EXERCISE 1-15A or 1-15B b. (cont.)

Balance Sheet As of December 31, 2013		
Assets		
Cash		
Total Assets		$
Liabilities		$
Stockholders' Equity		
Common Stock	$	
Retained Earnings		
Total Stockholders' Equity		
Total Liabilities and Stockholders' Equity		$

EXERCISE 1-15A or 1-15B (cont.)

c.

EXERCISE 1-16A or 1-16B

a.

Statement of Cash Flows **For the Year Ended December 31, 2013**		
Cash Flows From Operating Activities:		
Net Cash Inflow from Operating Activities		
Cash Flows From Investing Activities:		
Net Cash Outflow from Investing Activities		
Cash Flows From Financing Activities:		
Net Cash Outflow from Financing Activities		
Net Decrease in Cash		
Plus: Beginning Cash Balance		
Ending Cash Balance		

b.

c.

d.

EXERCISE 1-17A or 1-17B

a.

Event	Statement of Cash Flow Classification
1.	OA
2.	FA
3.	FA
4.	IA
5.	OA
6.	OA
7.	IA
8.	FA
9.	NA
10.	FA

b.

Statement of Cash Flows
For the Year Ended December 31, 2013

Cash Flows From Operating Activities:			
Net Cash Inflow from Operating Activities			
Cash Flows From Investing Activities:			
Net Cash Outflow from Investing Activities			
Cash Flows From Financing Activities:			
Net Cash Inflow from Financing Activities			
Net Increase in Cash			
Plus: Beginning Cash Balance			
Ending Cash Balance			

EXERCISE 1-18A

a.	Arnett Company:	
b.	Dan Arnett:	
c.	Arnett Company:	
d.	Dan Arnett:	

EXERCISE 1-18B

a.	Metal Works:	
b.	First State Bank:	
c.	Metal Works:	
d.	First State Bank:	

EXERCISE 1-19A or 1-19B

a.

		Accounting Equation for 2013						
	Assets			= Liabilities +		Stockholders' Equity		
Event	Cash	+ Land	=	Notes Payable	+	Com. Stock	+ Retained Earnings	Acct. Title/RE
Bal. 1/1/13								
1.								
2.								
3.								
4.								
5.								
6.								
7.								
8.								
Totals		+	=		+		+	

b.

Income Statement For the Year Ended December 31, 2013	
Service Revenue	$
Expenses:	
Net Income	$

EXERCISE 1-19A or 1-19B b. (cont.)

Statement of Changes in Stockholders' Equity For the Year Ended December 31, 2013		
Beginning Common Stock	$	
Plus: Common Stock Issued		
Ending Common Stock		$
Beginning Retained Earnings	$	
Plus: Net Income		
Less: Dividends		
Ending Retained Earnings		
Total Stockholders' Equity		$

Balance Sheet As of December 31, 2013		
Assets		
	$	
Total Assets		$
Liabilities		
Notes Payable	$	
Total Liabilities		$
Stockholders' Equity		
Common Stock	$	
Retained Earnings		
Total Stockholders' Equity		
Total Liabilities and Stockholders' Equity		$

EXERCISE 1-19A or 1-19B b. (cont.)

Statement of Cash Flows For the Year Ended December 31, 2013		
Cash Flows From Operating Activities:		
	$	
Net Cash Flow from Operating Activities		$
Cash Flows From Investing Activities:		
	$	
Net Cash Flow from Investing Activities		
Cash Flows From Financing Activities:		
	$	
Net Cash Flow from Financing Activities		
Net Increase in Cash		
Plus: Beginning Cash Balance		
Ending Cash Balance		$

c.   Percentage of assets provided by retained earnings:

EXERCISE 1-20A or 1-20B

a.

Cash Flows From Financing Activities:	
Net Cash Flow from Financing Activities	

b.

c.

Income Statement	
For the Year Ended December 31, 2013	
Revenue	
Expenses	
Net Income	

EXERCISE 1-20A or 1-20B c. (cont.)

Statement of Changes in Stockholders' Equity For the Year Ended December 31, 2013		
Beginning Common Stock		
Plus:		
Ending Common Stock		
Beginning Retained Earnings		
Plus:		
Less:		
Ending Retained Earnings		
Total Stockholders' Equity		

Balance Sheet As of December 31, 2013		
Assets		
Total Assets		
Liabilities		
Total Liabilities		
Stockholders' Equity		
Total Stockholders' Equity		
Total Liabilities and Stockholders' Equity		

EXERCISE 1-20A or 1-20B c. (cont.)

	Statement of Cash Flows	
For the Year Ended December 31, 2013		
Cash Flows From Operating Activities:		
Net Cash Flow from Operating Activities		
Cash Flows From Investing Activities:		
Net Cash Flow from Investing Activities		
Cash Flows From Financing Activities:		
Net Cash Flow from Financing Activities		
Net Decrease in Cash		
Plus: Beginning Cash Balance		
Ending Cash Balance		

EXERCISE 1-21A or 1-21B

a.

	Accounting Equation as of January 1, 2013						
	Assets		=	Liabilities	+	Stockholders' Equity	
			=	Notes		Common	Retained
Cash	+	Land	=	Payable	+	Stock	+ Earnings

Compute Retained Earnings:

b.

c.   Total Assets =

Percent of assets acquired from creditors:

d.   Percent of assets acquired from investors:

e.   Percent of assets acquired from retained earnings.

EXERCISE 1-21A or 1-21B (cont.)

f.

Accounting Equation as of January 1, 2013									
Assets			=	Liabilities	+	Stockholders' Equity			
				Notes		Common		Retained	
Cash	+	Land	=	Payable	+	Stock	+	Earnings	

g.

Accounting Equation as of December 31, 2013									
Assets			=	Liabilities	+	Stockholders' Equity			
				Notes		Common		Retained	
Cash	+	Land	=	Payable	+	Stock	+	Earnings	

Income Statement	
For the Year Ended December 31, 2013	
Revenue	
Expenses	
Net Income	

EXERCISE 1-21A or 1-21B g. (cont.)

Statement of Changes in Stockholders' Equity For the Year Ended December 31, 2013		
Beginning Common Stock		
Plus: Common Stock Issued		
Ending Common Stock		
Beginning Retained Earnings		
Plus: Net Income		
Less: Dividends		
Ending Retained Earnings		
Total Stockholders' Equity		

Balance Sheet As of December 31, 2013		
Assets		
Total Assets		
Liabilities		
Total Liabilities		
Stockholders' Equity		
Total Stockholders' Equity		
Total Liabilities and Stockholders' Equity		

EXERCISE 1-21A or 1-21b g. (cont.)

Statement of Cash Flows For the Year Ended December 31, 2013		
Cash Flows From Operating Activities:		
Net Cash Flow from Operating Activities		
Cash Flows From Investing Activities:		
Cash Flows From Financing Activities:		
Net Cash Flow from Financing Activities		
Net Increase in Cash		
Plus: Beginning Cash Balance		
Ending Cash Balance		

h.

i.

j.

EXERCISE 1-22A

Steps:

1.

Common Stock Issued	=	Change in Common Stock

2.

Change in Stockholders' Equity	=	Change in Comm. Stock	+	Change in Retained Earnings

3.

Increase in Retained Earnings	=	Net Income	–	Dividends

Alternate Solution:

From the Statement of Changes in Stockholders' Equity we know (with minor modifications):

Beginning Total Stk. Equity, 1/1/2013 (Common Stock + Retained Earnings)		
Plus: Common Stock Issued		
Plus: Net Income		
Less: Dividends		
Change in Stockholders' Equity		
Ending Total Stk. Equity, 12/31/2013		

Working backwards from the change in equity we can solve for net income:

Change in Stockholders' Equity, 2013	
Plus: Dividends	
Less: Common Stock Issued	
Net Income, 2013	

EXERCISE 1-22B

Steps:

1.

Change in Stockholders' Equity	=	Change in Comm. Stock	+	Change in Retained Earnings

2.

Increase in Retained Earnings	=	Net Income	−	Dividends

3.

Net Income	=	Revenues	−	Expenses

Alternate Solutions:

Working backwards from the change in equity we can solve for total revenue:

Computation of Total Revenues:	
Increase in Retained Earnings	
Plus: Dividends (given)	
Plus: Expenses (given)	
Total Revenues	

EXERCISE 1-23A or 1-23B

a.

Year	Cash Revenues	Cash Expenses	Net Income	Retained Earnings
2013				
2014				
2015				

b.

c.

Year	Cash Revenues	Cash Expenses	Net Income	Retained Earnings
2013				
2014				*
2015				*

*Hint: These amounts must be computed.

EXERCISE 1-24A or 1-24B

a.

b.

c.

d.

e.

EXERCISE 1-25A or 1-25B

a.

	Accounting Equation as of December 31, 2013		
Assets	=	Liabilities	+	Common Stock	+	Retained Earnings

Compute Retained Earnings:

b.

c.

EXERCISE 1-26A or 1-26B

a.

Event
1.
2.
3.
4.
5.
6.
7.

Horizontal Statements Model for 2013

Event No.	Balance Sheet									Income Statement				Statement of Cash Flows
	Assets			=	Liab.	+	Stockholders' Equity			Revenue	−	Expense	=	Net Inc.	
	Cash	+	Land	=	Notes Payable	+	Common Stock	+	Retained Earnings						
1	+			=				+			−		=	
2	+			=	+			+			−		=	
3	+			=	+			+			−		=	
4	+			=	+			+			−		=	
5	+			=	+			+			−		=	
6	+			=	+			+			−		=	
7	+			=	+			+			−		=	

1-38

EXERCISE 1-27A or 1 -27B

PROBLEM 1-28A or 1-28B

PROBLEM 1-29A or 1-29B

a. Entities mentioned:	b. Effect on the cash account:
1.	
2.	
3.	
4.	
5.	
6.	
7.	
8.	
9.	
10.	

PROBLEM 1-30A or 1-30B

Event No.	Type of Event	Effect on Total Assets
1.		
2.		
3.		
4.		
5.		
6.		
7.		
8.		
9.		
10.		
11.		
12.		
13.		
14.		
15.		

PROBLEM 1-31A

Item	Income Statement	Statement of Changes in Stk. Equity	Balance Sheet	Statement of Cash Flows
For the Period Ended (Date)				
Net Income				
Investing Activities				
Net Loss				
Ending Cash Balance				
Salary Expense				
Consulting Revenue				
Dividends				
Financing Activities				
Ending Common Stock				
Interest Expense				
As of (Date)				
Land				
Beginning Cash Balance				
Notes Payable				
Beginning Common Stock				
Service Revenue				
Utility Expense				
Cash from Stock Issue				
Operating Activities				

PROBLEM 1-31B

Components of Financial Statements	Income Statement	Statement of Changes in Stockholders' Equity	Balance Sheet	Statement of Cash Flows
1. Common Stock Ending Balance				
2. Common Stock Issued during the Period				
3. Liabilities				
4. Financing Activities				
5. Investing Activities				
6. Retained Earnings Beginning Balance				
7. Assets				
8. Expenses				
9. Retained Earnings Ending Balance				
10. Revenues				
11. Common Stock Beginning Balance				
12. Operating Activities				
13. Dividends				

PROBLEM 1-32A or 1-32B

a.

Accounting Equation for 2013

Event	Assets			=	Liabilities	+	Stockholders' Equity			
	Cash	+	Land	=	Notes Payable	+	Common Stock	+	Retained Earnings	Acct. Title/RE
Totals		+		=		+		+		

Accounting Equation for 2014

Event	Assets			=	Liabilities	+	Stockholders' Equity			
	Cash	+	Land	=	Notes Payable	+	Common Stock	+	Retained Earnings	Acct. Title/RE
Beg. Bal.										
Totals		+		=		+		+		

PROBLEM 1-32A or 1-32B (cont.)

b.

Income Statement
For the Period Ended December 31, 2013

Service Revenue	
Expenses	
Net Income	

Statement of Changes in Stockholders' Equity
For the Period Ended December 31, 2014

Beginning Common Stock		
Plus: Common Stock Issued		
Ending Common Stock		
Beginning Retained Earnings		
Plus: Net Income		
Ending Retained Earnings		
Total Stockholders' Equity		

Balance Sheet As of December 31, 2013		
Assets		
Total Assets		
Liabilities		
Stockholders' Equity		
Total Stockholders' Equity		
Total Liabilities and Stockholders' Equity		

Statement of Cash Flows For the Year Ended December 31, 2013		
Cash Flows From Operating Activities:		
Net Cash Flow from Operating Activities		
Cash Flows From Investing Activities:		
Net Cash Flow from Investing Activities		
Cash Flows From Financing Activities:		
Net Cash Flow from Financing Activities		
Net Increase in Cash		
Plus: Beginning Cash Balance		
Ending Cash Balance		$

Income Statement
For the Period Ended December 31, 2014

Service Revenue	
Expenses	
Net Income	

Statement of Changes in Stockholders' Equity
For the Period Ended December 31, 2014

Beginning Common Stock		
Plus:		
Ending Common Stock		
Beginning Retained Earnings		
Plus:		
Less:		
Ending Retained Earnings		
Total Stockholders' Equity		

Balance Sheet As of December 31, 2014		
Assets		
Total Assets		
Liabilities		
Stockholders' Equity		
Total Stockholders' Equity		
Total Liabilities and Stockholders' Equity		

	Statement of Cash Flows For the Year Ended December 31, 2014		
Cash Flows From Operating Activities:			
Net Cash Flow from Operating Activities			
Cash Flows From Investing Activities			
Cash Flows From Financing Activities:			
Net Cash Flow from Financing Activities			
Net Increase in Cash			
Plus: Beginning Cash Balance			
Ending Cash Balance			

c.

d.

e.

PROBLEM 1-33A

Note: The accounting equation is not required for 1-33A, but it is helpful.

	Accounting Equation							
	Assets	=	Liabilities	+	Stockholders' Equity			
		=		+	Common Stock	+	Retained Earnings	
					*			

*must be computed

a.

Income Statement For the Period Ended December 31, 2013	
Revenue	
Expenses	
Net Income	

PROBLEM 1-33B

a.

	Accounting Equation							
	Assets	=	Liabilities	+	Stockholders' Equity			
		=		+	Common Stock	+	Retained Earnings	
					*			
Revenue**								

* must be computed

**revenue must be computed:

_____

_____

_____

_____

Income Statement For the Period Ended December 31, 20___	
Revenue	
Expenses	
Net Income	

PROBLEM 1-33A or 1-33B a. (cont.)

Statement of Changes in Stockholders' Equity
For the Period Ended December 31, 20___

Beginning Common Stock

Plus:

Ending Common Stock

Beginning Retained Earnings

Plus:

Less:

Ending Retained Earnings

Total Stockholders' Equity

Balance Sheet
As of December 31, 20___

Assets

Total Assets

Liabilities

Stockholders' Equity

Total Stockholders' Equity

Total Liabilities and Stockholders' Equity

PROBLEM 1-33A or 1-33B a. (cont.)

Statement of Cash Flows For the Year Ended December 31, 20__		
Cash Flows From Operating Activities:		
Net Cash Flow from Operating Activities		
Cash Flows From Investing Activities		
Cash Flows From Financing Activities:		
Net Cash Flow from Financing Activities		
Net Increase in Cash		
Plus: Beginning Cash Balance		
Ending Cash Balance		

b. Percentage of assets provided by:

Creditors:	
Investors:	
Earnings:	

EXERCISE 1-34A or 1-34B

Horizontal Statements Model for 2013

	Balance Sheet								Income Statement				Statement of
	Assets		=	Liab.	+	Stockholders' Equity							Cash Flows
Event No.	Cash	+ Land	=	Notes Payable	+	Common Stock	+	Retained Earnings	Revenue	− Expense	= Net Inc.		
1													
2													
3													
4													
5													
6													
7													
8													
9													
Total	+		=		+		+			−	=		

b. Total Assets = _____

c.

Sources of Assets

Event	
Total Sources of Assets	

d.

e.

Operating Activities:	
Net Cash Flow from Operating Activities	

Investing Activities:	
Net Cash Flow from Investing Activities	

Financing Activities:	
Net Cash Flow from Financing Activities	

f.   Percentage of assets provided by:

Creditors:	
Investors:	
Earnings:	

g.

ATC 1-1

a.

b.

c.

d.

ATC 1-2

a.

b. ATC 1-2

a.

Income Statements (amounts given are in millions)

	2016	2015	2014	2013
Revenue	$ 860	$1,520	(a)	$1,200
Cost and Expenses	(a)	(a)	(2,400)	(860)
Income from Cont. Op.	(b)	450	320	(a)
Unusual Items	-0-	175	(b)	(b)
Net Income	$ 20	(b)	$ 175	$ 300
Balance Sheets				
Cash and Marketable Sec.	$ 350	$1,720	(c)	$ 940
Other Assets	1,900	(c)	2,500	(c)
Total Assets	$2,250	$2,900	(d)	$3,500
Liabilities	(c)	(d)	$1,001	(d)
Stockholders' Equity				
Common Stock	880	720	(e)	800
Retained Earnings	(d)	(e)	800	(e)
Total Stockholders' Equity	1,520	1,345	(f)	2,200
Total Liab. and Stk. Equity	$2,250	(f)	$3,250	$3,500

c.

ATC 1-4

a.

b.

c.

d.

Active Wilderness Adventures Income Statement For Year Ended December 31, 2015	
Revenue	
Operating Expenses	
Net Income from Continuing Operations	
Extraordinary Loss	
Net Income	

ATC 1-4 d. (cont.)

Active Wilderness Adventures Balance Sheet As of December 31, 2015		
Assets		
Liabilities		
Stockholders' Equity		
Common Stock		
Retained Earnings		
Total Stockholders' Equity		
Total Liabilities and Stockholders' Equity		

ATC 1-5

ATC 1-6 a.

Financial Statements	
Income Statement	
Revenue	
Expense	
Net Income	
Statement of Changes in Stockholders' Equity	
Beginning Common Stock	
Plus: Stock Issued	
Ending Common Stock	
Beginning Retained Earnings	
Plus: Net Income	
Less: Dividends	
Ending Retained Earnings	
Total Stockholders' Equity	
Balance Sheet	
Assets	
Cash	
Total Assets	
Stockholders' Equity	
Common Stock	
Retained Earnings	
Total Stockholders' Equity	
Statement of Cash Flows	
Net Cash Flow From Operating Activities:	
Inflow from Customers	
Outflow for Expenses	
Net Cash Flow from Operating Activities	
Net Cash Flow From Investing Activities	
Net Cash Flow From Financing Activities:	
Inflow from Stock Issue	
Outflow for Dividends	
Net Cash Flow from Financing Activities	
Net Change in Cash	
Plus: Beginning Cash Balance	
Ending Cash Balance	

ATC 1-6 (cont.)

b.

ACT 1-7

a.

b.

c.

d.

COMPREHENSIVE PROBLEM – CHAPTER 1

a.

	Assets			= Liabilities +		Stockholders' Equity		
Event	Cash	+	Land	= Notes Payable	+ Com. Stock	+ Retained Earnings	Acct. Title/RE
1. Issued stock		+		=	+	+	
2. Loan		+		=	+	+	
3. Provided Svc.		+		=	+	+	
4. Paid salaries		+		=	+	+	
5. Pur. land		+		=	+	+	
6. Paid expense		+		=	+	+	
7. Paid dividend		+		=	+	+	
8. No entry		+		=	+	+	
Totals		+		=	+	+	

Pacilio Security Service, Inc.
Accounting Equation for 2011

b.

Pacilio Security Services, Inc.
Income Statement
For the Year Ended December 31, 2011

Service Revenue	
Salaries Expense	
Other Operating Expense	
Net Income	

Pacilio Security Services, Inc.
Statement of Changes in Stockholders' Equity
For the Year Ended December 31, 2011

Beginning Common Stock		
Plus: Common Stock Issued		
Ending Common Stock		
Beginning Retained Earnings		
Plus: Net Income		
Less: Dividends		
Ending Retained Earnings		
Total Stockholders' Equity		

Pacilio Company
Balance Sheet
As of December 31, 2011

Assets		
Cash		
Land		
Total Assets		
Liabilities		
Notes Payable		
Total Liabilities		
Stockholders' Equity		
Common Stock		
Retained Earnings		
Total Stockholders' Equity		
Total Liabilities and Stockholders' Equity		$12,500

COMPREHENSIVE PROBLEM – CHAPTER 1 b. (cont.)

Pacilio Security Services, Inc. Statement of Cash Flows For the Year Ended December 31, 2011		
Cash Flows From Operating Activities:		
Cash Receipts from Customers		
Cash Payment for Salaries Expense		
Cash Payments for Other Operating Exp.		
Net Cash Flow from Operating Activities		
Cash Flows From Investing Activities:		
Cash Paid to Purchase Land		
Net Cash Flow from Investing Activities		
Cash Flows From Financing Activities:		
Cash Receipts from Stock Issue		
Cash Receipts from Loan		
Cash Payments for Dividends		
Net Cash Flow from Financing Activities		
Net Increase in Cash		
Plus: Beginning Cash Balance		
Ending Cash Balance		

CHAPTER 2

EXERCISE 2-1A or 2-1B

a.

General Ledger Accounts for the Year Ended December 31, 2013							
	Assets		**=**	**Liabilities**	**+**	**Stockholders' Equity**	
Event	Cash	Accounts Rec.	=	Salaries Pay.	+	Common Stock	Retained Earnings	Acct. Title for RE
Totals			=		+			

b.

Income Statement		
Revenue		
Expenses		
Total Expenses		
Net Income		

EXERCISE 2-1A or 2-1B b. (cont.)

Statement of Changes in Stockholders' Equity

Beginning Common Stock		
Plus: Common Stock Issued		
Ending Common Stock		
Beginning Retained Earnings		
Plus: Net Income		
Less: Dividends		
Ending Retained Earnings		
Total Stockholders' Equity		

Balance Sheet

Assets		
Total Assets		
Liabilities		
Total Liabilities		
Stockholders' Equity		
Total Stockholders' Equity		
Total Liab. and Stockholders' Equity		

EXERCISE 2-1A or 2-1B b. (cont.)

Statement of Cash Flows		
Cash Flow From Operating Activities		
Net Cash Flow from Operating Act.		
Cash Flow From Investing Activities		
Cash Flow From Financing Activities		
Net Cash Flow from Financing Act.		
Net Change in Cash		
Plus: Beginning Cash Balance		
Ending Cash Balance		

c.

EXERCISE 2-2A or 2-2B

Effect of Events on the 2013 Accounting Equation

	Assets			=	Liabilities	+	Stockholders' Equity		
Event	Cash	+	Accounts Rec.	=		+	Common Stock	+	Retained Earnings
		+		=		+		+	
		+		=		+		+	
Ending Balance		+		=		+		+	

a.	
b.	
c.	
d.	
e.	

EXERCISE 2-3A

a.

Crest Corporation Accounting Equation - 2013							
Event	Assets	=	Liabilities	+	Stockholders' Equity		
	Cash	=	Salaries Payable	+	Common Stock	+	Retained Earnings
Earned Rev.							
Accrued Sal.							

Crest Corporation Balance Sheet As of December 31, 2013		
Assets		
Total Assets		
Liabilities		
Total Liabilities		
Stockholders' Equity		
Retained Earnings		
Total Stockholders' Equity		
Total Liab. and Stockholders' Equity		

b.

Computation of Net Income	
Revenue	
Less: Expenses	
Net Income	

EXERCISE 2-3A (cont.)

c.

Cash Flow from Operating Activities	
Net Cash Flow from Operating Act.	

EXERCISE 2-3B

Chung Corporation Balance Sheet As of December 31, 2013		
Assets		
Total Assets		
Liabilities		
Total Liabilities		
Stockholders' Equity		
Retained Earnings		
Total Stockholders' Equity		
Total Liab. and Stockholders' Equity		

b.

Computation of Net Income	
Revenue	
Less: Expenses	
Net Income	

c.

Cash Flow from Operating Activities	
Cash from Revenue	
Net Cash Flow from Operating Act.	

d.

EXERCISE 2-4B or 2-4B

a. & c.

Event	Revenue	Expense	Statement of Cash Flows
1.			
2.			
3.			
4.			
5.			
6.			
7.			

b.

Computation of Net Income	
Revenue	
Less: Expenses	
Net Income	

d.

Cash Flow from Operating Activities	
Cash from Revenue	
Cash paid for expenses	
Net Cash Flow from Operating Act.	

e.

f.

EXERCISE 2-5A or 2-5B

a.

Statements Model for 2013

Event No.	Assets		=	Liabilities		+	S. Equity		Income Statement				Statement of Cash Flows
	Cash	+	Accts. Rec.	=	Acct. Payable	+	Sal. Pay.	+	Retained Earn.	Rev.	–	Exp.	=	Net Inc.	
1.														
2.														
3.														
4.														
5.														
6.														
7.														
8.														
Totals		+		=		+		+			–		=	

b.

c.

d.

e.

f.

g.

EXERCISE 2-6A or 2-6B

a.

Computation of Net Income	
Net Income	

b.

Computation of Cash Collected from Accounts Receivable	
Beginning balance of Accounts Receivable	
Cash collected from accounts receivable	

Computation of Cash Paid for Salaries Expense	
Beginning balance of Salaries Payable	
Cash paid for Salary Expense	

Cash Flow from Operating Activities	
Net Cash Flow from Operating Act.	

EXERCISE 2-7A or 2-7B

a.

	Effect of Events on the Accounting Equation				
	Assets		=	Liab.	+ Stk. Equity
Event	Cash	Supplies	=	Accounts Payable	Retained Earnings
1.					
2.					
3.					
Totals			=		

b.

Income Statement For the Year Ended December 31, 2013	
Net Income	

Balance Sheet As of December 31, 2013		
Assets		
Total Assets		
Liabilities		
Total Liabilities		
Stockholders' Equity		
Retained Earnings		
Total Stockholders' Equity		
Total Liab. and Stockholders' Equity		

Statement of Cash Flows For the Year Ended December 31, 2013			
Cash Flows From Operating Activities:			
Net Cash Flow from Operating Activities			
Cash Flows From Investing Activities			
Cash Flows From Financing Activities:			
Net Change in Cash			
Plus: Beginning Cash Balance			
Ending Cash Balance			

c.

d.

EXERCISE 2-8A or 2-8B

a.

Effect of Events on Financial Statements for 2013

Event No.	Assets			Liab.		Stockholders' Equity				Income Statement					Cash Flows
	Cash	+	Supplies	=	Accts. Pay.	+	Com. Stock	+	Retained Earnings	Rev.	−	Exp.	=	Net Income	
Beg. Bal.		+		=		+		+			−		=		
1.		+		=		+	+	+			−		=		
2.		+		=		+	+	+			−		=		
3.		+		=		+	+	+			−		=		
4.		+		=		+	+	+			−		=		
Totals		+		=		+	+	+			−		=		

b.

EXERCISE 2-9A or 2-9B

a.

	Effect of Events on the Accounting Equation				
		Assets		=	Stockholders' Equity
Event	Cash	Prepaid Rent		=	Retained Earnings
1.					
2.					
3.					
Totals				=	

b.

Income Statement
For the Year Ended December 31, 2013

Net Income		

Balance Sheet
As of December 31, 2013

Assets		
Total Assets		
Liabilities		-0-
Stockholders' Equity		
Retained Earnings		
Total Stockholders' Equity		
Total Liab. and Stockholders' Equity		

EXERCISE 2-9A or 2-9B b. (cont.)

Statement of Cash Flows For the Year Ended December 31, 2013		
Cash Flows From Operating Activities:		
Net Cash Flow from Operating Activities		
Cash Flows From Investing Activities		
Cash Flows From Financing Activities:		
Net Change in Cash		
Plus: Beginning Cash Balance		
Ending Cash Balance		

c.

EXERCISE 2-10A or 2-10B

a.

	Accounting Equation 2013							
	Assets		=	Liab.	+	Stockholders' Equity		
Event			=		+	Com. Stock	+	Retained Earnings
Totals			=		+		+	

b.

EXERCISE 2-11A or 2-11B

a.

			2013		
Event	Assets	=	Liabilities	+	Stockholders' Equity
	Cash	=	Unearned Revenue	+	Retained Earnings
event					
adjustment					
		=			

b.

Income Statement For the Year Ended December 31, 2013	
Revenue	
Expense	
Net Income	

Balance Sheet As of December 31, 2013		
Assets		
Total Assets		
Liabilities		
Total Liabilities		
Stockholders' Equity		
Retained Earnings		
Total Stockholders' Equity		
Total Liab. and Stockholders' Equity		

EXERCISE 2-11A or 2-11B b. (cont.)

| | Statement of Cash Flows | | |
	For the Year Ended December 31, 2013		
Cash Flows From Operating Activities:			
Net Cash Flow from Operating Activities			
Cash Flows From Investing Activities			
Cash Flows From Financing Activities:			
Net Change in Cash			
Plus: Beginning Cash Balance			
Ending Cash Balance			

c.

EXERCISE 2-12A or 2-12B

a.

Horizontal Statements Model for 2013

Event	Assets	=	Liabilities	+	Stk. Equity	Rev.	–	Exp.	=	Net Income	Statement of Cash Flows
	Cash	=	Unearned Revenue	+	Retained Earnings						
1.		=		+			–		=		
2.		=		+			–		=		
Totals		=		+			–		=		

b.

c.

EXERCISE 2-13A or 2-13B

EXERCISE 2-14A or 2-14B

Effect of Transactions on the Financial Statements for 2013

	Balance Sheet									Income Statement					Statement of Cash Flows
No.	Assets			=	Liabilities			+	S. Equity	Rev.	−	Exp.	=	Net Inc.	
	Cash	+	Supplies	=	Acct. Payable	+	Unearn. Revenue	+	Retained Earnings						
1.	+		+	=	+		+		+		−		=		
2.	+		+	=	+		+		+		−		=		
3.	+		+	=	+		+		+		−		=		
4.	+		+	=	+		+		+		−		=		
5.	+		+	=	+		+		+		−		=		
6.	+		+	=	+		+		+		−		=		
7.	+		+	=	+		+		+		−		=		
8.	+		+	=	+		+		+		−		=		
Totals	+		+	=	+		+		+		−		=		

EXERCISE 2-15A

a.

Event	Assets		=	Liabilities	+	Stockholders' Equity		
	Cash	Prepaid Rent	=		+	Common Stock	+	Retained Earnings
event								
Adj.								

Caldonia Company Accounting Equation - 2013 (table title)

b.

Event	Assets	=	Liabilities	+	Stockholders' Equity		
	Cash	=	Unearned Revenue	+	Common Stock	+	Retained Earnings
event							
Adj.							

East Alabama Rentals Accounting Equation - 2013 (table title)

EXERCISE 2-15B

a.

Josh Smith Attorney - 2013									
Event	Assets	=	Liabilities		+	Stockholders' Equity			
	Cash	=	Unearned Revenue		+	Common Stock		+	Retained Earnings
event									
Adj.									

b.

James Company - 2013									
Event	Assets		=	Liabilities	+	Stockholders' Equity			
	Cash	Prepaid Legal Fees	=		+	Common Stock		+	Retained Earnings
event									
Adj.									

EXERCISE 2-16A or 2-16B

					Stock. Equity		Income Statement				
Event	Type of Event	Assets	= Liab.	+	Com. Stock	+ Ret. Earn.	Rev.	– Exp.	= Net Inc.	Cash Flows
a.										
b.										
c.										
d.										
e.										
f.										
g.										
h.										
i.										
j.										
k.										
l.										
m.										
n.										
o.										
p.										
q.										

Horizontal Statements Model

EXERCISE 2-17A

a.

b.

Examples of costs that are assets:

c.

Examples of costs that are expenses:

EXERCISE 2-17B

a.

b.

	Asset	Expense
(1)		
(2)		
(3)		
(4)		
(5)		

EXERCISE 2-18A or 2-18B

	Type of Transaction
a.	
b.	
c.	
d.	
e.	
f.	
g.	
h.	
i.	
j.	
k.	

EXERCISE 2-19A or 2-19B

a.

Event	Requires year-end adjusting entry?
1.	
2.	
3.	
4.	
5.	
6.	
7.	
8.	
9.	
10.	

b.

EXERCISE 2-20A or 2-20B

a.

b.

c.

d.

EXERCISE 2-21A or 2-21B

a.

Event	Classification
1.	
2.	
3.	
4.	
5.	
6.	
7.	
8.	
9.	
10.	

b.

	Statement of Cash Flows For the Year Ended December 31, 2013		
Cash Flows From Operating Activities:			
Net Cash Flow from Operating Activities			
Cash Flows From Investing Activities			-0-
Cash Flows From Financing Activities:			
Net Cash Flow from Financing Activities			
Net Change in Cash			
Plus: Beginning Cash Balance			
Ending Cash Balance			

EXERCISE 2-22A or 2-22B

		Effect of Events on the General Ledger Accounts							
		Assets			=	Liabilities	+	Stockholders' Equity	
Event	Cash	Accounts Receivable	Land	=	Accounts Payable	+	Com. Stock	+	Retained Earnings
1.									
2.									
3.									
4.									
5.									
6.									
Totals				=		+		+	

a.

b.

c.

d.

e.

f.

g.

h.

EXERCISE 2-23A

Item/Account	Statement	Item/Account	Statement
a. Consulting Revenue		u. Rent Expense	
b. Market Value of Land		v. Salary Expense	
c. Supplies Expense		w. Total Stockholders' Equity	
d. Salaries Payable		x. Unearned Revenue	
		y. Cash Flow from Investing ctivities	
e. Notes Payable			
f. Ending Common Stock		z. Insurance Expense	
g. Beginning Cash Balance		aa. End. Retained Earn.	
h. Prepaid Rent		bb. Interest Revenue	
i. Net Change in Cash		cc. Supplies	
j. Land		dd. Beg. Retained Earn.	
k. Operating Expenses		ee. Utilities Payable	
l. Total Liabilities		ff. Cash Flow from Financing Activities	
m. "As of" Date Notation		gg. Accounts Receivable	
n. Salaries Expense		hh. Prepaid Insurance	
o. Net Income		ii. Ending Cash Balance	
p. Service Revenue		jj. Utilities Expense	
q. Cash Flow from Operating Activities		kk. Accounts Payable	
r. Operating Income		ll. Beg. Common Stock	
s. Interest Receivable		mm. Dividends	
t. Interest Revenue		nn. Total Assets	

EXERCISE 2-23B

	Item/Account	Statement		Item/Account	Statement
a.	Supplies	BS	u.	Rent Exp.	IS
b.	Cash Flow from Financing Act.	CF	v.	P/E Ratio	NA
c.	"As of" Date Notation	BS	w.	Taxes Payable	BS
d.	End Retained Earn.	BS/SE	x.	Unearned Revenue	BS
e.	Net Income	IS/SE	y.	Service Revenue	IS
e.	Dividends	SE/CF	z.	Cash Flow from Investing Activities	CF
g.	Net Change in Cash	CF	aa.	Consulting Revenue	IS
h.	"For the Period Ended"	IS, CF, SE	bb.	Utilities Expense	IS
i.	Land	BS	cc.	End. Common Stock	BS/SE
j.	Ending Common Stock	BS, SE	dd.	Total Liabilities	BS
k.	Salaries Expense	IS	ee.	Operating Cycle	NA
l.	Prepaid Rent	BS	ff.	Cash Flow from Operating Activities	CF
m.	Accounts Payable	BS	gg.	Operating Expenses	IS
n.	Total Assets	BS	hh.	Supplies Expense	IS
o.	Salaries Payable	BS	ii.	Beg. Retained Earn.	SE
p.	Insurance Expense	IS	jj.	Beg. Common Stock	SE
q.	Notes Payable	BS	kk.	Prepaid Insurance	BS
r.	Accounts Receivable	BS	ll.	Salary Expense	IS
s.	Interest Receivable	BS	mm.	Beginning Cash	CF
t.	Interest Revenue	IS	nn.	Ending Cash	BS/CF

EXERCISE 2-24A or 2-24B

Event No.	Net Income		Cash Flow from Operating Activities	
	Direction of Change	Amount of Change	Direction of Change	Amount of Change
a.				
b.				
c.				
d.				
e.				
f.				
g.				
h.				
i.				

EXERCISE 2-25A

a.

Permanent Accounts

Temporary (Nominal) Accounts

b.

Beginning Retained Earnings	
Ending Retained Earnings	

c.

Computation of Net Income	
Net Income	$1,500

d.

e.

EXERCISE 2-25B

a.

Accounts to be Closed to Retained Earnings	

b.

Beginning Retained Earnings	
Ending Retained Earnings	

c.

Computation of Net Income	
Net Income	

d.

e.

EXERCISE 2-26A or 2-26B

a.

Account	Classification
1.	
2.	
3.	
4.	
5.	
6.	
7.	
8.	
9.	
10.	

b.

EXERCISE 2-27A or 2-27B

a.

b.

c.

d.

EXERCISE 2-28A

a.	
b.	
c.	
d.	

EXERCISE 2-28B

a.

Examples of expenses that would be matched directly with revenue:

b.

Example of a period cost that is difficult to match with revenue:

EXERCISE 2-29A or 2-29B

a.

b.

c.

d.

e.

f.

g.

EXERCISE 2-30A or 2-30B

Event	Classification (Asset Source, Asset Use, Asset Exchange, Claims Exchange)
a.	
b.	
c.	
d.	
e.	
f.	
g.	
h.	
i.	
j.	

EXERCISE 2-31A or 2-31B

Event	Examples of Transactions:
a.	
b.	
c.	
d.	
e.	

EXERCISE 2-32A or 2-32B

EXERCISE 2-33A or 2-33B (Appendix)

a.

b.

c. (Exercise 2-33B)

c./d.

Statements Model for 2013

Event No.	Assets =		Liabilities		+	Stockholders' Equity		Income Statement			Statement of Cash Flows
	Cash	=	Notes Payable	+ Int. Payable	+	Common Stock	+ Ret. Earn.	Rev.	- Exp.	= Net Inc.	
1.											
2.											
3.											

EXERCISE 2-34A or 2-34B

a.

b.

Accounting Equation for 2013

Event	Assets					=	Liab.	+	Stockholders' Equity		
	Cash	+	Interest Rec.	+	CD	=		+	Common Stock	+	Retained Earnings
CD											
Accrue Int. Rev.											

c.

d.

e.

f.

g.

EXERCISE 2-35A (Appendix)

a.

	Accounting Equation for 2013						
	Assets			=	Stockholders' Equity		
Event			Accum. Depr.	=	Com. Stock	+	Retained Earnings
1.							
2.							
3.							
4.							
5.							
6.							
Totals				=		+	

Computation of depreciation expense:

b.

c.

d.

EXERCISE 2-35B (Appendix)

a.

				Accounting Equation for 2013				
	Assets			=	Stockholders' Equity			
Event			Accum. Depr.	=	Com. Stock	+	Retained Earnings	
1.								
2.								
3.								
4.								
5.								
Totals				=		+		

b.

Dill's Diner
Balance Sheet
As of December 31, 2013

Assets		
Total Assets		
Liabilities		
Stockholders' Equity		
Common Stock		
Retained Earnings		
Total Stockholders' Equity		
Total Liab. and Stockholders' Equity		

EXERCISE 2-35B (Appendix) b. (cont.)

Dills Diner Statement of Cash Flows For the Year Ended December 31, 2013		
Cash Flows From Operating Activities:		
Net Cash Flow from Operating Activities		
Cash Flows From Investing Activities:		
Net Cash Flow from Investing Activities		
Cash Flows From Financing Activities:		
Net Cash Flow from Financing Activities		
Net Change in Cash		
Plus: Beginning Cash Balance		
Ending Cash Balance		

c.

d.

e.

f.

EXERCISE 2-36A or 2-36B (Appendix)

a.

b.

c.

PROBLEM 2-37A or 2-37B

Effect of Events on the Financial Statements

Event	Balance Sheet										Income Statement					Stmt. of Cash Flows
	Assets		=	Liabilities	+	Stock. Equity					Rev.	−	Exp.	=	Net Inc.	
						Com. Stock	+	Ret. Earn.								
1.	+	+	=	+	+	+	+							=		
2.	+	+	=	+	+	+	+					−		=		
3.	+	+	=	+	+	+	+					−		=		
4.	+	+	=	+	+	+	+					−		=		
5.	+	+	=	+	+	+	+					−		=		
6.	+	+	=	+	+	+	+					−		=		
7.	+	+	=	+	+	+	+					−		=		
8.	+	+	=	+	+	+	+					−		=		
9.	+	+	=	+	+	+	+					−		=		
10.	+	+	=	+	+	+	+					−		=		
11.	+	+	=	+	+	+	+					−		=		
12.	+	+	=	+	+	+	+					−		=		
Bal.	+	+	=	+	+	+	+					−		=		

PROBLEM 2-38A or 2-38B

	The Accounting Equation							
	Total Assets			=	Liabilities	+	Stockholders' Equity	
Event/ Adjust.	Cash	+	Other Assets	=		+	Common Stock	+ Retained Earnings
a.								
a. Adj.[1]								
b.								
b. Adj.[2]								
c.								
c. Adj.[3]								
d.								
d. Adj.[4]								

EXERCISE 2-39A

a.

Bates Company Income Statement For the Year Ended December 31, 2013		
Net Income		

b.

Accounts to be Closed:
1.
2.
3.
4.
5.

c.

Computation of Retained Earnings:	
Beginning Retained Earnings	
Ending Retained Earnings	

d.

EXERCISE 2-39B

a.

Accounts to be Closed:

b.

Wathen Company		
Income Statement		
For the Year Ended December 31, 2013		

c.

Computation of Retained Earnings:	
Beginning Retained Earnings	
Ending Retained Earnings	

d.

EXERCISE 2-40A or 2-40B
(Not Required)

Accounting Equation

			Assets					Liabilities			Stk. Equity	
Date	Cash	Acc. Rec.	Pp. Rent	Supp.	Int. Rec.	Land	Acc. Pay.	Sal. Pay.	Unear. Rev.		Com. Stock	Ret. Earn.
Bal.											80,000	15,000
Bal.												

PROBLEM 2-40A or 2-40B (cont.)

a. The two transactions that need adjusting entries are as follows:

1.

2.

b.

c.

d.

e.

f.

g.

h.

i.

j.

k.

l.

m.

Financial Statements

Income Statement

Statement of Changes in Stockholders' Equity

	Balance Sheet			

PROBLEM 2-41A or 2-41B (cont.)

Statement of Cash Flows	
Cash Flow From Operating Activities	
Cash Flow From Investing Activities	
Cash Flow From Financing Activities	
Net Change in Cash	
Plus: Beginning Cash Balance	
Ending Cash Balance	

PROBLEM 2-42A

FOR THE YEARS	2013	2014	2015
Income Statements			
Revenue (cash)	$ 400	$ 500	$ 800
Expense (cash)	(250)	(l)	(425)
Net Income	(a)	$ 100	$ 375
Statements of Changes in Stockholders' Equity			
Beginning Common Stock	$ - 0-	(m)	$ 9,100
Plus: Common Stock Issued	(b)	1,100	310
Ending Common Stock	8,000	9,100	(s)
Beginning Retained Earnings	-0-	25	75
Plus: Net Income	(c)	100	375
Less: Dividends	(d)	(50)	(150)
Ending Retained Earnings	25	(n)	300
Total Stockholders' Equity	(e)	$ 9,175	(t)
Balance Sheets			
Assets			
Cash	(f)	(o)	(u)$
Land	-0-	(p)	2,500
Total Assets	$11,000	$11,650	$10,550
Liabilities	(g)	(q)	$ 840
Stockholders' Equity			
Common Stock	(h)	(r)	9,410
Retained Earnings	(i)	75	300
Total Stockholders' Equity	8,025	9,175	9,710
Total Liabilities and Stk. Equity	$11,000	$11,650	$10,550

PROBLEM 2-42A (cont.)

FOR THE YEARS	2013	2014	2015
Statements of Cash Flows			
Cash Flows From Oper. Activities:			
Cash Receipts from Revenue	(j)	$ 500	(v)
Cash Payments for Expenses	(k)	(400)	(w)
Net Cash Flows from Oper. Act.	150	100	375
Cash Flows From Invest. Activities:			
Cash Payments for Land	-0-	(5,000)	-0-
Cash Receipt from Sale of Land	-0-	-0-	2,500
Net Cash Flows from Invest. Act.	-0-	(5,000)	2,500
Cash Flows From Fin. Activities:			
Cash Rec. from Borrowed Funds	2,975	-0-	-0-
Cash Payments to Reduce Debt	-0-	(500)	(x)
Cash Receipts from Stock Issue	8,000	1,100	(y)
Cash Payments for Dividends	(125)	(50)	(z)
Net Cash Flows from Fin. Activities	10,850	550	(1,475)
Net Change in Cash	11,000	(4,350)	1,400
Plus: Beginning Cash Balance	-0-	11,000	6,650
Ending Cash Balance	$11,000	$ 6,650	$ 8,050

PROBLEM 2-42B

FOR THE YEARS	2013	2014	2015
Income Statements			
Revenue (cash)	$ 700	$ 1,300	$ 2,000
Expense (cash)	(a)	(700)	(1,300)
Net Income (Loss)	$ 200	(m)	$ 700
Statements of Changes in Stockholders' Equity			
Beginning Common Stock	$ -0-	(n)	$ 6,000
Plus: Common Stock Issued	5,000	1,000	2,000
Ending Common Stock	5,000	6,000	(t)
Beginning Retained Earnings	-0-	100	200
Plus: Net Income (Loss)	(b)	(o)	700
Less: Dividends	(c)	(500)	(300)
Ending Retained Earnings	100	(p)	600
Total Stockholders' Equity	(d)	$ 6,200	$ 8,600
Balance Sheets			
Assets			
Cash	(e)	(q)	(u)$
Land	-0-	(r)	8,000
Total Assets	(f)	$11,200	$10,600
Liabilities	(g)	$ 5,000	$ 2,000
Stockholders' Equity			
Common Stock	(h)	(s)	8,000
Retained Earnings	(i)	200	600
Total Stockholders' Equity	(j)	6,200	8,600
Total Liab. and Stk. Equity	$8,100	$11,200	$10,600

PROBLEM 2-42B (cont.)

FOR THE YEARS	2013	2014	2015
Statements of Cash Flows			
Cash Flows From Oper. Activities:			
Cash Receipts from Revenue	(k)$	$1,300	(v)
Cash Payments for Expenses	(l)	(700)	(w)
Net Cash Flows from Oper. Act.	200	600	700
Cash Flows From Invest. Activities:			
Cash Payments for Land	-0-	(8,000)	-0-
Cash Flows From Fin. Activities:			
Cash Receipts from Loan	3,000	3,000	-0-
Cash Payments to Reduce Debt	-0-	(1,000)	(x)
Cash Receipts from Stock Issue	5,000	1,000	(y)
Cash Payments for Dividends	(100)	(500)	(z)
Net Cash Flows from Fin. Activities	7,900	2,500	(1,300)
Net Change in Cash	8,100	(4,900)	(600)
Plus: Beginning Cash Balance	-0-	8,100	3,200
Ending Cash Balance	$8,100	$3,200	$2,600

PROBLEM 2-43A or 2-43B

a.

Accounting Equation for 2013

| Event | Type of Event | Assets | | | | | = | Liabilities | | | + | Stk. Equity | |
		Cash	Accts. Rec.	Supp.	Prepd. Rent	Land	=	Accts. Pay.	Salaries Payable	Unearn. Rev.	+	Com. Stock	Retained Earnings
1.													
2.													
3.													
4.													
5.													
6.													
7.													
8.													
9.													
Totals							=				+		

PROBLEM 2-43A or 2-43B a. (cont.)

Accounting Equation for 2014

Event	Type of Event	Assets						=	Liabilities			+	Stk. Equity	
		Cash	Accts. Rec.	Supp.	Prepd. Rent	Land	=	Accts. Pay.	Salaries Payable	Unearn. Revenue	+	Com. Stock	Retained Earnings
Bal.														
1.														
2.														
3.														
4.														
5.														
6.														
7.														
8.														
9.														
10.														
11.														
12.														
13.														
14.*														
15.*														
16.*														
Totals							=				+		

*2-43A only

b.

Financial Statements
For the Years Ended December 31, 2013 and 2014

Income Statements

	2013	2014
Net Income		

Statements of Changes in Stockholders' Equity

	2013	2014
Beginning Common Stock		
Plus:		
Ending Common Stock		
Beginning Retained Earnings		
Plus:		
Less:		
Ending Retained Earnings		
Total Stockholders' Equity		

	Balance Sheets As of December 31, 2013 and 2014	
	2013	**2014**
Assets		
Total Assets		
Liabilities		
Total Liabilities		
Stockholders' Equity		
Total Stockholders' Equity		
Total Liab. and Stockholders' Equity		

	Statements of Cash Flows For the Years Ended December 31, 2013 and 2014		
		2013	2014
Cash Flows From Operating Activities:			
Net Cash Flow from Operating Activities			
Cash Flows From Investing Activities:			
Net Cash Flow From Investing Activities			
Cash Flows From Financing Activities:			
Net Cash Flow From Financing Activities			
Net Change in Cash			
Plus: Beginning Cash Balance			
Ending Cash Balance			

PROBLEM 2-44A or 2-44B

PROBLEM 2-45A or 2-45B
(Not required)

Accounting Equation

| | Assets | | | | | | | | | | Liabilities | | | | | Stk. Equity | |
Date	Cash	Acc. Rec.	Pp. Rent	Supp	CD	Int. Rec.	Van	Acc. Depr.	Land		Acc. Pay.	Sal. Pay.	Note Pay.	Int. Pay.	Unear. Rev.		Com. Stock	Ret. Earn.
Bal.																		
1/1																		
1/1																		
3/1																		
4/1																		
6/1																		
7/1																		
8/1																		
9/1																		
10/1																		
11/1																		
12/31																		
12/31																		
12/31																		
12/31																		
12/31																		
12/31a1																		
12/31a2																		
12/31a3																		
12/31a4																		
12/31a5																		
Bal.																		

Computations:

PROBLEM 2-45A or 2-45B (cont.)

a. The five transactions that need adjusting entries are:

b.

c.

d.

e.

f.

g.

h.

i.

j.

k.

l.

m.

n.

ATC 2-1   (All dollar amounts are in millions.)

a.

b.

c.

d.

ATC 2-2

a. 1. (in millions)

	2010	2009	2008
Revenue			
Less: Operating Costs			
Net Income			

2.

3.

ATC 2-3

Dollar amounts are in thousands.

a.

	2010	2009
Revenues		
Expenses		
Net income		
Beg. retained earnings		
+ Net income		
- Dividends		
End. Retained earnings		

b.

Revenue increased by:

Net income decreased by:

c.

d.

ATC 2-4

Dollar amounts in thousands.

a. and b.

	2010	2009
Cash from operating activities		
Cash from investing activities		
Cash from financing activities		
Net change in cash		
+ Beg. cash balance		
= End. Cash balance		

c.

ATC 2-5

Dollar amounts are in thousands.

a.

	Aeropostale	American Eagle Outfitters
Revenues		
Expenses		
Net income		
Beg. retained earnings		
+ Net income		
- Dividends		
End. Retained earnings		

b. Aeropostale:

American Eagle:

c.

ATC 2-6

Dollar amounts in thousands.

a. and b.

	H&R Block	Jackson Hewitt
Revenues		
Expenses		
Net income		
Cash from operating activities		
Cash from investing activities		
Cash from financing activities		
Net change in cash		
+ Beg. cash balance		
= End. Cash balance		

c.

d.

ATC 2-7

a.

Income Statement		Balance Sheet	
Service Revenue	$	Assets:	$
Operating Exp.			
Net Income	$	Liabilities:	$
		Stockholders' Equity:	
		Common Stock	
		Retained Earnings	
		Total Stk Equity	
		Total Liab. and Stk. Equity	$

Computations for Income Statement Items:

Computations for Balance Sheet Items:

b.

c.

ATC 2-8

a. Netflix's accrual accounts are:

_____

_____

_____

_____

_____

b. Netflix's deferral accounts are:

_____

_____

_____

_____

_____

_____

_____

_____

_____

_____

COMPREHENSIVE PROBLEM – CHAPTER 2

Pacilio Security Services, Inc.

Event	Cash	+	Acct. Rec.	+	Supp.	+	Pp. Rent	+	Land	=	Accts. Pay	+	Sal. Pay.	+	Unear. Rev.	+	Notes Pay.	+	Com. Stock	+	Ret. Earn.	Acct. Titles
B. Bal.	8,500	+		+		+		+	4,000	=		+		+		+	5,000	+	6,000	+	1,500	
1.																						
2.																						
3.																						
4.																						
5.																						
6.																						
7.																						
8.																						
9.																						
10.																						
11.																						
12.																						
13.*																						
14.																						
15.[1]																						
16.[2]																						
17.																						
Bal.		+		+		+		+		=		+		+		+		+		+		

b.

Pacilio Security Services, Inc. Income Statement For the Year Ended December 31, 2012		
Service Revenue		
Expenses		
Total Expenses		
Net Income		

Pacilio Security Services, Inc. Statement of Changes in Stockholders' Equity For the Year Ended December 31, 2012		
Beginning Common Stock		
Plus: Common Stock Issued		
Ending Common Stock		
Beginning Retained Earnings		
Plus: Net Income		
Less: Dividends		
Ending Retained Earnings		
Total Stockholders' Equity		

Pacilio Security Services, Inc. Balance Sheet As of December 31, 2012		
Assets		
Total Assets		
Liabilities		
Total Liabilities		
Stockholders' Equity		
Total Stockholders' Equity		
Total Liabilities and Stockholders' Equity		

Pacilio Security Services, Inc. Statement of Cash Flows For the Year Ended December 31, 2012		
Cash Flows From Operating Activities:		
Net Cash Flow from Operating Activities		
Cash Flows From Investing Activities:		
Cash Flows From Financing Activities:		
Cash Receipts from Stock Issue		
Cash Payments on Loan		
Cash Payments for Dividends		
Net Cash Flow from Financing Activities		
Net Increase in Cash		
Plus: Beginning Cash Balance		
Ending Cash Balance		

WORKING PAPERS – CHAPTER 3

EXERCISE 3-1A

Account Category	Used to Increase This Account	Used to Decrease This Account
Accounts Receivable		
Accounts Payable		
Common Stock		
Land		
Unearned Revenue		
Service Revenue		
Retained Earnings		
Insurance Expense		
Rent Expense		
Prepaid Rent		
Interest Revenue		

EXERCISE 3-1B

Accounting Elements	Used to Increase This Element	Used to Decrease This Element
Assets		
Liabilities		
Common Stock		
Retained Earnings		
Revenue		
Expense		
Dividends		

EXERCISE 3-2A or 3-2B

EXERCISE 3-3A

Account	Normal Balance
a. Common Stock	
b. Prepaid Rent	
c. Supplies	
d. Accounts Payable	
e. Interest Revenue	
f. Rent Expense	
g. Unearned Revenue	
h. Service Revenue	
i. Dividends	
j. Land	
k. Accounts Receivable	

EXERCISE 3-3B

Account	Normal Balance
a. Salaries Payable	
b. Cash	
c. Prepaid Insurance	
d. Common Stock	
e. Interest Revenue	
f. Rent Expense	
g. Salaries Expense	
h. Consulting Revenue	
i. Unearned Revenue	
j. Accounts Payable	
k. Dividends	
l. Land	

EXERCISE 3-4A or 3-4B

a.

	Event	Account Debited	Account Credited
1.			
2.			
3.			
4.			
5.			
6.			
7.			
8.			
9.			

b.

No.	Assets	=	Liab.	+	Equity	Rev.	–	Exp.	=	Net Inc.	Cash Flow
1.											
2.											
3.											
4.											
5.											
6.											
7.											
8.											
9.											

EXERCISE 3-5A or 3-5B

Event Number	Account Debited	Account Credited
a.		
b.		
c.		
d.		
e.		
f.		
g.		
h.		
i.		
j.		
k.		
l.		
m.		
n.		

EXERCISE 3-6 or 3-6B

Event No.	Type of Event	Assets	=	Liabilities	+	Stockholders' Equity Common Stock	+	Retained Earnings
a.								
b.								
c.								
d.								
e.								
f.								
g.								
h.								
i.								
j.								
k.								
l.								
m.								
n.								

EXERCISE 3-7A

Assets		=	Liabilities		+	Stockholders' Equity	
Debit	Credit		Debit	Credit		Debit	Credit

Revenue	
Debit	Credit

Expense	
Debit	Credit

EXERCISE 3-7B

Cash	
Debit	Credit

Accounts Payable	
Debit	Credit

Common Stock	
Debit	Credit

Accounts Receivable	
Debit	Credit

Salaries Payable	
Debit	Credit

Dividends	
Debit	Credit

Supplies	
Debit	Credit

Service Revenue	
Debit	Credit

Other Operating Exp.	
Debit	Credit

EXERCISE 3-8A or 3-8B

a.

Debit	Credit		Debit	Credit

b.

Debit	Credit		Debit	Credit

c.

Debit	Credit		Debit	Credit

d.

Debit	Credit		Debit	Credit

EXERCISE 3-9A or 3-9B

a. e. & f.

Assets = Stockholders' Equity

Cash

Accounts Rec.

Retained Earnings

2013

2013

2013

Bal.
2014

Bal.
2014

Bal.

Bal.

Service Revenue

2013

Bal.
2014

b. & g.

Effect of Transactions on the Financial Statements for 2013 and 2014

No.	Assets		=	Liab.	+	Stockholders' Equity			Rev.	–	Exp.	=	Net Inc.	Cash Flows
	Cash	+ Acct. Rec.	=		+	Com. Stock	+	Ret. Earn.						
2013														
1.														
2.														
Bal.		+	=		+		+			–		=		
2014														
3.														
Bal.		+	=		+		+			–		=		

EXERCISE 3-9A or 3-9B (cont.)

c.

d.

e.

f.

g.

h.

EXERCISE 3-10A or 3-10B

a. b. & e.

| Assets | = | Liabilities | + | Stockholders' Equity |

Accounts Rec.

Debit	Credit

Accounts Pay.

Debit	Credit

Retained Earnings

Debit	Credit

Supplies

Debit	Credit

Service Revenue

Debit	Credit

Supplies Expense

Debit	Credit

EXERCISE 3-10A or 3-10B (cont.)

c.

Effect of Transactions on the Financial Statements for 2013

No.	Assets				Liab.		Stockholders' Equity			Revenue	Exp.		Net Inc.	Cash Flows
	Accts. Rec.	+	Supplies	=	Accts. Pay.	+	Common Stock	+	Ret. Earn.		–	=		
a1.														
a2.														
b.														
Bal.		+		=		+		+			–	=		

d.

EXERCISE 3-10A or 3-10B (cont.)

e.

General Journal			
Date	Account Titles	Debit	Credit
	Closing Entries		

Post closing entries to T-accounts in part a.

Post-Closing Trial Balance December 31, 2013		
Account Titles	Debit	Credit

EXERCISE 3-11A or 3-11B

a. & b.

Assets	=	Liabilities	+ Stockholders' Equity
Cash		Unearned Revenue	Service Revenue

c.

	Effect of Transactions on Financial Statements							
	Balance Sheet				Income Statement			Statement of Cash Flows
Date	Assets	= Liab.	+	S. Equity	Rev.	− Exp.	= Net Inc.	
Bal.		=	+			−	=	

d.

Revenue	
Expense	
Net Income	

Cash Flow From Operating Activities	
Net Cash Flow from Operating Activities	

e. _____

EXERCISE 3-12A or 3-12B

Accounts Receivable

Debit	Credit
Beg. Bal	Coll.
Rev.	
End. Bal.	

EXERCISE 3-13A or 3-13B

Accounts Payable

Debit	Credit
	Beg. Bal.
Paid	Exp.
	End Bal.

EXERCISE 3-14A or 3-14B

a.

Account Title	Debit	Credit

Assets	=	Liab.	+	Equity	Rev.	–	Exp.	=	Net Inc.	Cash Flow

b.

Account Title	Debit	Credit

Assets	=	Liab.	+	Equity	Rev.	–	Exp.	=	Net Inc.	Cash Flow

c.

Account Title	Debit	Credit

Assets	=	Liab.	+	Equity	Rev.	–	Exp.	=	Net Inc.	Cash Flow

d.

Account Title	Debit	Credit

Assets	=	Liab.	+	Equity	Rev.	–	Exp.	=	Net Inc.	Cash Flow

e.

Account Title	Debit	Credit

Assets	=	Liab.	+	Equity	Rev.	–	Exp.	=	Net Inc.	Cash Flow

f.

Account Title	Debit	Credit

Assets	=	Liab.	+	Equity	Rev.	–	Exp.	=	Net Inc.	Cash Flow

g.

Account Title	Debit	Credit

Assets	=	Liab.	+	Equity	Rev.	–	Exp.	=	Net Inc.	Cash Flow

h.

Account Title	Debit	Credit

Assets	=	Liab.	+	Equity	Rev.	–	Exp.	=	Net Inc.	Cash Flow

EXERCISE 3-14A or 3-14B (cont.)

i.

Account Title	Debit	Credit

Assets	=	Liab.	+	Equity	Rev.	–	Exp.	=	Net Inc.	Cash Flow

EXERCISE 3-15A

a.

	Debit	Credit

b.

Assets	=	Liab. Sal. Pay.	+	Equity Ret. Earn.	Rev.	–	Exp.	=	Net Inc.	Cash Flow

c.

Computation of Net Income:	
Cash Flow From Operating Activities:	

d.

EXERCISE 3-15B

a. & b.

Southern Company
Journal Entries for 2013

Date	Account Titles	Debit	Credit
a. 3/1			
b. 12/31			

c.

Southern Company
Horizontal Statements Model

	Assets			Liab.	=	Stockholders' Equity				Income Statement					Cash Flows
	Cash	+	Prepaid Rent	=		Comm. Stock	+	Retained Earn.		Rev.	−	Exp.	=	Net Inc.	
1.															
2.															
3.															
adj															
Bal.															

EXERCISE 3-15B (cont.)

d.

Computation of Net Income:

Cash Flow From Operating Activities:

e. Prepaid Rent: _____

EXERCISE 3-16A

a. & b.

	Washington Mining Journal Entries for 2013		
Date	Account Titles	Debit	Credit
a. 3/1			
b. 12/31			

EXERCISE 3-16A (cont.)

c.

Washington Mining
Horizontal Statements Model for 2013

Event	Assets			=	Liab.	+	Stk. Equity			Income Statement			Statement of Cash Flows
	Cash	+	Prepaid Rent	=		+	Comm. Stock	+	Ret. Earn	Revenue	− Expense	= Net Inc.	
1.													
2.													
3.													
Adj.													
Bal.													

d.

Computation of Net Income:

Cash Flow From Operating Activities:

e. Prepaid Rent: _____

EXERCISE 3-16B

a.

Debit	Credit

b.

Assets	=	Liab.	+	Equity	Rev.	−	Exp.	=	Net Inc.	Cash Flow
		Sal. Pay.		Ret. Earn.						

c.

Revenue	
Expense	
Net Income	

Cash Flow From Operating Activities	
Net Cash Flow from Operating Activities	

d. Salaries Payable: _____

EXERCISE 3-17A or 3-17B

a.

Closing Entries	Debit	Credit

b.

Retained Earnings, 2013	
Beginning Retained Earnings	
Add: Revenue	
Less: Expenses	
Less: Dividends	
Ending Retained Earnings	

EXERCISE 3-18A or 3-18B

a.

	General Journal, 2013		
Event	Account Titles	Debit	Credit
1.			
2.			
3.			
4.			
5.			
6.			
7.			
8.			

EXERCISE 3-18A or 3-18B (cont.)

b.

Assets	=	Liabilities	+	Stockholders' Equity

Cash   **Accounts Payable**   **Common Stock**

Dividends

Accounts Receivable   **Service Revenue**

Supplies (3-18A only)

Salaries Expense

Supp. Exp./Oper. Expense

c. ....

d. ....

EXERCISE 3-19A or 3-19B

	Trial Balance December 31, 2013	
Account Titles	Debit	Credit
Totals		

EXERCISE 3-20A or 3-20B

a.

b.

c.

d.

e.

EXERCISE 3-21A

a.

General Journal, 2013			
Event	Account Titles	Debit	Credit
1.			
2.			
3.			
4.			
5.			
6.			
7.			
8.			
9.			
10.			
11.			
12.			
13.			

EXERCISE 3-21A b. or 3-21B

a.

T-Accounts, 2013

ASSETS = LIABILITIES + STOCKHOLDERS' EQUITY

Cash		Accounts Payable		Common Stock		Retained Earnings	
Debit	Credit	Debit	Credit	Debit	Credit	Debit	Credit

Unearned Revenue		Dividends	
Debit	Credit	Debit	Credit

Salaries Pay.
(3-21B)

Service Revenue

Accounts Rec.			Debit	Credit
Debit	Credit			

Interest Revenue	
Debit	Credit

Supplies	
Debit	Credit

Operating Expense

Debit	Credit

Interest Rec.	
Debit	Credit

Salaries Exp.
(3-21B)

Debit	Credit

Land (3-21A only)

Debit	Credit

Supplies Expenses

Debit	Credit

EXERCISE 3-21A c. or 3-21B (cont.)

b.

	Debit	Credit
Trial Balance		
As of December 31, 2013		
Account Titles	Debit	Credit

EXERCISE 3-22A or 3-22B

a.

	General Journal, 20__		
Date	Account Titles	Debit	Credit
1.			
2.			
3.			
4.			
5.			
6.			

EXERCISE 3-22A or 3-22B (cont.)

b. and d.

T-Accounts, 20___							

Assets = **Liabilities** + **Stockholders' Equity**

Cash
Debit	Credit

Accounts Payable
Debit	Credit

Common Stock
Debit	Credit

Accounts Receivable
Debit	Credit

Retained Earnings
Debit	Credit

Dividends
Debit	Credit

Service Revenue
Debit	Credit

Operating Expenses
Debit	Credit

Salaries Expense
Debit	Credit

EXERCISE 3-22A or 3-22B (cont.)

C.

Effect of Transactions on the Financial Statements for 20___

	Balance Sheet									Income Statement					Statement of Cash Flows
	Assets			=	Liab.	+	Stockholders' Equity				Rev.	−	Exp.	=	Net Inc.	
No.	Cash	+	Accts. Rec.	=	Acc. Pay.	+	Comm. Stock	+	Ret. Earn.							
Bal.																
1.																
2.																
3.																
4.																
5.																
6.																
Bal.		+		=		+		+				−		=		

3-35

EXERCISE 3-22A or 3-22B (cont.)

d.

Event	Account Titles	Debit	Credit
	Closing Entries		

e.

f.

Trial Balance As of December 31, 2013		
Account Titles	Debit	Credit

EXERCISE 3-23A or 3-23B

a.

Company	Total Debt	÷	Total Assets	=	Debt to Assets Ratio
		÷		=	
		÷		=	

b.

EXERCISE 3-24A or 3-24B

PROBLEM 3-25A or 3-25B

No.	Account	Balance	No.	Account	Balance
a.			k.		
b.			l.		
c.			m.		
d.			n.		
e.			o.		
f.			p.		
g.			q.		
h.			r.		
i.			s.		
j.			t.		
			u.*		

*3-25B

PROBLEM 3-26A or 3-26B

Event	Type of Event	Account Debited	Account Credited
1.			
2.			
3.			
4.			
5.			
6.			
7.			
8.			
9.			
10.			
11.			
12.			
13.			
14.			
15.			

PROBLEM 3-27A or 3-27B

a.

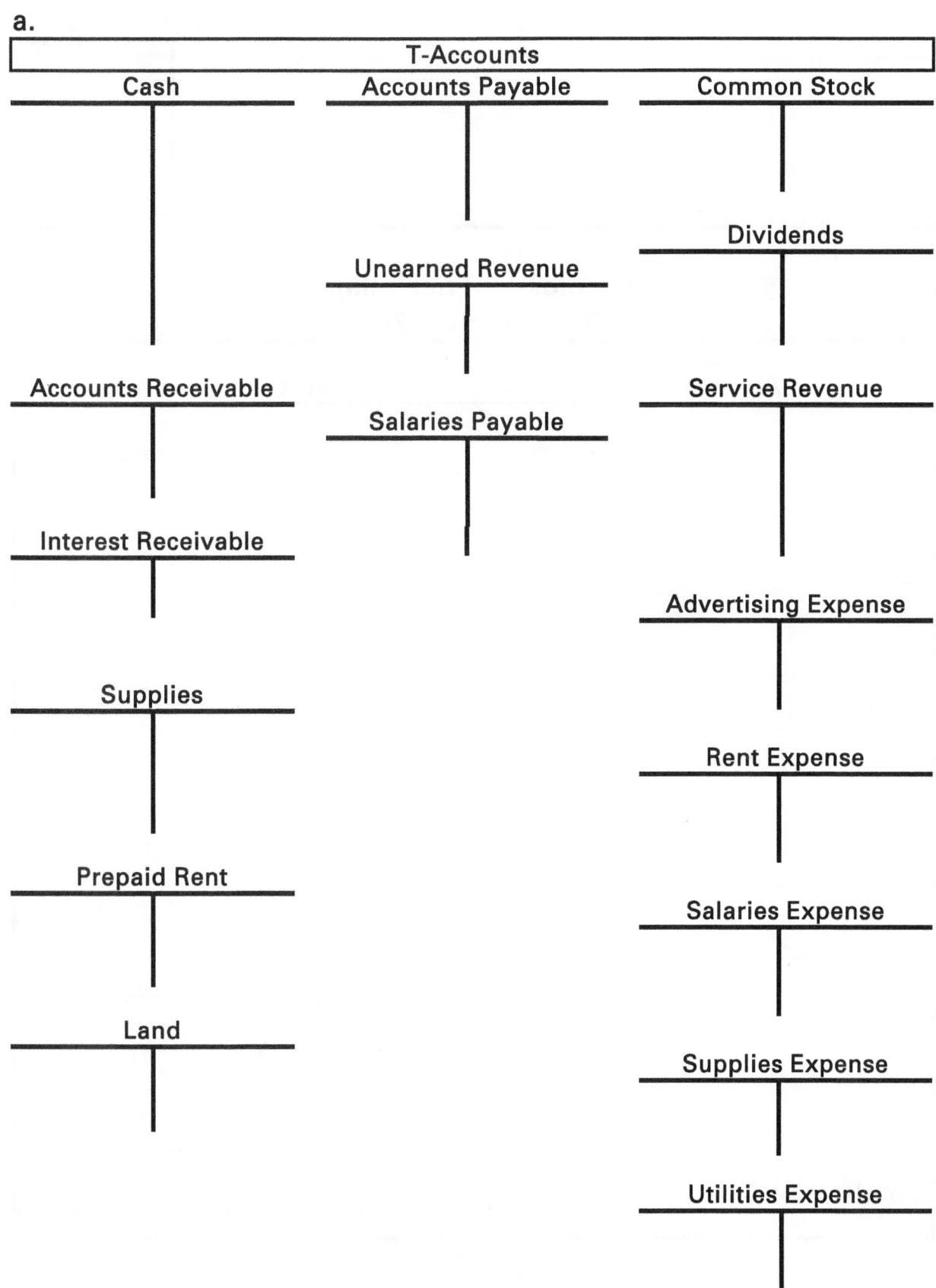

T-Accounts		
Cash	**Accounts Payable**	**Common Stock**
		Dividends
	Unearned Revenue	
Accounts Receivable	**Salaries Payable**	**Service Revenue**
Interest Receivable		
		Advertising Expense
Supplies		
		Rent Expense
Prepaid Rent		**Salaries Expense**
Land		**Supplies Expense**
		Utilities Expense

PROBLEM 3-27A or 3-27B a. (cont.)

Interest Revenue
_____|_____
          |
          |
          |
          |
          |

b.

Post-Closing Trial Balance December 31, 20__		
Account Titles	Debit	Credit
Totals		

PROBLEM 3-27A or 3-27B

c.

	Effect of Transactions on Financial Statements							
	Balance Sheet			**Income Statement**			**Stmt. of**
						Net	**Cash**
Event	Assets	= Liab.	+ S. Equity	Rev.	– Exp.	= Inc.	Flows
1.							
2.							
3.							
4.							
5.							
6.							
7.							
8.							
9.							
10.							
11.							
12.							
13.							
14.							
15.							
16.							
17.							
18.							
19.							

PROBLEM 3-28A or 3-28B

	Effect of Transactions on Financial Statements								
	Balance Sheet				**Income Statement**				**Stmt. of**
Event	**Assets**	**= Liab.**	**+ S. Equity**		**Rev.**	**– Exp.**	**=**	**Net Inc.**	**Cash Flows**
1.									
2.									
3.									
4.									
5.									
6.									
7.									
8.									
9.									
10.									
11.									
12.									
13.									

PROBLEM 3-29A or 3-29B

Entry Date	Description of Transaction

PROBLEM 3-30A or 3-30B

No.	Date	Account Titles	Debit	Credit
a.				
b.				
c.				
d.				

General Journal

PROBLEM 3-31A

a.

b.

Event No.	Assets	=	Liabilities	+	Stk. Equity
1.					
2.					
3.					
4.					
5.					
6.					

c.

Trial Balance As of May 31, 2013		
Account Titles	Debit	Credit
Cash		
Accounts Receivable		
Supplies		
Prepaid Insurance		
Land		
Accounts Payable		
Common Stock		
Retained Earnings		
Dividends		
Service Revenue		
Rent Expense		
Salaries Expense		
Operating Expenses		
Utilities Expense		
Totals		

PROBLEM 3-31B

Corrections:

Corrected Trial Balance:

Zumba Company Trial Balance As of April 30, 2013		
Account Titles	Debit	Credit
Cash		
Accounts Receivable		
Supplies		
Prepaid Insurance		
Land		
Accounts Payable		
Common Stock		
Retained Earnings		
Dividends		
Service Revenue		
Rent Expense		
Salaries Expense		
Operating Expense		
Totals		

PROBLEM 3-32A or 3-32B

a.

General Journal, 20__			
Date	Account Titles	Debit	Credit

PROBLEM 3-32A or 3-32B a. (cont.)

Date	Account Titles	Debit	Credit
	General Journal (continued)		

b.

Sky Training Company T-Accounts

Cash	Accounts Payable	Common Stock

Accounts Receivable	Unearned Revenue	Retained Earnings

	Salaries Payable	Dividends

Prepaid Rent

Service Revenue

Supplies

Rent Expense

Salaries Expense

Supplies Expense

c.

	Debit	Credit
Trial Balance		
December 31, 20__		

Account Titles	Debit	Credit
Totals		

d.

	Financial Statements		
For the Year Ended December 31, 20__			

Income Statement

Statement of Changes in Stockholders' Equity

PROBLEM 3-32A or 3-32B d. (cont.)

	Balance Sheet		
	As of December 31, 20__		

Statement of Cash Flows		
For the Year Ended December 31, 20__		

PROBLEM 3-32A or 3-32B (cont.)

e.

Date	Account Titles	Debit	Credit
	Closing Entries		

Post closing entries to T-accounts in part b.

f.

	Post-Closing Trial Balance December 31, 20__	
Account Titles	Debit	Credit
Totals		

PROBLEM 3-33A or 3-33B

a.

	General Journal, 2013		
Event	Account Titles	Debit	Credit

PROBLEM 3-33A or 3-33B (cont.)

b.

	T-Accounts – 2013	

| Assets | = | Liabilities | + | Stockholders' Equity |

Cash

Accounts Pay.

Common Stock

Service Revenue

Salaries Payable

Accounts Receivable

Unearned Rev.
(3-33A)

Operating Expenses

Prepaid Rent

Rent Expense

Salaries Expense

c.

	Trial Balance December 31, 2013		
Account Titles		Debit	Credit
Totals			

d.

	Financial Statements For the Year Ended December 31, 2013		
Income Statement			
Statement of Changes in Stockholders' Equity			
Beginning Common Stock			
Plus: Stock Issued			
Ending Common Stock			
Beginning Retained Earnings			
Plus: Net Income			
Ending Retained Earnings			
Total Stockholders' Equity			

PROBLEM 3-33A or 3-33B d. (cont.)

	Balance Sheet		
	As of December 31, 2013		

	Statement of Cash Flows For the Year Ended December 31, 2013			
Cash Flows From Operating Activities:			
Cash Flows From Investing Activities			
Cash Flows From Financing Activities:			
Net Change in Cash			
Plus: Beginning Cash Balance			
Ending Cash Balance			

PROBLEM 3-33A or 3-33B (cont.)

e.

Date	Account Titles	Debit	Credit
	Closing Entries		

Post closing entries to T-accounts in part b.

PROBLEM 3-33A or 3-33B (cont.)

f.

Post-Closing Trial Balance December 31, 2013		
Account Titles	Debit	Credit

PROBLEM 3-33A or 3-33B (cont.)

g.

	General Journal, 2014		
Event	Account Titles	Debit	Credit

PROBLEM 3-33A or 3-33B g. (cont.)

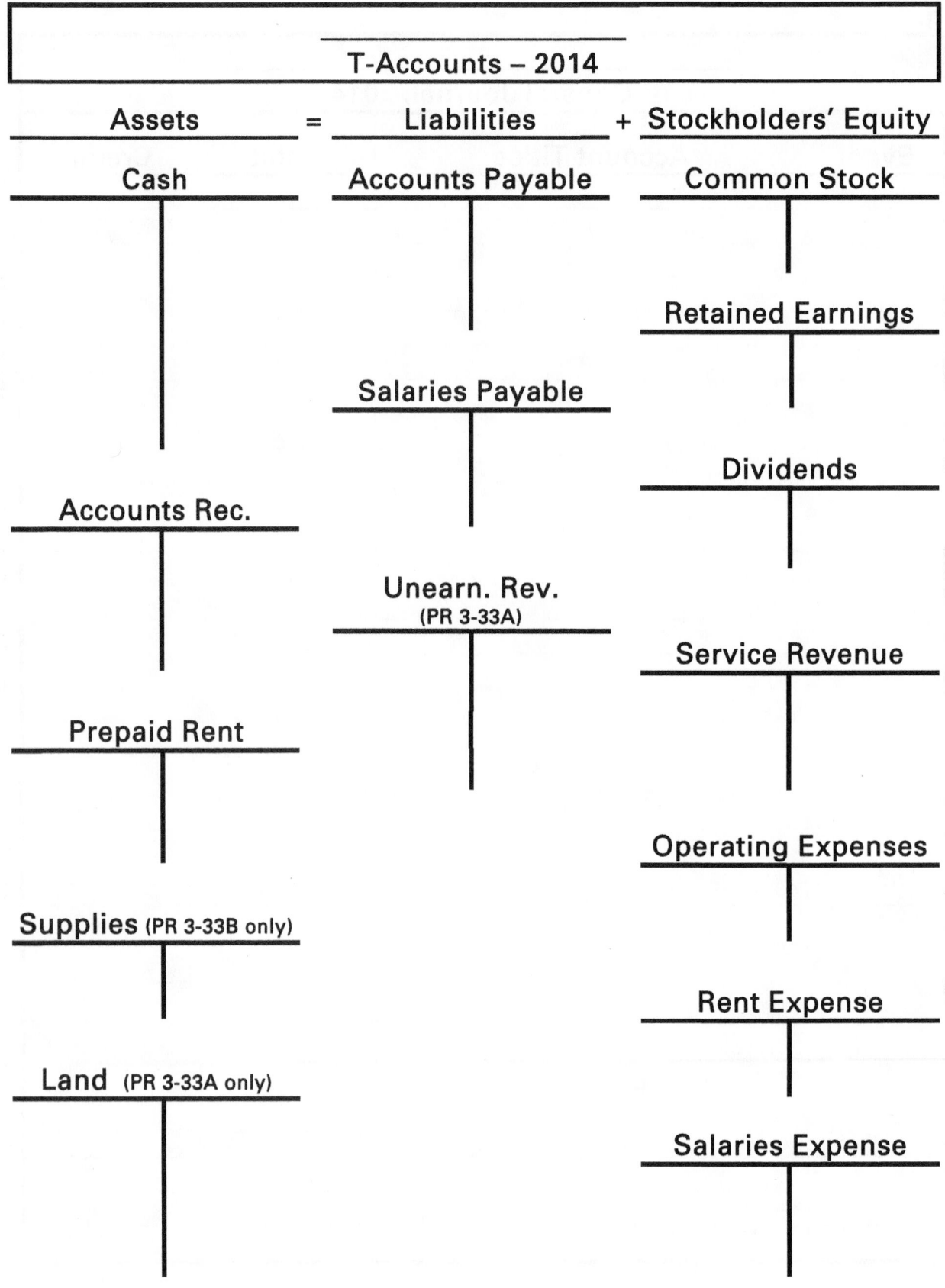

	T-Accounts – 2014	
Assets =	**Liabilities** +	**Stockholders' Equity**
Cash	Accounts Payable	Common Stock
	Salaries Payable	Retained Earnings
Accounts Rec.		Dividends
	Unearn. Rev. (PR 3-33A)	Service Revenue
Prepaid Rent		Operating Expenses
Supplies (PR 3-33B only)		Rent Expense
Land (PR 3-33A only)		Salaries Expense

PROBLEM 3-33A or 3-33B g. (cont.)

Supplies Exp.
(PR 3-33B)

Trial Balance
December 31, 2014

Account Titles	Debit	Credit
Totals		

Financial Statements
For the Year Ended December 31, 2014

Income Statement

Statement of Changes in Stockholders' Equity

Beginning Common Stock		
Plus: Stock Issued		
Ending Common Stock		
Beginning Retained Earnings		
Plus: Net Income		
Less: Dividends		
Ending Retained Earnings		
Total Stockholders' Equity		

Balance Sheet		
As of December 31, 2014		

Statement of Cash Flows
For the Year Ended December 31, 2014

Cash Flows From Operating Activities:

Cash Flows From Investing Activities

Cash Flows From Financing Activities:

Net Change in Cash

Plus: Beginning Cash Balance

Ending Cash Balance

PROBLEM 3-33A or 3-33B g. (cont.)

Date	Account Titles	Debit	Credit
	Closing Entries		

Note: Post closing entries to the T-accounts in part g.

PROBLEM 3-33 or 3-33B g. (cont.)

	Post-Closing Trial Balance December 31, 2014	
Account Titles	Debit	Credit
Totals		

PROBLEM 3-34A or 3-34B

a.

Debt to Assets Ratio:

Company	Total Debt	÷ Total Assets	= Debt to Assets Ratio

Return on Equity Ratio:

Company	Net Income	÷	Equity	= Return on Equity Ratio

b.

c.

d.

e.

PROBLEM 3-35A or 3-35B

	General Journal, 20__		
Event	Account Titles	Debit	Credit

PROBLEM 3-36A or 3-36B

| | General Journal, 20__ | | |
Event	Account Titles	Debit	Credit

T-Accounts – 2013

Assets	=	Liabilities	+	Stockholders' Equity

Cash

Unearned Revenue

Common Stock

Retained Earnings

Prepaid Insurance

Service Revenue

Supplies

Salaries Expense

Depreciation Expense

Rent/Insurance Expense

Accumulated Depr.

Supplies Expense

PROBLEM 3-36A or 3-36B (cont.)

b.

	Financial Statements For the Year Ended December 31, 2013	
Income Statement		

PROBLEM 3-36A or 3-36B b. (cont.)

Balance Sheet			
As of December 31, 2013			

Statement of Cash Flows
For the Year Ended December 31, 2013

ATC 3-2

a.

Miller Company
T-Accounts, 2013

Assets	=	Liabilities	+	Stockholders' Equity

Cash

Accounts Pay.

Common Stock

Retained Earnings

Accounts Receivable

Service Revenue

Prepaid Rent

Operating Expenses

Land

Rent Expense

ATC 3-2 a. (cont.)

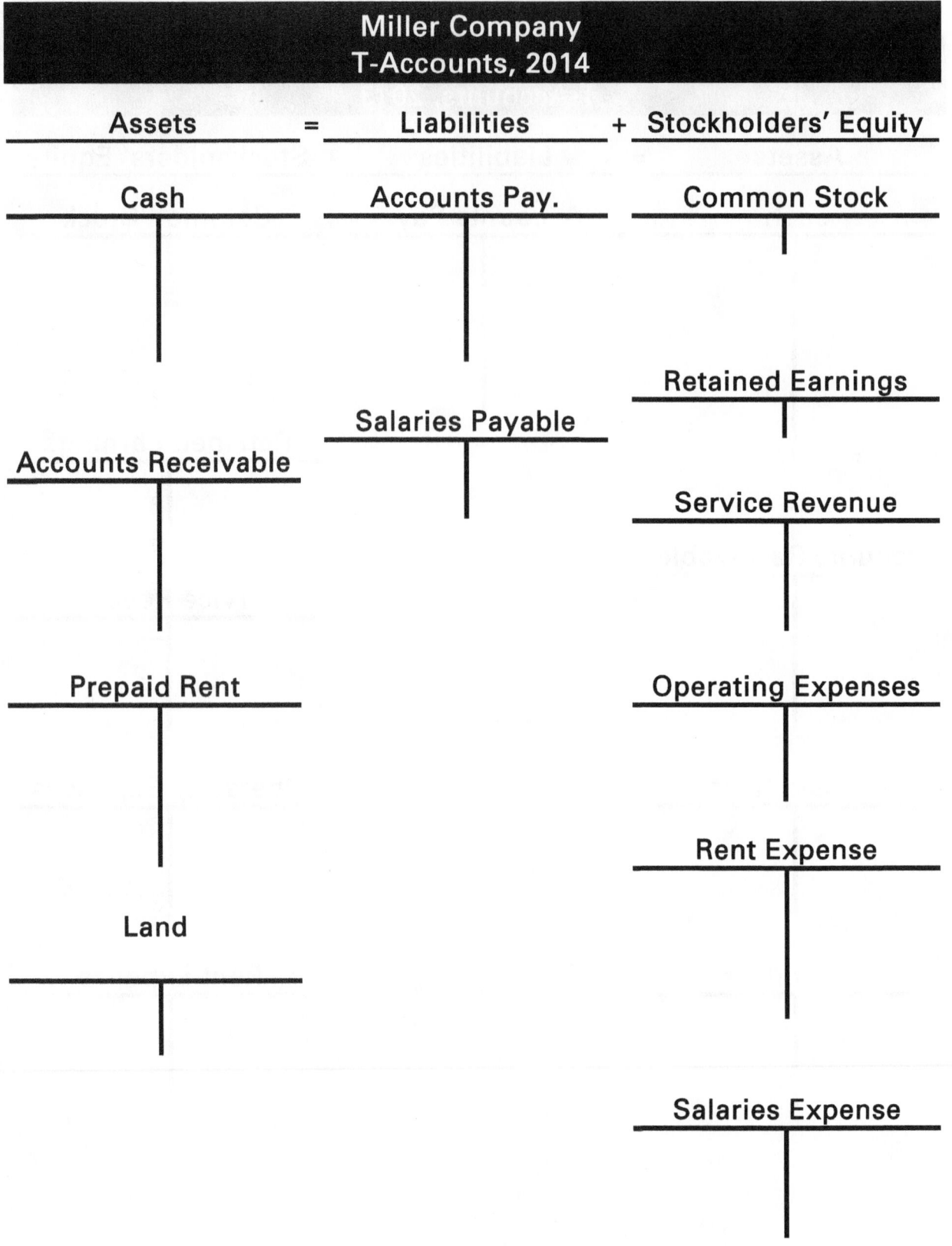

Miller Company
T-Accounts, 2014

| Assets | = | Liabilities | + | Stockholders' Equity |

Cash

Accounts Pay.

Common Stock

Retained Earnings

Salaries Payable

Accounts Receivable

Service Revenue

Prepaid Rent

Operating Expenses

Rent Expense

Land

Salaries Expense

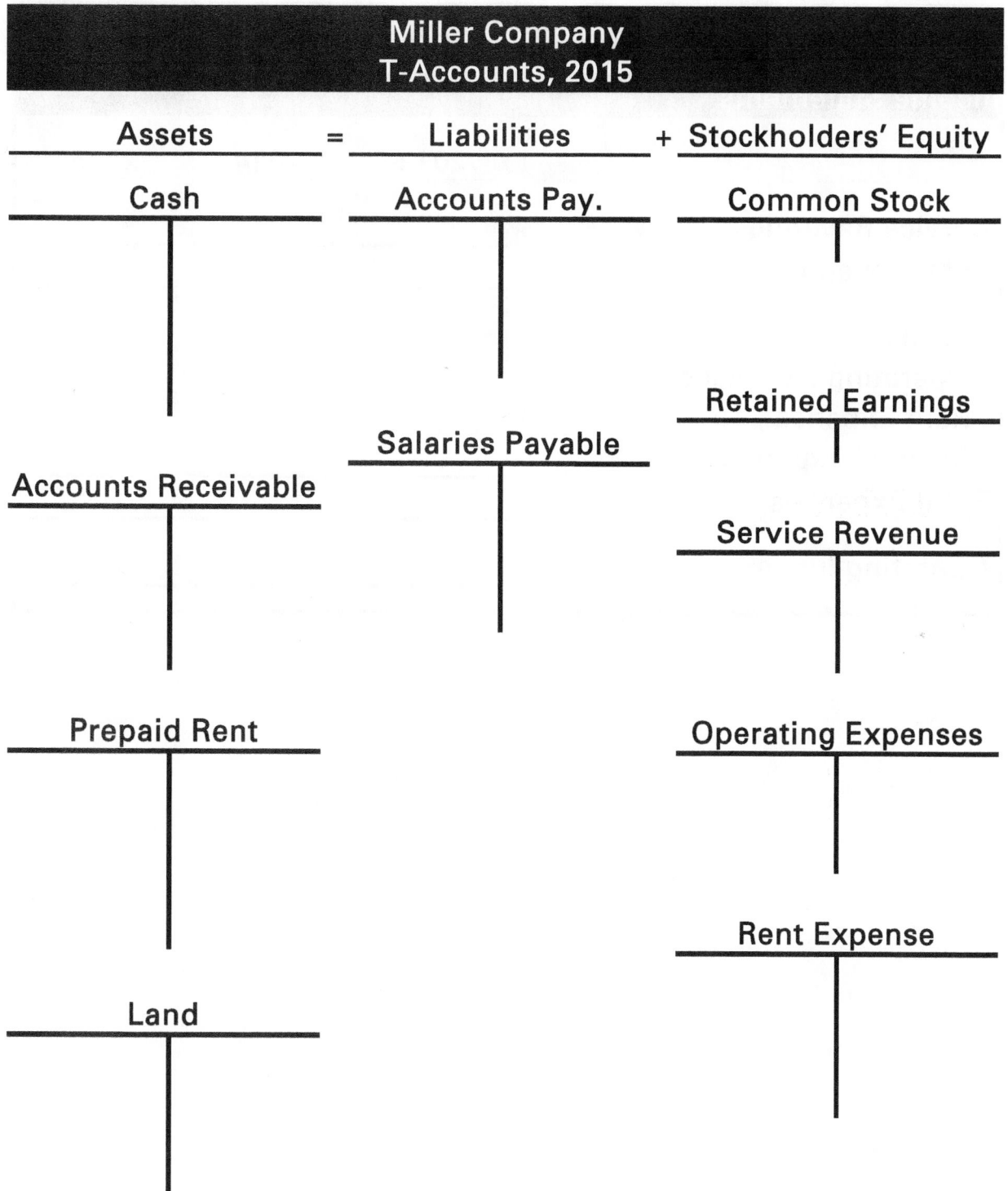

Miller Company
T-Accounts, 2015

| Assets | = | Liabilities | + | Stockholders' Equity |

Cash

Accounts Pay.

Common Stock

Retained Earnings

Salaries Payable

Accounts Receivable

Service Revenue

Prepaid Rent

Operating Expenses

Rent Expense

Land

ATC 3-2 a. (cont.)

Miller Company			
Income Statements			
	2013	**2014**	**2015**
Service Revenue			
Total Revenue			
Expenses			
Operating Expenses			
Rent Expense			
Salaries Expense			
Total Expenses			
Operating Income			

Miller Company			
Balance Sheets			
	2013	**2014**	**2015**
Assets			
Total Assets			
Liabilities			
Total Liabilities			
Stockholders' Equity			
Total Stockholders' Equity			
Total Liab. and Stockholders' Equity			

ATC 3-2 a. (cont.)

Miller Company			
Statements of Cash Flows			
	2013	2014	2015
Cash Flow from Operating Act.			
Net Cash Flow from Operating Act.			
Cash Flow From Investing Act.			
Net Cash Flow from Investing Act.			
Cash Flow From Financing Act.			
Net Change in Cash			
Add Beginning Cash			
Ending Cash Balance			

b.

c.

d.

ATC 3-3

ATC 3-3 (cont.)

ATC 3-4

a. **First compute Netflix's liabilities:**

	Assets	–	Stockholders' Equity	=	Liabilities
2010:					
2009:					

Debt to assets:
    2010:
    2009:

Return on assets:
    2010:
    2009:

Return on equity:
    2010:
    2009:

b.

c.

d.

ATC 3-5

a. **Debt to Assets Ratio:**   Total debt ÷ Total assets

   Biogen Idec
   Amgen

   Return on Assets Ratio: Net Income ÷ Assets

   Biogen Idec
   Amgen

   Return on Equity Ratio: Net income ÷ Equity

   Biogen Idec
   Amgen

b.

c.

d.

ATC 3-6

ATC 3-7

a. This answer represents one acceptable solution out of many possible alternatives. Eight identifiable events for Argon and seven for Rogan are shown below under accounting equations. The financial statements on the following pages are drawn from the information contained in the equations. Note that the unit of measure is "sheep" rather than "dollars." The value of the land provided by the father's initial contribution had to be estimated. Since Argon purchased additional land at a price of 2 sheep per acre, the father's contribution, which occurred on the same day, was assumed to have the same value (i.e., 2 sheep per acre).

		ARGON													
		ASSETS					=	LIABILITIES		+	STK. EQUITY				
	Explanation	Sheep	+	Land	+	Fence	=	Sheep Pay.	+	Int. Pay	+	Com. Stock	+	Ret. Ear.	
1.	Acq.from Owner														
2.	Purchase Land														
3.	Sold Land														
4.	Sheep Revenue														
5.	Purchase Fence														
6.	Loan														
7.	Interest Expense														
8.	Fence Used														
	Ending Balances		+		+		=		+		+		+		

		ROGAN							
		ASSETS			=	LIAB.	+	STK. EQUITY	
1.	Explanation	Sheep	+	Land	=		+	Com Stk	+ Ret. Ear.
2.	Acq. from Owner								
3.	Sheep Revenue								
4.	Dead Sheep Expense								
5.	Predator Expense								
6.	Acquired from Wife								
7.	Sheep Revenue								
	Ending Balances		+		=		+		+

ARGON
FINANCIAL STATEMENTS

Income Statement	Balance Sheet	Sheep Flow Statement
Rev.	Assets:	Operating Act.
Gain	Sheep	Inflow from Rev.
Int. Exp.	Fence	Investing Act.
Fence Exp.	Land	Purchased Land
Net Inc.	Total Assets	Built Fence
		Sold Land
	Liabilities	Net from Inv.
	Sheep Pay.	Financing Act.
	Int. Pay.	Owner Invest.
	Stk. Equity	Borrowing
	Com. Stock	Net from Fin.
	Ret. Ear.	Net Change in Sheep
	Total Liab. & S. Eq.	

ROGAN
FINANCIAL STATEMENTS

Income Statement	Balance Sheet	Sheep Flow Statement
Rev.	Assets:	Operating Act.
Dead S. Ex.	Sheep	Inflow from Rev.
Pred. Exp.	Land	Outflow for Exp.
Net Inc.	Total Assets	Net from Oper.
	Stk. Equity	Financing Activity
	Com. Stock	Acq. from Owner
	Ret. Earn.	Acq. from Owner Wife
	Total Liab. & Eq.	Net Change in Sheep

ATC 3-7 (cont.)

ATC 3-7 (cont.)

ATC 3-8

SOLUTION TO COMPREHENSIVE PROBLEM – CHAPTER 3

a.

	Pacilio Security Services, Inc. General Journal, 2013		
Event	Account title	Debit	Credit
1.			
2.			
3.			
4.			
5.			
6.			
7.			
8.			
9.			
10.			
11.			
12.			

Event	Account title	Debit	Credit
13.	No Entry		
14.			
15.			
16.			
17.			

**Pacilio Security Services, Inc.
General Journal, 2013**

b.

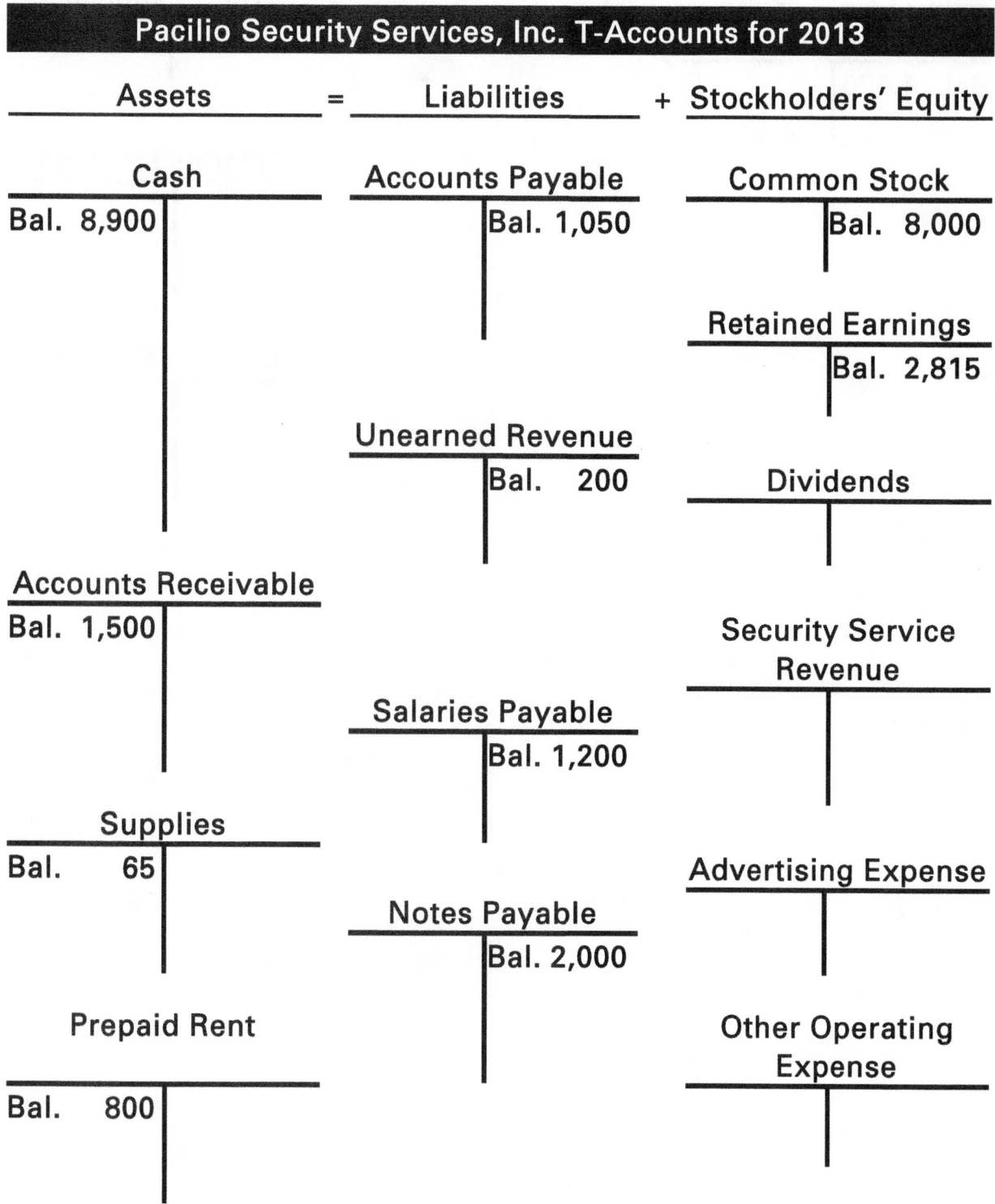

Pacilio Security Services, Inc. T-Accounts for 2013		

Assets = **Liabilities** + **Stockholders' Equity**

Cash
Bal. 8,900 |

Accounts Payable
| Bal. 1,050

Common Stock
| Bal. 8,000

Retained Earnings
| Bal. 2,815

Unearned Revenue
| Bal. 200

Dividends

Accounts Receivable
Bal. 1,500 |

Security Service Revenue

Salaries Payable
| Bal. 1,200

Supplies
Bal. 65 |

Advertising Expense

Notes Payable
| Bal. 2,000

Prepaid Rent
Bal. 800 |

Other Operating Expense

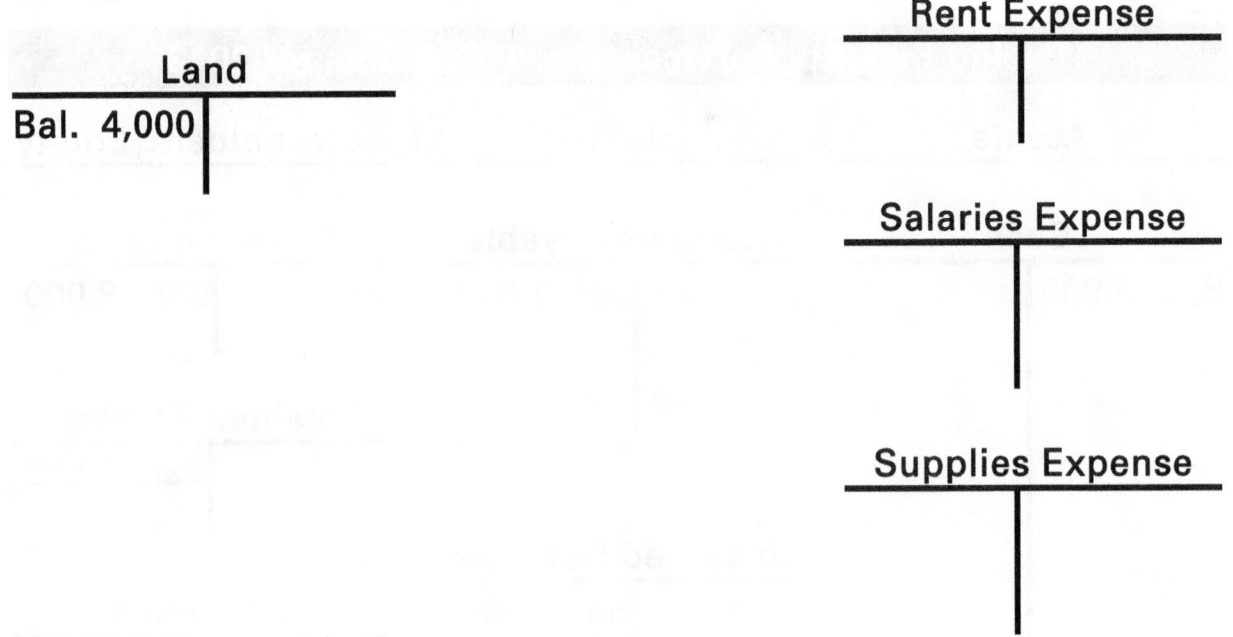

Land

Bal. 4,000

Rent Expense

Salaries Expense

Supplies Expense

COMPREHENSIVE PROBLEM – CHAPTER 3 (cont.)

c.

Pacilio Security Services, Inc. Trial Balance December 31, 2013		
Cash		
Accounts Receivable		
Supplies		
Prepaid Rent		
Land		
Unearned Revenue		
Salaries Payable		
Common Stock		
Retained Earnings		
Dividends		
Security Service Revenue		
Advertising Expense		
Other Operating Expense		
Rent Expense		
Salaries Expense		
Supplies Expense		
Totals		

d.

Pacilio Security Services, Inc. Income Statement For the Year Ended December 31, 2013		

Pacilio Security Services, Inc. Statement of Changes in Stockholders' Equity For the Year Ended December 31, 2003		
Beginning Common Stock		
Plus: Common Stock Issued		
Ending Common Stock		
Beginning Retained Earnings		
Plus: Net Income		
Less: Dividends		
Ending Retained Earnings		
Total Stockholders' Equity		

Pacilio Security Services, Inc.
Balance Sheet
As of December 31, 2013

Pacilio Security Services, Inc. Statement of Cash Flows For the Year Ended December 31, 2013		
Cash Flows From Operating Activities:		
Cash Receipts from Customers[1]		
Cash Payment for Expenses[2]		
Net Cash Flow from Operating Activities		
Cash Flows From Investing Activities:		
Cash Flows From Financing Activities:		
Net Cash Flow from Financing Activities		
Net Increase in Cash		
Plus: Beginning Cash Balance		
Ending Cash Balance		

[1]Cash Receipts from Customers:	
Total Cash from Customers	
[2]Cash Payment for Expenses	
Total Cash Payment for Expenses	

COMPREHENSIVE PROBLEM – CHAPTER 3 (cont.)

e.

Date	Account Titles	Debit	Credit
	Closing Entries		

Post closing entries to T-accounts in part b.

f.

Pacilio Security Services, Inc. Post-Closing Trial Balance December 31, 2013		
Totals		

EXERCISE 4-1A or 4-1B

a.

Income Statement		
Revenue		
Net Income		

Balance Sheet		
Assets		
Total Assets		
Liabilities		
Total Liabilities		
Stockholders' Equity		
Retained Earnings		
Total Stockholders' Equity		
Total Liab. and Stockholders' Equity		

EXERCISE 4-1A or 4-1B a. (cont.)

Statement of Cash Flows For the Year Ended 2013		
Cash Flows From Operating Activities:		
Net Cash Flow from Operating Activ.		
Cash Flows From Investing Activities		-0-
Cash Flows From Financing Activities:		
Net Cash Flow from Financing Activ.		
Net Increase in Cash		
Plus: Beginning Cash Balance		
Ending Cash Balance		

EXERCISE 4-1A or 4-1B a. (cont.)

Income Statement

Net Sales		
Cost of Goods Sold		
Gross Margin		
Expenses		
Operating Expenses		
Net Income		

Balance Sheet

Assets		
Cash		
Merchandise Inventory		
Total Assets		
Liabilities		
Notes Payable		
Total Liabilities		
Stockholders' Equity		
Retained Earnings		
Total Stockholders' Equity		
Total Liab. and Stockholders' Equity		

Statement of Cash Flows		
Cash Flows From Operating Activities:		
Net Cash Flow from Operating Activities		
Cash Flows From Investing Activities		
Cash Flows From Financing Activities:		
Inflow from Loan		
Net Cash Flow from Financing Activities		
Net Increase in Cash		
Plus: Beginning Cash Balance		
Ending Cash Balance		

b.

c.

d.

EXERCISE 4-2A or 4-2B

a.

	General Journal, 20___		
Date	Account Titles	Debit	Credit
1.			
2.			
3a.			
3b.			

b.

T-Accounts

Assets   =   Stockholders' Equity

Cash

Merchandise Inventory

Common Stock

Sales Revenue

Cost of Goods Sold

EXERCISE 4-2A or 4-2B (cont.)

c.

Income Statement		
For the Year Ended December 31, 20__		
Net Sales		
Cost of Goods Sold		
Gross Margin		
Operating Expenses		
Net Income		

4-2A

d. Total assets:

4-2B

d.

Cash Flows from Operating Activities:		

EXERCISE 4-3A or 4-3B

a.

Effect of Events on the Financial Statements

	Balance Sheet							Income Statement					Cash Flows
	Assets			=	Liab.	+	Stkholders' Equity						
Events	Cash	+ A. Rec.	+ Mdse. Inv.	=	A. Pay.	+	C. Stk.	+ Ret. Ear.	Rev.	– Exp.	= Net Inc.		
Beg. Bal.	+	+	+	=	+			+					
1.	+	+	+	=	+			+	–	=			
2a.	+	+	+	=	+			+	–	=			
2b.	+	+	+	=	+			+	–	=			
3.	+	+	+	=	+			+	–	=			
4.	+	+	+	=	+			+	–	=			
5.	+	+	+	=	+			+	–	=			
End. Bal.	+	+	+	=	+			+	–	=			

b.

c.

d.

Computation of Net Income

e.

Cash Flows from Operating Activities:

EXERCISE 4-3A or 4-3B (cont.)

f.

EXERCISE 4-4A or 4-4B

a.

	General Journal for 2013		
Date	Account Titles	Debit	Credit
1.			
2.			
3a.			
3b.			
4.			

b.

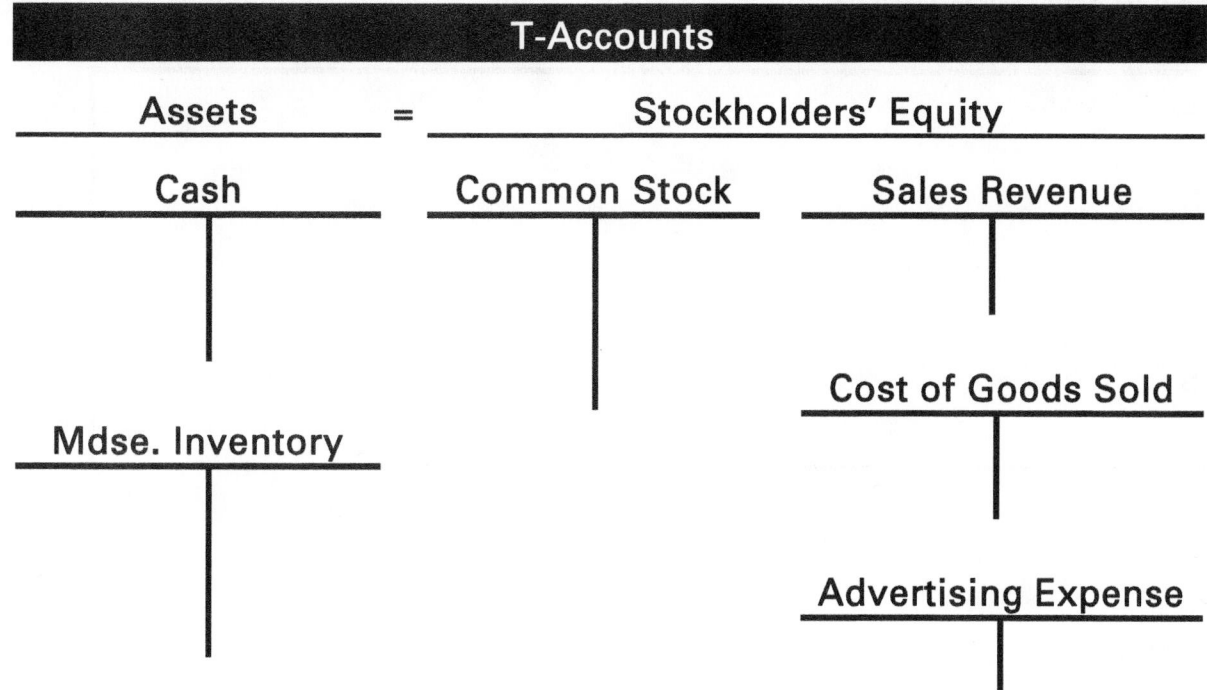

T-Accounts

Assets = Stockholders' Equity

Cash   Common Stock   Sales Revenue

Mdse. Inventory   Cost of Goods Sold

Advertising Expense

EXERCISE 4-4A or 4-4B (cont.)

c.

Account Titles	Debit	Credit
Trial Balance		
December 31, 20__		
Totals		

EXERCISE 4-5A or 4-5B

a.	
b.	
c.	
d.	

EXERCISE 4-6A

a.

Calculation of Ending Inventory	
Beginning balance in inventory	
From item 1:	
From item 2	
Total cost of inventory	
Cost of inventory sold	
Ending balance in inventory	

b.

_____

_____

_____

_____

c.

Net Sales	
Cost of goods sold	
Gross Margin	

EXERCISE 4-6B

a. & b.

Computation of Ending Inventory		
	Mona's Dress Shop	Ben's Boap Shop
Beginning balance in inventory		
Plus: Purchases		
Less: Purchase Returns and Allow.		
Less: Purchases Discounts		
Plus: Transportation-In Costs		
Cost of Goods Available for Sale		
Less: Cost of Goods Sold		
Ending Inventory		

EXERCISE 4-7A or 4-7B

a.

	General Journal for 2013		
Date	Account Titles	Debit	Credit
1.			
2.			
3.			
4.			
5a.			
5b.			
6.			
7.			

b.

| T-Accounts |

Assets = Liabilities + Stockholders' Equity

Cash | Accounts Payable | Common Stock

Retained Earnings

Mdse. Inventory | Sales Revenue

Cost of Goods Sold

Transportation-out

EXERCISE 4-7A (cont.)

c.

Income Statement		
Net Sales		
Cost of Goods Sold		
Gross Margin		
Operating Expenses		
Net Income		

Statement of Cash Flows		
Cash Flows From Operating Activities:		
Net Cash Flow from Operating Activities		
Cash Flows From Investing Activities		-0-
Cash Flows From Financing Activities		-0-
Net Change in Cash		
Plus: Beginning Cash Balance		
Ending Cash Balance		

d.

EXERCISE 4-7B (cont.)

c.

Austin's Shoe Shop Financial Statements		
Income Statement		
Net Sales		
Cost of Goods Sold		
Gross Margin		
Operating Expenses		
Transportation-out		
Net Income		
Balance Sheet		
Assets		
Total Assets		
Liabilities		
Stockholders' Equity		
Total Stockholders' Equity		
Total Liab. and Stockholders' Equity		

EXERCISE 4-7B c. (cont.)

Austin's Auto Shop Statement of Cash Flows		
Cash Flows From Operating Activities:		
Net Cash Flow from Operating Activities		
Cash Flows From Investing Activities		-0-
Cash Flows From Financing Activities		-0-
Net Change in Cash		
Plus: Beginning Cash Balance		
Ending Cash Balance		

d.

EXERCISE 4-8A or 4-8B

Transaction	Debited to Inventory
a.	
b.	
c.	
d.	
e.	
f.	

EXERCISE 4-9A or 4-9B

a.

Transaction	Period Costs	Product Costs	Not Applicable
1.			
2.			
3.			
4.			
5.			
6.			
7.			
8.			
9.			
10.			

EXERCISE 4-9A or 4-9B (cont.)

b.

Statements Model for 2013

	Balance Sheet								Income Statement			Statement of Cash Flows
	Assets			=	Liab.	+	Stkholders' Equity		Rev.	– Exp.	= Net Inc.	
	Cash	+ A. Rec.	+ Mdse. Inv.	=	A. Pay.	+	C. Stk.	+ Ret. Ear.				
1.	+	+	+	=	+	+	+	+		–	=	
2.	+	+	+	=	+	+	+	+		–	=	
3.	+	+	+	=	+	+	+	+		–	=	
4.	+	+	+	=	+	+	+	+		–	=	
5a.	+	+	+	=	+	+	+	+		–	=	
5b.	+	+	+	=	+	+	+	+		–	=	
6.	+	+	+	=	+	+	+	+		–	=	
7.	+	+	+	=	+	+	+	+		–	=	
8.	+	+	+	=	+	+	+	+		–	=	
9.	+	+	+	=	+	+	+	+		–	=	
10.	+	+	+	=	+	+	+	+		–	=	
End. Bal.	+	+	+	=	+	+	+	+		–	=	

EXERCISE 4-10A or 4-10B

a. Computation of net amount due:

b.

Events	Balance Sheet								Income Statement			Stmt. of Cash Flows
	Assets			Liab.	+	Stkholders' Equity			Rev.	–	Exp. = Net Inc.	
	Cash	+	Mdse. Inv.	= A. Pay.	+	C. Stk.	+	Ret. Ear.				
1.		+	+	= +			+	+				
2.		+	+	= +			+	+			=	
3a. Disc.		+	+	= +			+	+	–		=	
3b. Pd. AP											=	

c. Computation of amount of cash paid:

4-20

EXERCISE 4-10A or 4-10B (cont.)

d.

Events	Balance Sheet					Income Statement			Stmt. Of Cash Flows
	Assets		Liab.	+	Stkholders' Equity	Rev.	– Exp.	= Net Inc.	
	Cash	+ Mdse. Inv.	= A. Pay.	+	C. Stk. + Ret. Ear.				
3. Pd. AP	+	+	=		+	+		–	=	

e.

EXERCISE 4-11A

Event No.	Event Type	Assets	= Liab.	+ S. Equity	Rev.	– Exp.	= Net Inc.	Cash Flow
1.								
2a.								
2b.								
3.								
4.								
5.								
6.								
7a.								
7b.								
8.								
9.								
10.								

EXERCISE 4-11B

Event No.	Event Type	Assets	=	Liab.	+	S. Equity	Rev.	−	Exp.	=	Net Inc.	Cash Flow
1.												
2a.												
2b.												
3.												
4.												
5a.												
5b.												
6.												
7.												
8.												
9.												
10.												

EXERCISE 4-12A or 4-12B

a.

Income Statement		
Sales Revenue		
Cost of Goods Sold		
Gross Margin		
Expenses		
Operating Expenses		
Net Operating Income		
Non-Operating Items		
Gain on the Sale of Land		
Net Income		

b.

Income Statement		
Sales Revenue		
Cost of Goods Sold		
Gross Margin		
Expenses		
Operating Expenses		
Net Operating Income		
Non-Operating Items		-0-
Net Income		

EXERCISE 4-12A or 4-12B (cont.)

c.

d.

EXERCISE 4-13A

a. Determine Cost of Inventory:

Sawyer Merchandisers	
Cost of inventory purchase	
Minus Purchase returns	
Minus Purchase discounts	
Total cost of the inventory	

b.

Sawyer Merchandisers Income Statement	
Net Sales	
Cost of Goods Sold	
Gross Margin	
Operating Expenses	
Operating Income	
Nonoperating items	
Net Income	

c.

d.

e.

EXERCISE 4-13B

a. Compute Net Sales:

Foster Merchandisers	
Gross Sales	
Less: Sales Returns	
Less: Sales discounts	
Net Sales	

b.

Foster Merchandisers Income Statement	
Net Sales	
Cost of Goods Sold*	
Gross Margin	
Operating Expenses	
Operating Income	
Nonoperating items	
Net Income	

c.

d.

e.

EXERCISE 4-14A

a.

Financial Statements Model

Event No.	Cash	+	Inv.	+	Land	+	Accts. Pay.	=	Common Stock	+	Retained Earnings		Rev./ Gain	−	Exp.	=	Net Inc.		Cash Flow
Bal.	+		+			+		=		+	+			−		=			
1.	+		+					=		+	+			−		=			
2.	+		+					=		+	+			−		=			
3.	+							=		+	+			−		=			
4a.	+		+					=		+	+			−		=			
4b.	+		+					=		+	+			−		=			
5a.	+		+					=		+	+			−		=			
5b.	+		+					=		+	+			−		=			
6.	+		+					=		+	+			−		=			
7.	+							=		+	+			−		=			
8.	+		+					=		+	+			−		=			
Bal.	+		+					=		+	+			−		=			

4-28

EXERCISE 4-14A (cont.)

b.

The Wedding Shop Income Statement				
Net Sales				
Cost of Goods Sold				
Gross Margin				
Operating Expenses				
Total Operating Expenses				
Operating Income				
Non-Operating Items				
Net Income				

c.

d.

a.

Financial Statements Model

Event No.	Cash	+	Accts. Rec	+	Inv.	+	Land	=	Common Stock	+	Retained Earnings		Rev./Gain	−	Exp.	=	Net Inc.	Cash Flow
Bal.	+	+		+	+		+	=		+								
1.	+	+	+	+	+	+	+	=	=	+	+		•		•	=		
2.	+	+	+	+	+	+	+	=	=	+	+		•		•	=		
3a.	+	+	+	+	+	+	+	=	=	+	+		•		•	=		
3b.	+	+	+	+	+	+	+	=	=	+	+		•		•	=		
4a.	+	+	+	+	+	+	+	=	=	+	+		•		•	=		
4b.					+			=	=		+							
5.	+	+	+	+	+	+	+	=	=	+	+		•		•	=		
6a*	+	+	+	+	+	+	+	=	=	+	+		•		•	=		
6b.	+	+	+	+	+	+	+	=	=	+	+		•		•	=		
7.	+	+	+	+	+	+	+	=	=	+	+		•		•	=		
8.	+	+	+	+	+	+	+	=	=	+	+		•		•	=		
Bal.	+	+	+	+	+	+	+	=	=	+	+							

b.

Power Buys Calculation of Net Sales For the Year Ended December 31, 2013		
Sales		
Less: Sales Returns		
Less: Sales Discounts		
Net Sales		

c.

Power Buys Income Statement			
Net Sales			
Cost of Goods Sold*			
Gross Margin			
Operating Expenses			
Total Operating Expenses			
Operating Income			
Non-Operating Items			
Net Income			

d.

e.

EXERCISE 4-15A or 4-15B

Single-Step Income Statement:

Income Statement			
Net Sales			
Expenses			
Total Expenses			
Net Income (Loss)			

Multistep Income Statement:

Income Statement			
Net Sales			
Cost of Goods Sold			
Gross Margin			
Operating Expenses			
Total Operating Expenses			
Operating Income (Loss)			
Non-Operating Expenses			
Net Income (Loss)			

EXERCISE 4-16A or 4-16B

a.

T-Accounts for 2013

Assets	=	Stockholders' Equity

Cash	Common Stock	Sales Revenue

Mdse. Inventory		Cost of Goods Sold

b.

Income Statement	
Net Sales	
Cost of Goods Sold	
Gross Margin	
Operating Expenses	
Net Income	

EXERCISE 4-16A or 4-16B b. (cont.)

	Balance Sheet			
Assets				
Total Assets				
Liabilities				
Stockholders' Equity				
Total Stockholders' Equity				
Total Liab. And Stockholders' Equity				

c.

EXERCISE 4-17A or 4-17B

a.

	General Journal for 2013		
Date	Account Titles	Debit	Credit
1a.			
1b.			
2.			
3a.			
3b.			
4.			
5.			

EXERCISE 4-17A or 4-17B (cont.)

b.

	T-Accounts for 2013	

Assets = **Stockholders' Equity**

Cash	Common Stock	Retained Earnings

Accounts Receivable

Sales Revenue

Mdse. Inventory

Cost of Goods Sold

Transportation-out

c.

Financial Statements		
Income Statement		
Net Income		
Balance Sheet		

Financial Statements		
Statement of Cash Flows		

d.

EXERCISE 4-18A or 4-18B

Gross Margin Percentages:	
Company	Percentage

Return on Sales Ratio:	
Company	Ratio

....

....

....

....

b.

Return-on-Equity Ratios:	
Company	Ratio

....

....

....

....

EXERCISE 4-19A or 4-19B

a.

Common Size Income Statements				
Company:		%		%
Sales				
Cost of Goods Sold				
Gross Margin				
Operating Expenses				
Net Income				

b.

Company	
Return on Assets:	
Return on Equity:	

Company	
Return on Assets:	
Return on Equity:	

c.

d.

EXERCISE 4-20A or 4-20B (Appendix)

Beginning Mdse. Inventory	
Plus: Merchandise Purchased	
Goods Available for Sale	
Less: Ending Mdse. Inventory	
Cost of Goods Sold	

a.	Goods Available for Sale	
b.	Cost of Goods Sold	
c.	Merchandise Inventory on year-end balance sheet	

EXERCISE 4-21A or 4-21B (Appendix)

a.

Schedule of Cost of Goods Sold For the Year Ended 20___	
Beginning Merchandise Inventory	
Plus: Purchases	
Plus: Transportation-in	
Less: Purchase Returns and Allowances	
Cost of Goods Available for Sale	
Less: Ending Merchandise Inventory	
Cost of Goods Sold	

b.

Income Statement		
Net Sales Revenue*		
Cost of Goods Sold		
Gross Margin		
Operating Expenses		
Net Income		

*net sales must be computed.

EXERCISE 4-22A or 4-22B (Appendix)

a.

	General Journal for 20____		
Date	Account Titles	Debit	Credit
1.			
2.			
3.			
4.			
5.			
6.			
7.			
8. (adj.)			

Cost of Goods Sold Calculation:	
Beginning Merchandise Inventory	
Owner Contribution	
Purchases	
Goods Available for Sale	
Less: Ending Merchandise Inventory	
Cost of Goods Sold	

EXERCISE 4-22A or 4-22B (Appendix) (cont.)

b.

T-Accounts for 20_____

Assets	=	Liabilities	+	Stockholders' Equity

Cash	Accounts Payable	Common Stock

Merchandise Inventory

Sales Revenue

Cost of Goods Sold

Purchases

Advertising Expense

Salaries Expense

EXERCISE 4-22A or 4-22B (Appendix) (cont.)

c.

Financial Statements		
For the Year Ended December 31, 20____		
Income Statement		
Net Sales		
Cost of Goods Sold		
Gross Margin		
Operating Expenses		
Total Operating Expenses		
Net Income		
Statement of Changes in Stockholders' Equity		
Beginning Common Stock		
Plus: Stock Issued		
Ending Common Stock		
Beginning Retained Earnings		
Plus: Net Income		
Ending Retained Earnings		
Total Stockholders' Equity		

EXERCISE 4-22A or 4-22B (Appendix) c. (cont.)

Financial Statements

Balance Sheet

Statement of Cash Flows

EXERCISE 4-22A or 4-22B (Appendix) (cont.)

d.

	General Journal		
Date	Account Titles	Debit	Credit
	Closing Entries		

EXERCISE 4-22A or 4-22B (Appendix) d. (cont.)

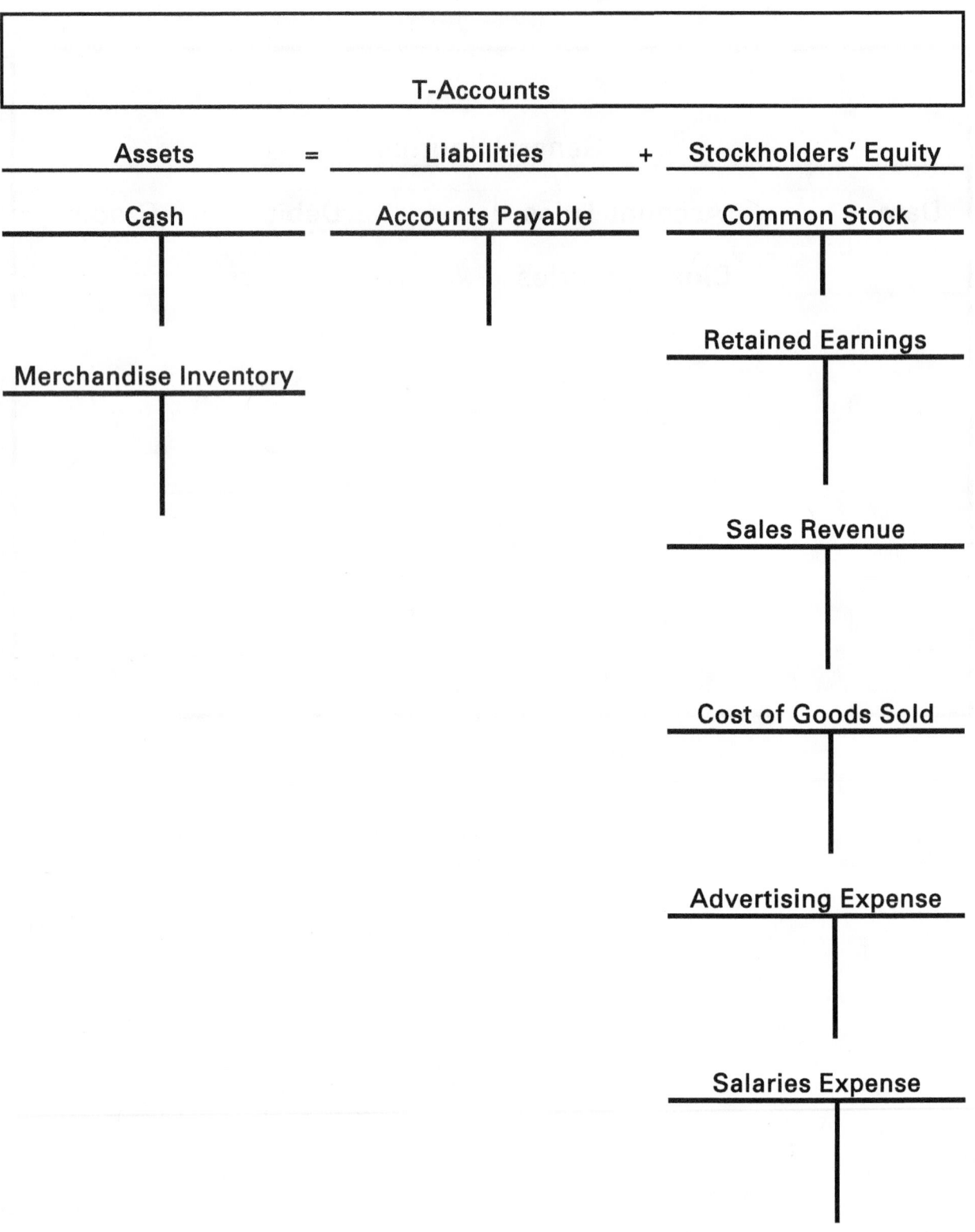

T-Accounts		
Assets =	Liabilities +	Stockholders' Equity
Cash	Accounts Payable	Common Stock
Merchandise Inventory		Retained Earnings
		Sales Revenue
		Cost of Goods Sold
		Advertising Expense
		Salaries Expense

EXERCISE 4-22A or 4-22B (Appendix) (cont.)

e.

Post-Closing Trial Balance As of December 31, 20___		
Account Titles	Debit	Credit

f.

g.

PROBLEM 4-23A or 4-23B

T-accounts are not required but may be useful in working the problem

T-Accounts 2013, 2014, and 2015

Assets	=	Stockholders' Equity

Cash

Common Stock

Retained Earnings

Sales Revenue

Merchandise Inv.

Cost of Goods Sold

Selling and Adm. Exp.

PROBLEM 4-23A or 4-23B (cont.)

Financial Statements

Income Statements

	2013	2014	2015
Net Income			

Balance Sheets

	2013	2014	2015

PROBLEM 4-24A or 4-24B

Event	Freight Costs Paid	Period/Product
a.		
b.		
c.		
d.		

PROBLEM 4-25A or 4-25B

Event	Product Costs	Period Costs
a.		
b.		
c.		
d.		
e.		
f.		
g.		
h.		
i.		
j.		

ROBLEM 4-26A or 4-26B

a. & b.

Common Size Income Statements				
	20__	%	20__	%
Net Sales				
Cost of Goods Sold				
Gross Margin				
Operating Expenses				
Selling and Adm. Exp.				
Operating Income				
Non Operating Items:				
Net Income				

c.

PROBLEM 4-27A or 4-27B

Effect of Events on the Financial Statements for 2013

Event No.	Event Type	Balance Sheet			Income Statement			Statement of Cash Flows
		Assets	= Liab.	+ S. Equity	Rev.	− Exp.	= Net Inc.	
1a.								
1b.								
2.								
3a. Disc								
3b. Pay								
4a. Sale								
4b. Cost								
5a. Ret								
5b. Ret								
6.								
7a. Disc								
7b. Coll								
8.								
9.								
10. Adj								

PROBLEM 4-27A or 4-27B (cont.)

b.

	General Journal -2013		
Date	Account Titles	Debit	Credit
1a.			
1b.			
2.			
3a.			
3b.			
4a.			
4b.			
5a.			
5b.			
6.			
7a.			
7b.			

PROBLEM 4-27A or 4-27B b. (cont.)

Date	Account Titles	Debit	Credit
8.			
9.			
10.			

c.

	T-Accounts for 2013	

Assets	=	Liabilities	+	Stockholders' Equity
Cash		Accounts Payable		Common Stock

Merchandise Inventory

Retained Earnings

Sales Revenue

Accounts Receivable

Cost of Goods Sold

Interest Receivable

Transportation-out

PROBLEM 4-27A or 4-27B c. (cont.)

Land

Interest Revenue

Gain on Sale of Land

PROBLEM 4-27A or 4-27B

d.

Financial Statements
For the Year Ended December 31, 2013

Income Statement

Statement of Changes in Stockholders' Equity

Financial Statements		
Balance Sheet		
Statement of Cash Flows For the Year Ended December 31, 2013		

PROBLEM 4-27A or 4-27B (cont.)

e.

Date	Account Titles	Debit	Credit
	Closing Entries		

Post closing entries to T-Accounts in part c.

	Post Closing Trial Balance **December 31, 2013**		
	Account Titles	Debit	Credit

PROBLEM 4-28A or 4-28B (Appendix)

a.

Schedule of Cost of Goods Sold For Year Ended December 31, 2013	

b.

Income Statement		

c.

Income Statement		

PROBLEM 4-29A or 4-29B (Appendix)

a.

	General Journal, 2013		
Event	Account Titles	Debit	Credit

PROBLEM 4-29A or 4-29B (Appendix) a. (cont.)

	General Journal, 2013		
Event	Account Titles	Debit	Credit

Computation of Cost of Goods Sold:

b.

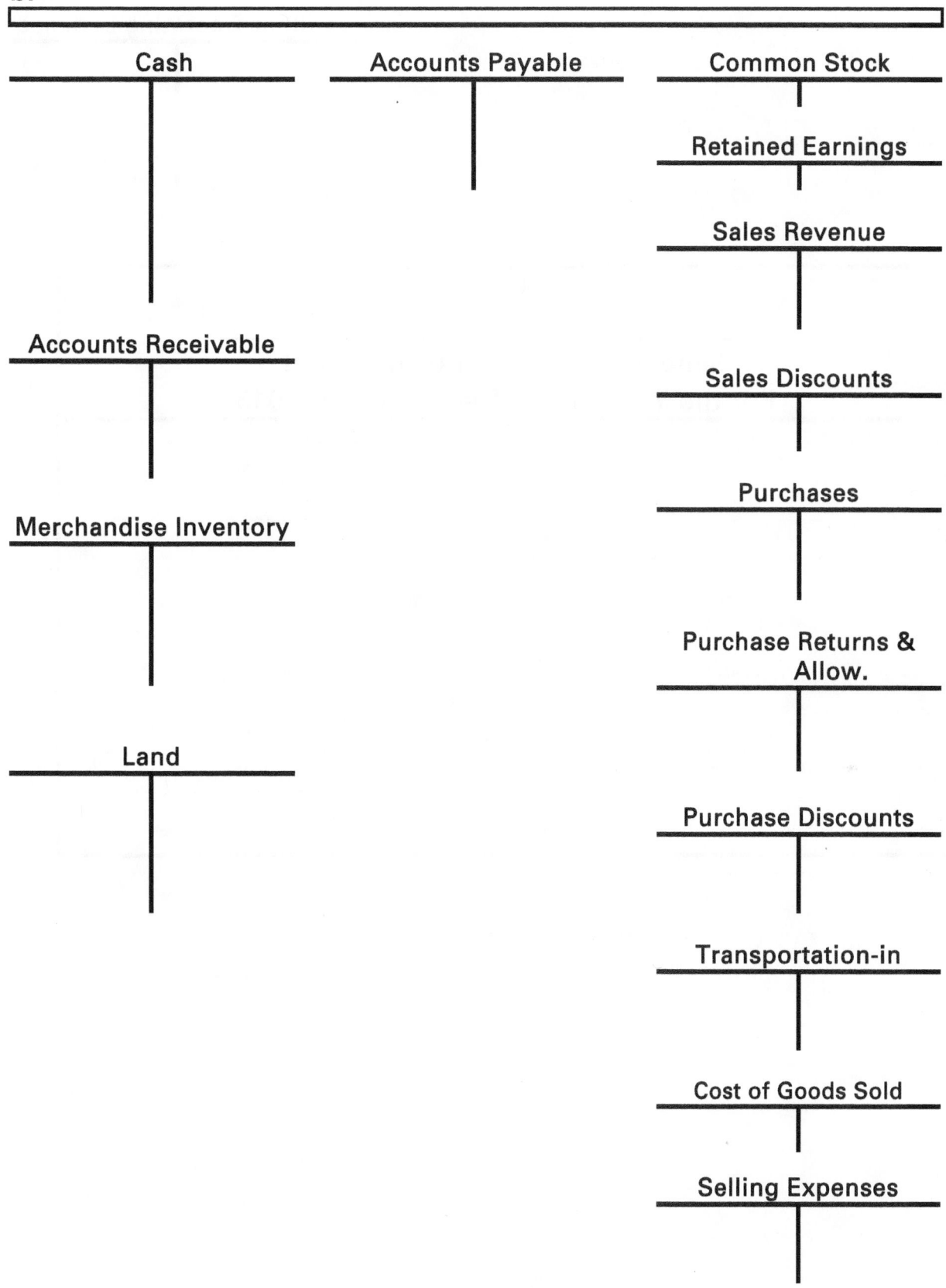

Cash

Accounts Payable

Common Stock

Retained Earnings

Sales Revenue

Accounts Receivable

Sales Discounts

Merchandise Inventory

Purchases

Purchase Returns & Allow.

Land

Purchase Discounts

Transportation-in

Cost of Goods Sold

Selling Expenses

PROBLEM 4-29A or 4-29B (Appendix) b. (cont.)

Other Operating Expense

c.

	Schedule of Cost of Goods Sold For the Year Ended December 31, 2013		

Income Statement			
For the Year Ended December 31, 20___			

Statement of Changes in Stockholders' Equity
For the Year Ended December 31, 20___

| | Balance Sheet | | | |
| | As of December 31, 20____ | | | |

PROBLEM 4-29A or 4-29B (Appendix) c. (cont.)

	Statement of Cash Flows For the Year Ended December 31, 20____		

ATC 4-1

a. Compute Gross Margin:
(All amounts are in thousands)

	Sales	–	Cost of Sales	=	Gross Margin
2010		–		=	
2009		–		=	
		–			

	Gross Margin	÷	Sales	=	Gross Margin %
2010		÷		=	
2009		÷		=	

b.

	Net Income	÷	Sales	=	Return on Sales %
2010		÷		=	
2009		÷		=	

c.

ATC 4-2

a. (1)
Calculate cost of goods sold:

	First Quarter	Second Quarter	Third Quarter	Fourth Quarter
Sales				
Less gross margin				
Cost of goods sold				

Calculate operating expenses:

	First Quarter	Second Quarter	Third Quarter	Fourth Quarter
Gross margin				
Less net income				
Operating expenses				

Multistep income statements

	First Quarter	Second Quarter	Third Quarter	Fourth Quarter
Sales				
Less Cost of goods sold				
Gross margin				
Less operating expenses				
Net income				

a. (2)
Gross margin percentage:

Quarter	Gross Margin	÷	Sales	=	Gross margin %
First		÷		=	
Second		÷		=	
Third		÷		=	
Fourth		÷		=	

ATC 4-2 a. (2) (cont.)

Cost of goods sold percentage:

Quarter	1 – Gross margin %	=	Cost of goods sold %
First		=	
Second		=	
Third		=	
Fourth		=	

b.

ATC 4-3

Sales	A	B	C	D
Cost of Goods Sold				
Gross Margin				

Company

RATIO:	A	B	C	D
Gross Margin				
Return-on-Sales				
Return-on-Assets				

ATC 4-3 (cont.)

ATC 4-4

a. Gross Margin Percentages:

b. Return-on-Sales Ratios:

c.

d.

ATC 4-5

a.

b. Compute Gross Margin Percentages:

Supervalu:

Whole Foods:

c. Compute Return On Sales

d.

ATC 4-6

ATC 4-6 (cont.)

ATC 4-7

ATC 4-7 (cont.)

ATC 4-8

COMPREHENSIVE PROBLEM – CHAPTER 4

a.

	Pacilio Security Services, Inc. General Journal, 2014		
Event	Account title	Debit	Credit
1.			
2.			
3.			
4.			
5.			
6.			
7a.			
7b.			
8.			
9.			
10.			
11.			

	Pacilio Security Services, Inc. General Journal, 2014		
Event	Account Titles	Debit	Credit
12.			
13.			
14.			
15.			
16.			
17.			
18.			
19.			
20.			

COMPREHENSIVE PROBLEM – CHAPTER 4 (cont.)

b.

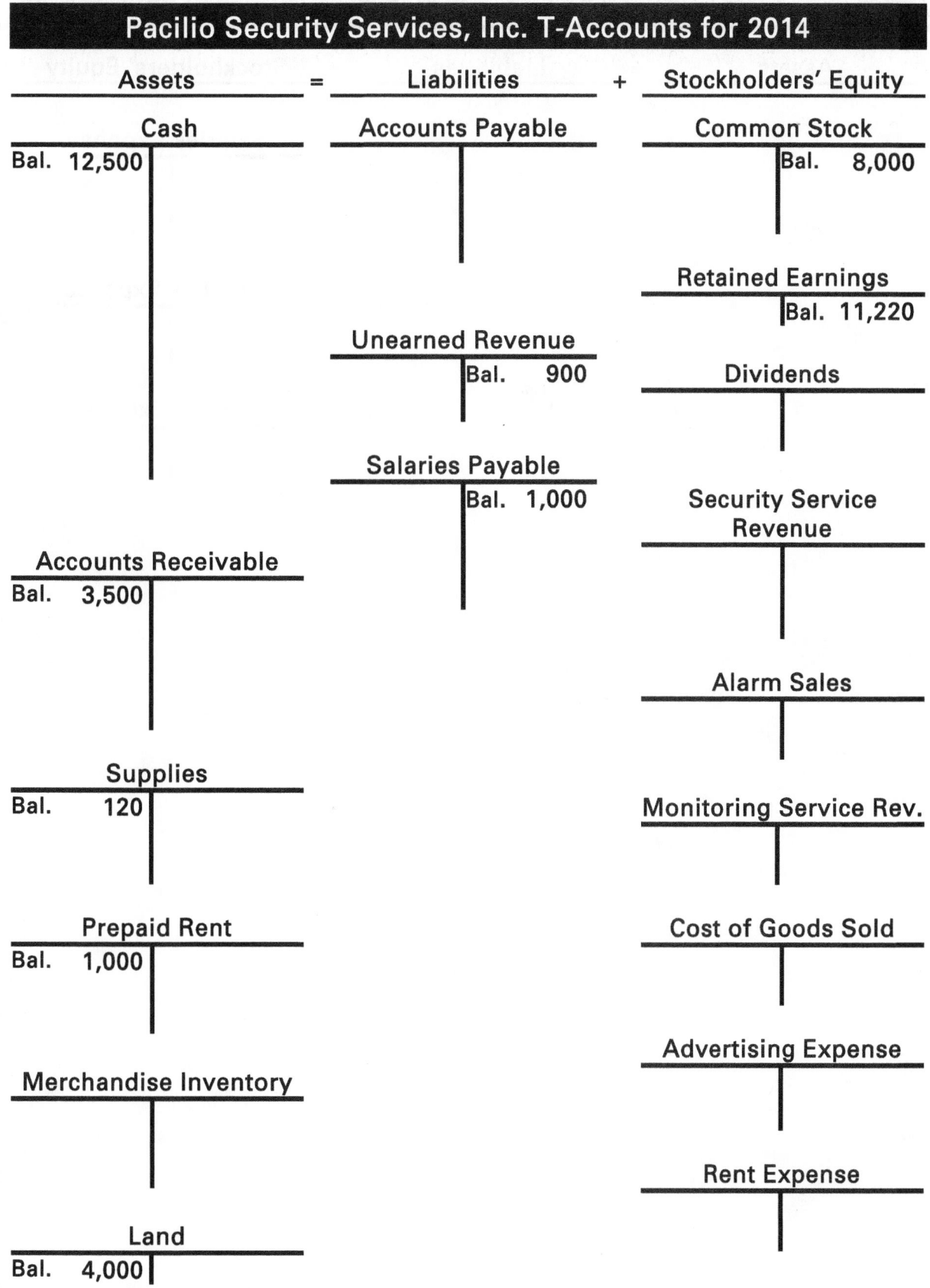

Pacilio Security Services, Inc. T-Accounts for 2014

Assets	=	Liabilities	+	Stockholders' Equity

Cash
Bal. 12,500

Accounts Payable

Common Stock
Bal. 8,000

Retained Earnings
Bal. 11,220

Unearned Revenue
Bal. 900

Dividends

Salaries Payable
Bal. 1,000

Security Service Revenue

Accounts Receivable
Bal. 3,500

Alarm Sales

Supplies
Bal. 120

Monitoring Service Rev.

Prepaid Rent
Bal. 1,000

Cost of Goods Sold

Advertising Expense

Merchandise Inventory

Rent Expense

Land
Bal. 4,000

COMPREHENSIVE PROBLEM – CHAPTER 4 b. (cont.)

Pacilio Security Services, Inc. T-Accounts for 2014

Assets	=	Liabilities	+	Stockholders' Equity

Salaries Expense

Supplies Expense

Utilities Expense

c.

Pacilio Security Services, Inc. Trial Balance December 31, 2014		
Cash		
Accounts Receivable		
Supplies		
Prepaid Rent		
Merchandise Inventory		
Land		
Accounts Payable		
Salaries Payable		
Common Stock		
Retained Earnings		
Dividends		
Security Service Revenue		
Alarm Sales		
Monitoring Service Revenue		
Cost of Goods Sold		
Advertising Expense		
Rent Expense		
Salaries Expense		
Supplies Expense		
Utilities Expense		
Totals		

d.

Pacilio Security Services, Inc. Income Statement For the Year Ended December 31, 2014		

COMPREHENSIVE PROBLEM – CHAPTER 4 d. (cont.)

Pacilio Security Services, Inc. Statement of Changes in Stockholders' Equity For the Year Ended December 31, 2014		
Beginning Common Stock		
Plus: Common Stock Issued		
Ending Common Stock		
Beginning Retained Earnings		
Plus: Net Income		
Less: Dividends		
Ending Retained Earnings		
Total Stockholders' Equity		

Pacilio Security Services, Inc.
Balance Sheet
As of December 31, 2014

Pacilio Security Services, Inc.
Statement of Cash Flows
For the Year Ended December 31, 2014

Cash Flows From Operating Activities:		
Cash Receipts from Customers[1]		
Cash Payment for Expenses[2]		
Cash Payment for Interest		
Net Cash Flow from Operating Activities		
Cash Flows From Investing Activities:		
Cash Flows From Financing Activities:		
Cash from Issue of Common Stock		
Cash Payments for Dividends		
Net Cash Flow from Financing Activities		
Net Increase in Cash		
Plus: Beginning Cash Balance		
Ending Cash Balance		

Cash Receipts from Customers:	
Cash Sales	
Collection of Accounts Receivable	
Total Cash from Customers	

Cash Payment for Expenses:	
Payment of Prepaid Rent	
Payment of Salaries	
Payment of Accounts Payable	
Payment of Advertising	
Payment for Supplies	
Payment for Utilities	
Total Cash Payment for Expenses	

e.

Date	Account Titles	Debit	Credit
	Closing Entries		

COMPREHENSIVE PROBLEM – CHAPTER 4 (cont.)

f.

Pacilio Security Services T-Accounts for 2014
T-Accounts with Closing Entries

Assets	=	Liabilities	+	Stockholders' Equity

Cash
Bal.

Accounts Payable
Bal.

Common Stock
Bal.

Accounts Receivable
Bal.

Salaries Payable
Bal.

Retained Earnings
Bal.

Supplies
Bal.

Prepaid Rent
Bal.

Dividends
Bal.

Security Service Revenue
Bal.

Merchandise Inventory
Bal.

Alarm Sales Revenue
Bal.

Land
Bal.

Monit. Service Revenue
Bal.

Cost of Goods Sold
Bal.

Advertising Expense
Bal.

Rent Expense
Bal.

Pacilio Security Services T-Accounts for 2014
T-Accounts with Closing Entries

Assets	=	Liabilities	+	Stockholders' Equity

Salaries Expense

Bal. |

Supplies Expense

Bal. |

Utilities Expense

Bal. |

Pacilio Security Systems Sales and Service After-Closing Trial Balance December 31, 2014		
Account Titles	Debit	Credit
Cash		
Accounts Receivable		
Supplies		
Prepaid Rent		
Merchandise Inventory		
Land		
Accounts Payable		
Salaries Payable		
Common Stock		
Retained Earnings		
Totals		

WORKING PAPERS – CHAPTER 5

EXERCISE 5-1A or 5-1B

(Note: Exercise 5-1A does not use f, g, and h)

	Inventory Method
a.	
b.	
c.	
d.	
e.	
f.	
g.	
h.	

EXERCISE 5-2A or 5-2B

_____Co.		
First Purchase		
Second Purchase		
Total		

	(a) FIFO	(b) LIFO	(c) W. AVG.
Cost of Goods Sold			
Ending Inventory			

*Average Cost per Unit:

EXERCISE 5-3A or 5-3B

Inventory Purchases					
Beginning Inventory		@		=	
First Purchase		@		=	
Second Purchase		@		=	
Goods Available for Sale					

a. Cost of Goods Sold:

FIFO	Units	Unit Cost	Cost of Goods Sold

Ending Inventory:

FIFO	Units	Unit Cost	Ending Inventory

b. Cost of Goods Sold

LIFO	Units	Unit Cost	Cost of Goods Sold

Ending Inventory

LIFO	Units	Unit Cost	Ending Inventory

c.

Weighted Average:			
Total Cost	÷ Total Units	=	Cost per Unit

Cost of Goods Sold			
Ending Inventory:			

EXERCISE 5-4A or 5-4B

a. (1)

FIFO			
Sales			
Cost of Goods Sold:			
Gross Margin			

a. (2)

LIFO			
Sales			
Cost of Goods Sold:			
Gross Margin			

a. (3)

Weighted Average			
Sales			
Cost of Goods Sold:			
Gross Margin			

b. (5-4A only)

EXERCISE 5-4A (cont.)

c.

	FIFO	LIFO	W. Avg.
Cash Flows From Operating Activities:			
Cash Inflow from Customers			
Cash Outflow for Inventory			
Net Cash Flow from Operating Act.			

EXERCISE 5-4B (cont.)

b.

	FIFO	LIFO	Weighted Avg.
Sales			
Cost of Goods Sold			
Gross Margin			
Operating Expenses			
Net Income			

c.

Ending Inventory:

	Units @ unit cost	=	Ending Inventory
FIFO		=	
LIFO		=	
Weighted Average		=	

EXERCISE 5-5A or 5-5B

Summary of Purchase Transactions					
1/20	Purchased Units		@	=	
4/21	Purchased Units		@	=	
7/25	Purchased Units		@	=	
9/19	Purchased Units		@	=	
	Available for Sale				

a. (1)

FIFO	Units	Cost per Unit	
Ending Inventory			
Total Ending Inventory			

a. (2)

LIFO	Units	Cost per Unit	
Ending Inventory			
Total Ending Inventory			

a. (3)

Weighted Average				
Total Cost	÷	Total Units	=	Cost per Unit
	÷		=	
Ending Inventory				

EXERCISE 5-5A or 5-5B (cont.)

b.

Note: The purchase entries are the same for all three methods.

	General Journal		
Date	Account Title	Debit	Credit
Jan. 20			
Apr. 21			
July 25			
Sept. 19			
(1) FIFO Sales and Cost of Goods Sold			
20___	Cash		
	Sales Revenue		
20___	Cost of Goods Sold		
	Merchandise Inventory		
(2) LIFO Sales and Cost of Goods Sold			
20___	Cash		
	Sales Revenue		
20___	Cost of Goods Sold		
	Merchandise Inventory		
(3) Weighted Average Sales and Cost of Goods Sold			
20___	Cash		
	Sales Revenue		
20___	Cost of Goods Sold		
	Merchandise Inventory		

EXERCISE 5-5A or 5-5B b. (cont.)

(1) FIFO

Cash		Sales Revenue

	Cost of Goods Sold

Merchandise Inventory

(2) LIFO

Cash		Sales Revenue

	Cost of Goods Sold

Merchandise Inventory

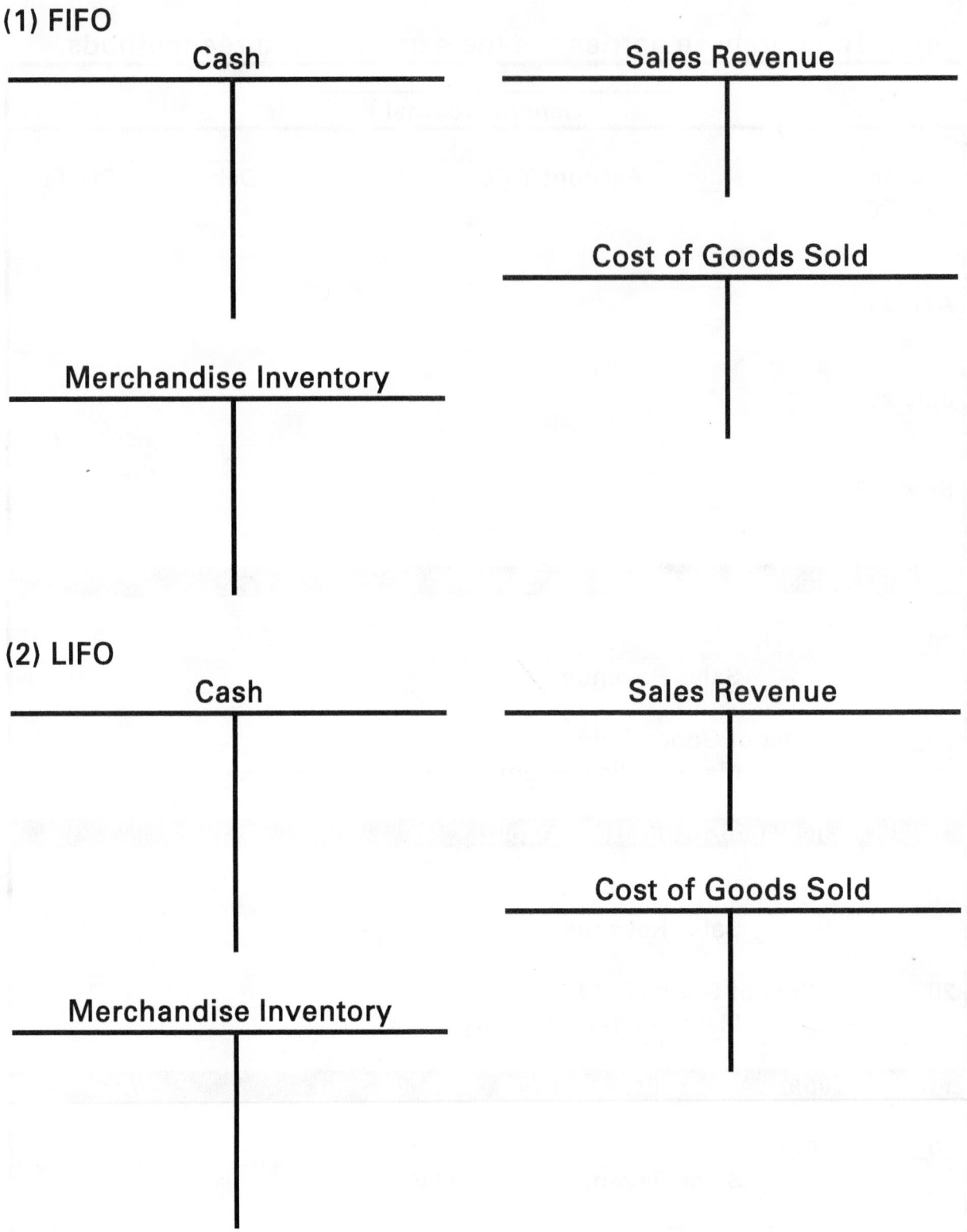

EXERCISE 5-5A or 5-5B b. (cont.)

(3) Weighted Average

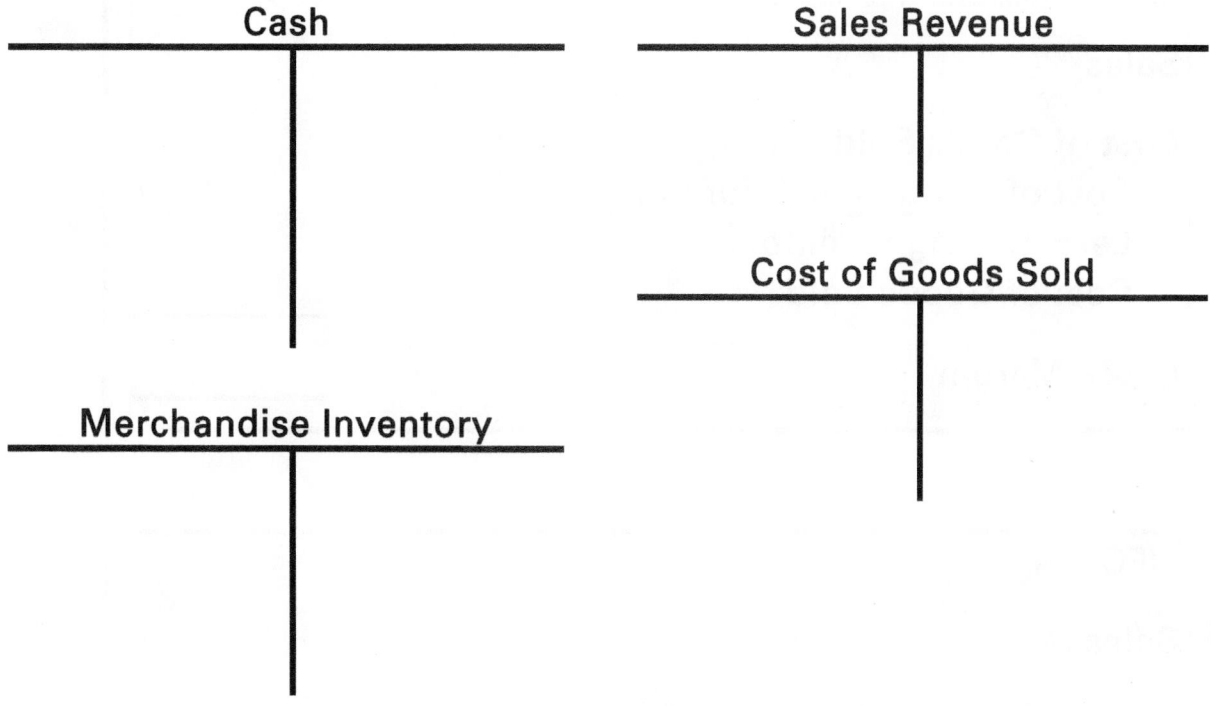

Cash

Sales Revenue

Cost of Goods Sold

Merchandise Inventory

EXERCISE 5-5A or 5-5B (cont.)

c.

FIFO		
Sales		
Cost of Goods Sold		
Cost of Goods Avail. for Sale*		
Less: Ending Inventory		
Cost of Goods Sold		
Gross Margin		

LIFO		
Sales		
Cost of Goods Sold		
Cost of Goods Avail. for Sale*		
Less: Ending Inventory		
Cost of Goods Sold		
Gross Margin		

EXERCISE 5-6A or 5-6B

a. (1) FIFO

Date	Account Title	Debit	Credit
Apr. 1			
Oct. 1			
Sales			
Cost of Sales			
Op. Exp.			
Tax Exp.			

Cost of Goods Sold Computation:	

EXERCISE 5-6A or 5-6B a. (cont.)

(1) FIFO

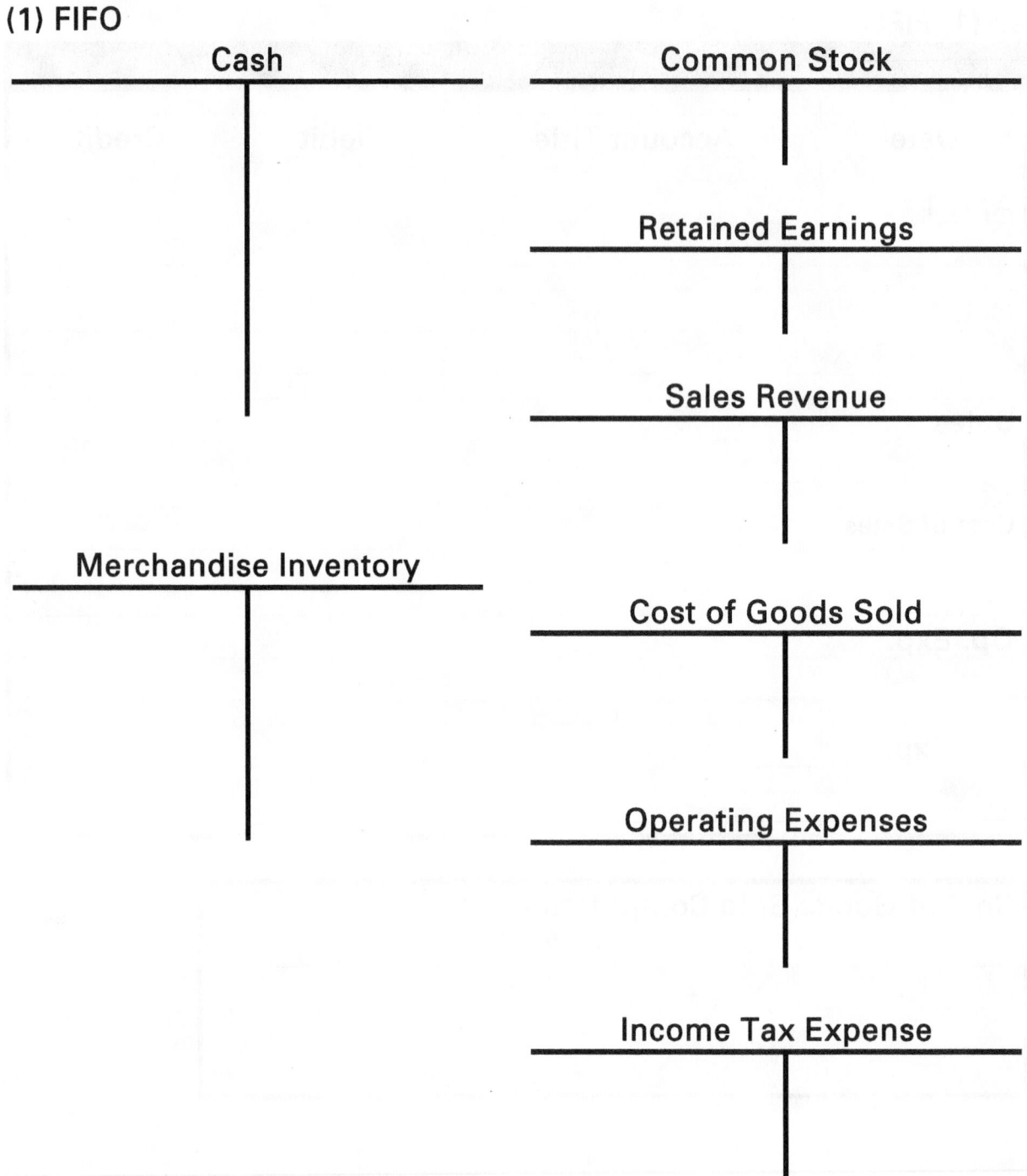

Cash

Common Stock

Retained Earnings

Sales Revenue

Merchandise Inventory

Cost of Goods Sold

Operating Expenses

Income Tax Expense

EXERCISE 5-6A or 5-6B a. (cont.)

a. (2) LIFO

Date	Account Title	Debit	Credit
Apr. 1			
Oct. 1			
Sales			
Cost of Sales			
Op. Exp.			
Tax Exp.			

Cost of Goods Sold Computation	

EXERCISE 5-6A or 5-6B a. (cont.)

(2) LIFO

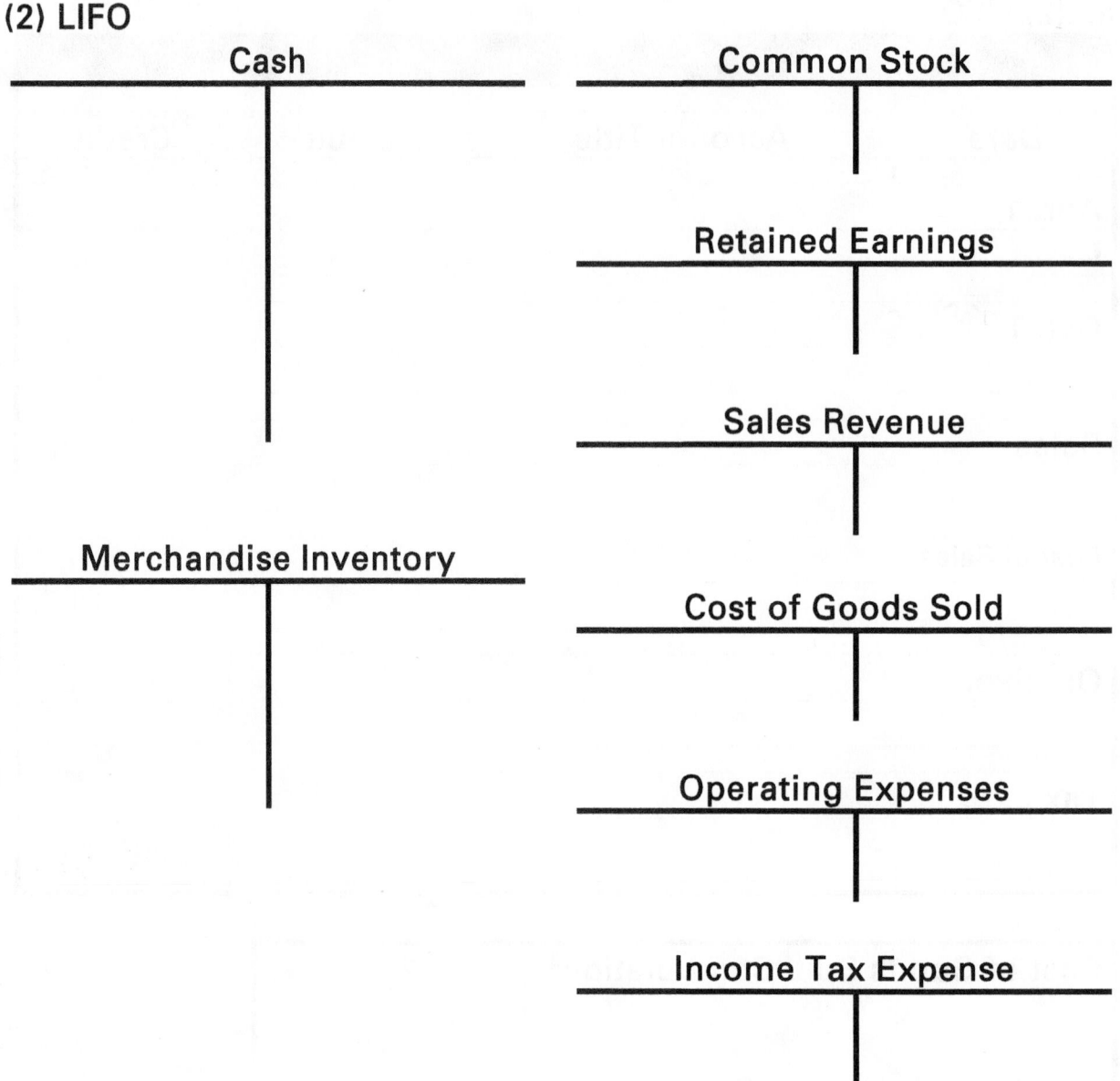

Cash

Merchandise Inventory

Common Stock

Retained Earnings

Sales Revenue

Cost of Goods Sold

Operating Expenses

Income Tax Expense

EXERCISE 5-6A or 5-6B (cont.)

b.

	Income Statements			
FIFO				
Sales				
Cost of Goods Sold:	(computations)			
Gross Margin				
Operating Expenses				
Income Before Tax				
Income Tax Expense				
Net Income				
LIFO				
Sales				
Cost of Goods Sold:	(computations)			
Cost of Goods Sold				
Gross Margin				
Operating Expenses				
Income Before Tax				
Income Tax Expense				
Net Income				

EXERCISE 5-6A or 5-6B (cont.)

c.

d.

Cash Flows from Operating Activities		
	FIFO	LIFO
Cash Flows From Operating Activities:		
Net Cash Flow from Operating Activities		

*Computation of cash paid for inventory:

e.

EXERCISE 5-7A or 5-7B

a.

Effect of Events on Financial Statements

Panel 1: FIFO Cost Flow

Event	Cash	+	Inv.	=	C. Stk.	+	Ret. Ear.		Rev.	−	Exp.	=	Net Inc.		Cash Flows
1.		+		=		+	+					=			
2.		+		=		+	+					=			
3.		+		=		+	+					=			
4.		+		=		+	+					=			
5.		+		=		+	+					=			
Bal.		+		=		+	+					=			

Panel 2: LIFO Cost Flow

Event	Cash	+	Inv.	=	C. Stk	+	Ret. Ear.		Rev.	−	Exp.	=	Net Inc.		Cash Flows
1.		+		=		+	+					=			
2.		+		=		+	+					=			
3.		+		=		+	+					=			
4.		+		=		+	+					=			
5.		+		=		+	+					=			
Bal.		+		=		+	+					=			

EXERCISE 5-7A or 5-7B a. (cont.)

Cost of Goods Sold — FIFO:

Income Tax Expense:

Cost of Goods Sold — LIFO:

Income Tax Expense

EXERCISE 5-7A or 5-7B (cont.)

b.

c.

d.

e.

EXERCISE 5-8A or 5-8B

a.

	General Journal		
Date	Account Titles	Debit	Credit
1/1			
4/1a			
4/1b			
8/1			
12/1a			
12/1b			

*Cost of Goods Sold:

5-8A b. Ending Inventory:

5-8B b. Total Cost of Goods Sold:

EXERCISE 5-9A or 5-9B

a.

Date	Purchased			Sold			Inventory Balance		
	Units	Cost	Total	Units	Cost	Total	Units	Cost	Total
1/1 Beg. Inv.								=	
3/15 Pur.		=						=	
5/30 Sold					=				
					=			=	
8/10 Pur		=						=	
11/20 Sold					=				
					=			=	

Ending Inventory:

b.

EXERCISE 5-10A or 5-10B

a.

a.	b.	c.	d.	e.	f.	g.
Item	Quantity	Cost Per Unit	Mkt. Val. per Unit	Total Cost	Total Market	Ind. Item Lower Cost/Mkt.
				(b x c)	(b x d)	(b x e)

1. Ending inventory using the individual item method:

2. Ending inventory using the aggregate method:

b.

Date	Account Titles	Debit	Credit
1.			
2.			

EXERCISE 5-11A or 5-11B

a.

a. Item	b. Quantity	c. Cost Per Unit	d. Market Per Unit	e. Unit Lower Cost/Mkt.	f. Total Cost	g. Total Lower Cost/Mkt.
Totals						

b.

Account Title	Debit	Credit

EXERCISE 5-12A or 5-12B

a. Gross Margin:

b. Cost of Goods Sold:

c. Computation of Ending Inventory:

Beginning Inventory	
Plus: Purchases	
Goods Available for Sale	
Less: Cost of Goods Sold (Est.)	
Ending Inventory (Est.)	

d. Lost Inventory:

e. (5-12A)

EXERCISE 5-13A or 5-13B

June 14 Inventory Account Balance	
Less: Cost of Unrecorded Sale	
Balance in the Warehouse	
Less: 5% Shrinkage	
Less: Amount of Inventory in Showroom	
Inventory Lost	

EXERCISE 5-14A or 5-14B

EXERCISE 5-15A or 5-15B

Item Number	Year	Amount Affected	Effect
1.			
2.			
3.			
4.			
5.			
6.			
7.			
8.			
9.			
10.			
11.			
12.			

EXERCISE 5-16A or 5-16B

EXERCISE 5-17A or 5-17B

PROBLEM 5-18A or 5-18B

	Inventory Purchases		
	Units	Cost per Unit	
Beginning Inventory		@	=
First Purchase		@	=
Second Purchase		@	=
Total			

a. Cost of Goods Sold:

FIFO	Units	Cost per Unit	Cost of Goods Sold

Ending Inventory:

FIFO	Units	Cost per Unit	Ending Inventory

Cost of Goods Sold:

LIFO	Units	Cost per Unit	Cost of Goods Sold

PROBLEM 5-18A or 5-18B a. (cont.)

Ending Inventory:

LIFO				

Weighted Average				
Total Cost	÷	Total Units	=	Cost per Unit
	÷		=	

Weighted Average			
Cost of Goods Sold:	@		=
Ending Inventory:	@		=

b.

Computation of Net Income:			
	FIFO	LIFO	Weighted Average

PROBLEM 5-18A or 5-18B b. (cont.)

b. (1) FIFO

Date	Account Title	Debit	Credit
1.			
2.			
3a.			
3b.			
4.			
5.			

PROBLEM 5-18A or 5-18B b. (cont.)

b. (1) FIFO

Cash

Common Stock

Retained Earnings

Sales Revenue

Merchandise Inventory

Cost of Goods Sold

Operating Expenses

Income Tax Expense

PROBLEM 5-18A or 5-18B b. (cont.)

b. (2) LIFO

Date	Account Title	Debit	Credit
1.			
2.			
3a.			
3b.			
4.			
5.			

PROBLEM 5-18A or 5-18B b. (cont.)

b. (2) LIFO

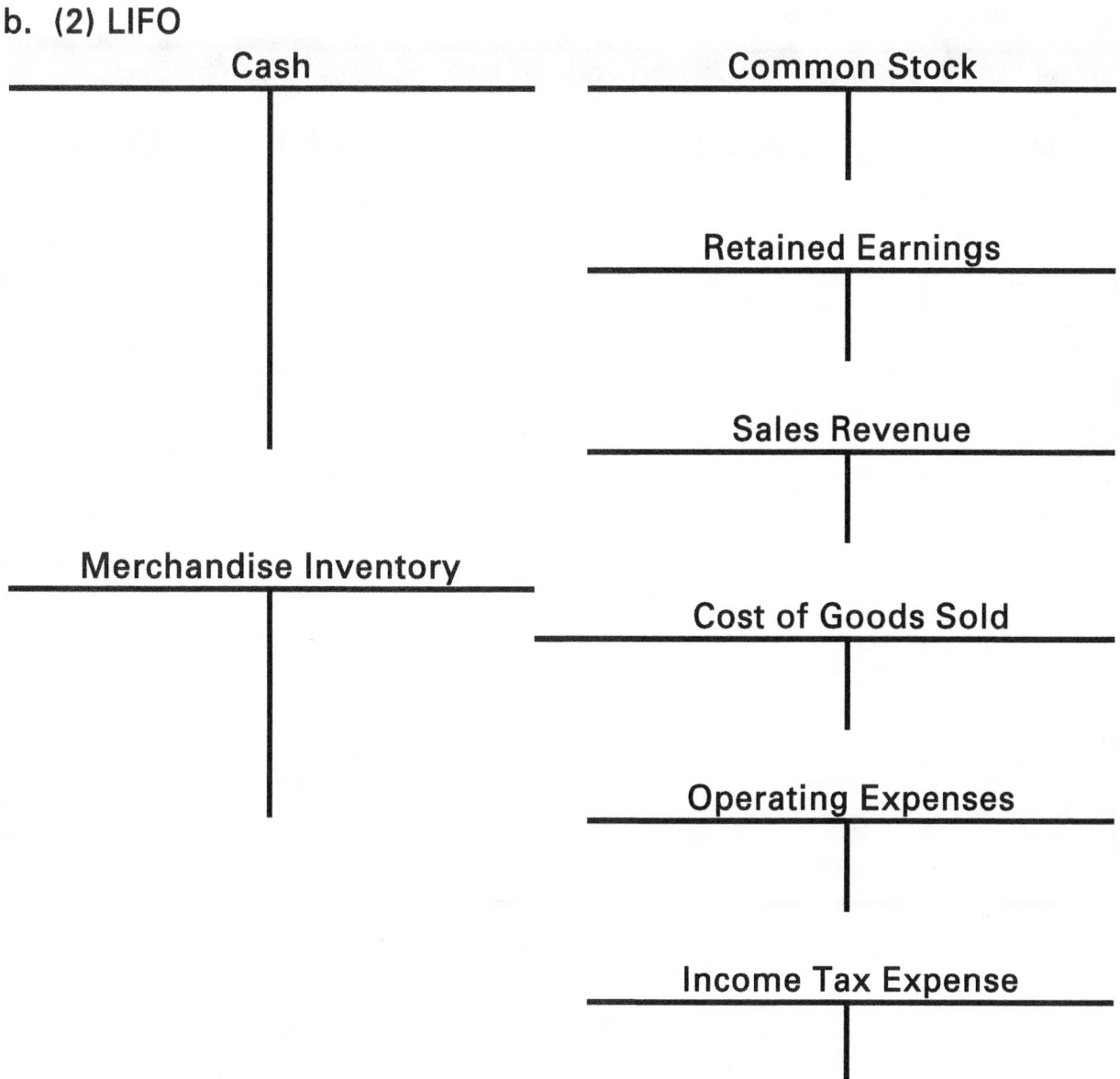

PROBLEM 5-18A or 5-18B b. (cont.)

b. (3) Weighted Average

Date	Account Title	Debit	Credit
1.			
2.			
3a.			
3b.			
4.			
5.			

b. (3) Weighted Average

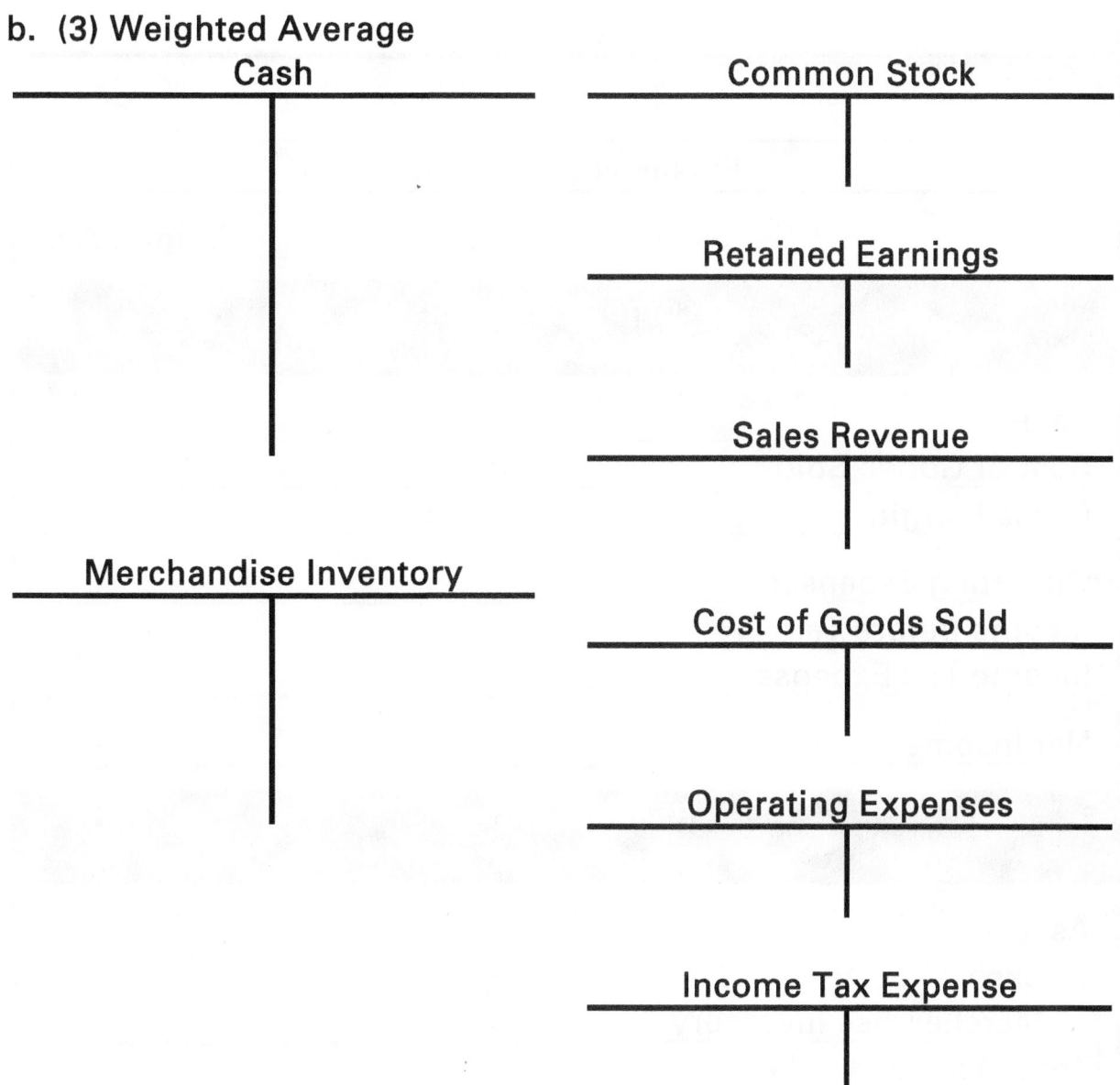

Cash

Merchandise Inventory

Common Stock

Retained Earnings

Sales Revenue

Cost of Goods Sold

Operating Expenses

Income Tax Expense

PROBLEM 5-18A or 5-18B (cont.)

c.

	FIFO	LIFO	Weight. Av.
Financial Statements			
Income Statements **For Year Ended December 31, 2013**			
Sales			
Cost of Goods Sold			
Gross Margin			
Operating Expenses			
Income Before Tax			
Income Tax Expense			
Net Income			
Balance Sheets **As of December 31, 2013**			
Assets			
Cash			
Merchandise Inventory			
Total Assets			
Stockholders' Equity			
Common Stock			
Retained Earnings			
Total Stockholders' Equity			

PROBLEM 5-18A or 5-18B c. (cont.)

Statements of Cash Flows
For the Year Ended December 31, 2013

	FIFO	LIFO	Weight. Av.
Cash Flows From Operating. Act.:			
Cash Inflow from Customers			
Cash Outflow for Inventory			
Cash Outflow for Oper. Exp.			
Cash Outflow for Income Tax			
Net Cash Flow from Oper. Act.			
Cash Flows From Investing Act.			
Cash Flows From Financing Act.			
Net Change in Cash			
Plus: Beginning Cash Balance			
Ending Cash Balance			

PROBLEM 5-19A or 5-19B
Not required

Sales and Purchase Transactions for 2013

Date	Sales			Purchases			Cost of Goods Sold			Inventory		
	Units	Price Per Unit	Total	Units	Cost Per Unit	Total	Units	Cost per Unit	Total	Units	Cost per Unit	Total
1/1											=	
3/5											=	
4/10											=	
6/19											=	
9/16						=					=	
11/28											=	
Totals			=						=			

PROBLEM 5-19A or 5-19B (cont.)

a.

	General Journal, 2013		
Date	Account Titles	Debit	Credit
3/5			
4/10			
4/10			
6/19			
6/19			
9/16			
11/28			
11/28			

b.

Sales	
Cost of Goods Sold	
Gross Margin	

c. Ending Inventory:

Item	Quantity	Unit Cost	Unit Market	Total Cost	Total Market	Individual Item Lower of Cost or Market
						Total

a.

b.

Account Title	Debit	Credit

c.

d.

e. (5-20B)

PROBLEM 5-21A or 5-21B

a. 1. Estimated Gross Margin:

2. Estimated Cost of Goods Sold:

3. Estimated Inventory at _____ **:**

b. Loss:

	Total Inventory	$
	Less: Undamaged	_____
	Total Loss	$_____

c.

PROBLEM 5-22A or 5-22B

	20__	20__	Total
Net Sales			
Cost of Goods Sold			
Gross Margin			

Gross Margin %	÷	=	
Cost of Goods Sold %	÷	=	

a. Computation of Cost of Goods Sold:

Sales	
Average Cost of Goods Sold %	
Cost of Goods Sold	

b. Computation of Ending Inventory:

Beginning Inventory	
Plus: Purchases	
Plus: Transportation-In	
Goods Available for Sale	
Less: Cost of Goods Sold	
Ending Inventory	

c. Estimate Inventory Shortage:

Estimated Ending Inventory	
Less, Actual Good Inventory	
Inventory Shortage	

PROBLEM 5-23A

Error No.1	Amount of Error	Effect
Sales, 2013		
Ending Inventory, 12/31/13		
Gross Margin, 2013		
Beginning Inventory, 1/1/14		
Cost of Goods Sold, 2013		
Net Income, 2013		
Retained Earnings, 12/31/13		
Total Assets, 12/31/13		

Error No. 2	Amount of Error	Effect
Sales, 2013		
Ending Inventory, 12/31/13		
Gross Margin, 2013		
Beginning Inventory, 1/1/14		
Cost of Goods Sold, 2013		
Net Income, 2013		
Retained Earnings, 12/31/13		
Total Assets, 12/31/13		

Error No. 3	Amount of Error	Effect
Sales, 2013		
Ending Inventory, 12/31/13		
Gross Margin, 2013		
Beginning Inventory, 1/1/14		
Cost of Goods Sold, 2013		
Net Income, 2013		
Retained Earnings, 12/31/13		
Total Assets, 12/31/13		

PROBLEM 5-23B

Error No.1	Amount of Error	Effect
Sales, 2013		
Ending Inventory, 12/31/13		
Gross Margin, 2013		
Beginning Inventory, 1/1/14		
Cost of Goods Sold, 2013		
Net Income, 2013		
Retained Earnings, 12/31/13		
Total Assets, 12/31/13		

Error No. 2	Amount of Error	Effect
Sales, 2013		
Ending Inventory, 12/31/13		
Gross Margin, 2013		
Beginning Inventory, 1/1/14		
Cost of Goods Sold, 2013		
Net Income, 2013		
Retained Earnings, 12/31/13		
Total Assets, 12/31/13		

Error No. 3	Amount of Error	Effect
Sales, 2013		
Ending Inventory, 12/31/13		
Gross Margin, 2013		
Beginning Inventory, 1/1/14		
Cost of Goods Sold, 2013		
Net Income, 2013		
Retained Earnings, 12/31/13		
Total Assets, 12/31/13		

PROBLEM 5-24A or 5-24B

a. First the company's gross margins must be calculated:

Sales			
Cost of Goods Sold			
Gross Margin			

Compute Gross Margin %:

Company	Gross Margin	÷	Sales	=	Gross Margin %

b. Inventory turnover ratios:

Company	Cost of Goods Sold	÷	Ending Inventory	=	Inventory Turnover Ratio

Average days to Sell Inventory

Company	365	÷	Inventory Turnover	=	Average days to sell inventory

PROBLEM 5-24A or 5-24B (cont.)

c.

ATC 5-1

a.

Compute Inventory Turnover:

2010:

2009:

Compute Average Days to Sell Inventory:

2010:

2009:

b.

c.

ATC 5-2

a.

Blue Bird Company Inventory Purchases					
Beginning Inventory	100	@	$50	=	$ 5,000
	70	@	55	=	3,850
First Purchase	100	@	54	=	5,400
Second Purchase	250	@	58	=	14,500
Total	520				$28,750

FIFO
Cost of Goods Sold:

FIFO	Units		Cost per Unit		Cost of Goods Sold
		@		=	
		@		=	
		@		=	
		@		=	

Ending Inventory:

LIFO
Cost of Goods Sold:

LIFO	Units		Cost per Unit		Cost of Goods Sold
		@		=	
		@		=	
		@		=	

Ending Inventory:

ATC 5-2 a. (cont.)

Weighted Average					
Total Cost	÷	Total Units	=	Cost per Unit	
	÷		=		

Cost of Goods Sold		@		=	
Ending Inventory		@		=	

Blue Bird Company			
Income Statements	FIFO	LIFO	Weighted Average
Sales			
Cost of Goods Sold			
Gross Margin			
Operating Expenses			
Income Before Tax			
Income Tax (30%)			
Net Income			

b.

ATC 5-3

a. Compute Gross Margin Percentage:

Gross Margin ÷ Sales = Gross Margin %

2010

2009

b. Compute Inventory Turnover:

Cost of Goods Sold ÷ Ending Inventory = Inventory Turnover

2010

2009

Compute Average Days to Sell Inventory:

Days in the Year ÷ Inventory Turnover = Average days to Sell

2010

2009

c.

ACT 5-4

a.

Compute Inventory Turnover:

Cost of Goods Sold ÷ Ending Inventory = Inventory Turnover

2010

2009

b. Compute Average Days to Sell Inventory:

Days in the Year ÷ Inventory Turnover = Average days to sell

2010

2009

c.

ATC 5-5

a.

b. Compute Inventory Turnover:

       Cost of Goods Sold ÷ Ending Inventory = Inventory Turnover

   Ruby Tuesday's

   Zale Corporation

c. Compute Average Days to Sell Inventory:

       Days in the Year ÷ Inventory Turnover = Average days to sell

   Ruby Tuesday's

   Zale Corporaton

d.

ATC 5-6

ATC 5-7

ATC 5-8

COMPREHENSIVE PROBLEM – CHAPTER 5

a.

	Pacilio Security Services, Inc. General Journal, 2015		
Event	Account title	Debit	Credit
1.			
2. 1/15			
3. 2/1			
4. 3/1			
5. 5/1			
6.			
7. 8/1			
8. 9/5			
9a.			
9b.			

Cost of Goods Sold:	

Event	Account Titles	Debit	Credit
10a.			
10b.			
11.			
12.			
13.			
14.			
15.			
16.			
17.			
18.			
19.			
20.			

Pacilio Security Services, Inc.
General Journal, 2015

	Pacilio Security Services, Inc. General Journal, 2015		
Event	Account Title	Debit	Credit
21.			
22.			

b.

Pacilio Security Services, Inc. T-Accounts for 2015

Assets	=	Liabilities	+	Stockholders' Equity

Cash

Bal.	62,860	

Accounts Payable

	Bal.	980

Common Stock

	Bal.	50,000

Unearned Revenue

Retained Earnings

	Bal.	39,190

Salaries Payable

	Bal.	1,500

Dividends

Alarm Sales

Accounts Receivable

Bal.	20,500	

Monitoring Service Rev

Supplies

Bal.	150	

Cost of Goods Sold

Advertising Expense

Prepaid Rent

Bal.	2,000	

Rent Expense

Salaries Expense

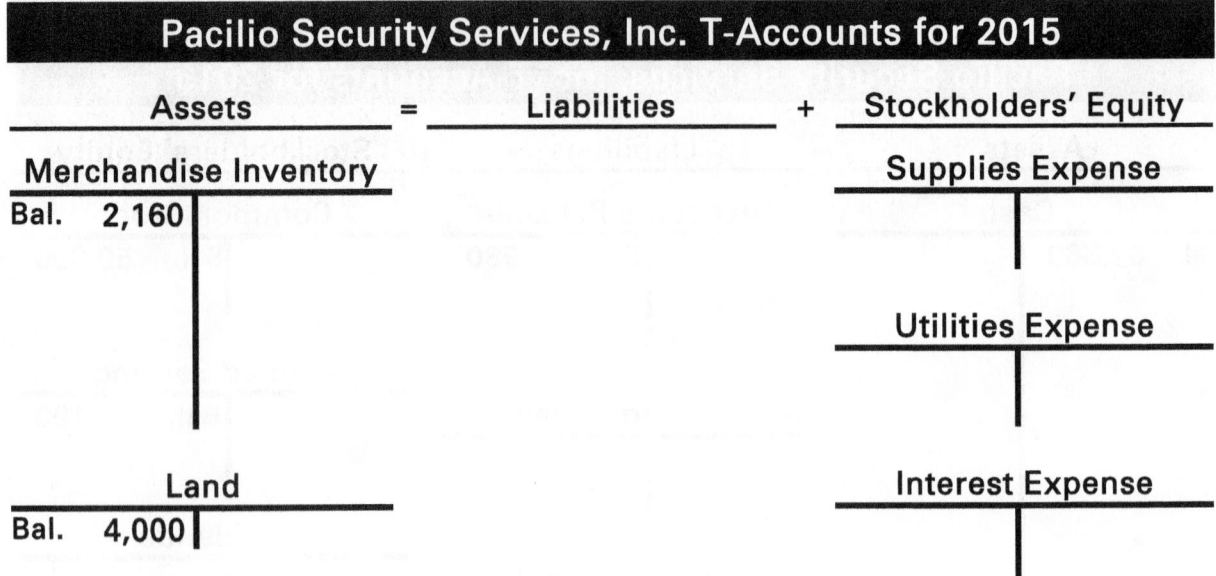

Pacilio Security Services, Inc. T-Accounts for 2015

| Assets | = | Liabilities | + | Stockholders' Equity |

Merchandise Inventory

Bal. 2,160

Land

Bal. 4,000

Supplies Expense

Utilities Expense

Interest Expense

c.

Pacilio Security Services, Inc. Trial Balance December 31, 2015		

d.

Pacilio Security Services, Inc. Income Statement For the Year Ended December 31, 2015			

Pacilio Security Services, Inc. Statement of Changes in Stockholders' Equity For the Year Ended December 31, 2015		
Beginning Common Stock		
Plus: Common Stock Issued		
Ending Common Stock		
Beginning Retained Earnings		
Plus: Net Income		
Less: Dividends		
Ending Retained Earnings		
Total Stockholders' Equity		

Pacilio Security Services, Inc.		
Balance Sheet		
As of December 31, 2015		

Pacilio Security Services, Inc. Statement of Cash Flows For the Year Ended December 31, 2015		
Cash Flows From Operating Activities:		
Cash Receipts from Customers[1]		
Cash Payment for Expenses[2]		
Net Cash Flow from Operating Activities		
Cash Flows From Investing Activities:		
Cash Flows From Financing Activities:		
Cash Payments for Dividends		
Net Cash Flow from Financing Activities		
Net Increase in Cash		
Plus: Beginning Cash Balance		
Ending Cash Balance		

Cash Receipts from Customers:	
Total Cash from Customers	

Cash Payment for Expenses:	
Total Cash Payment for Expenses	

e.

Date	Account Titles	Debit	Credit
	Closing Entries		

f.

Pacilio Security Services T-Accounts for 2015
T-Accounts with Closing Entries

Assets	=	Liabilities	+	Stockholders' Equity

Cash
Bal.

Accounts Payable
Bal.

Common Stock
Bal.

Accounts Receivable
Bal.

Salaries Payable
Bal.

Retained Earnings
Bal.

Supplies
Bal.

Unearned Revenue
Bal.

Prepaid Rent
Bal.

Dividends
Bal.

Alarm Sales Revenue
Bal.

Merchandise Inventory
Bal.

Mont. Service Revenue
Bal.

Land
Bal.

Cost of Goods Sold
Bal.

Advertising Expense
Bal.

Rent Expense
Bal.

Salaries Expense
Bal.

Pacilio Security Services T-Accounts for 2015
T-Accounts with Closing Entries

Assets	=	Liabilities	+	Stockholders' Equity

Supplies Expense

Bal
.

Utilties Expense

Bal.

Interest Expense

Bal.

Pacilio Security Systems Sales and Service After-Closing Trial Balance December 31, 2015		
Account Titles	Debit	Credit

EXERCISE 6-1A or 6-1B

EXERCISE 6-2A or 6-2B

EXERCISE 6-3A or 6-3B

EXERCISE 6-4A or 6-4B

EXERCISE 6-5A or 6-5B

EXERCISE 6-6A or 6-6B

EXERCISE 6-7A or 6-7B

a. & c.

						Statements Model					
	Assets		=	Liab.	+	S. Equity	Rev.	−	Exp.	= Net Inc.	Cash Flow
Cash	+	Acct. Rec.	=		+						
	+		=		+			−		=	
	+		=		+			−		=	
	+		=		+			−		=	

b.

d.

e.

Event	Account Titles	Debit	Credit

EXERCISE 6-8A

Reconciling Items:	Book Balance Adjusted?	Added or Subtracted?
Automatic Debit for Utility Bill		
Charge for Printing New Checks		
NSF Check from Customer		
ATM Fee		
Outstanding Checks		
Interest Revenue Earned on the Account		
Deposits in Transit		
Service Charge		

EXERCISE 6-8B

Reconciling Items:	Book Balance Adjusted?	Added or Subtracted?
Charge for Checks		
NSF Check from Customer		
Note Receivable Collected by Bank		
Outstanding Checks		
Credit Memo		
Interest Revenue		
Deposits in Transit		
Debit Memo		
Service Charge		

EXERCISE 6-9A

Reconciling Items:	Bank Balance Adjusted?	Added or Subtracted?
Credit Memo		
ATM Fee		
Petty Cash Voucher		
NSF Check from Customer		
Interest Revenue		
Bank Service Charge		
Outstanding Checks		
Deposits in Transit		
Debit Memo		

EXERCISE 6-9B

Reconciling Items:	Bank Balance Adjusted?	Added or Subtracted?
Certified Checks		
Petty Cash Voucher		
NSF Check from Customer		
Interest Revenue		
Bank Service Charge		
Outstanding Checks		
Deposits in Transit		
Debit Memo		
Credit Memo		

EXERCISE 6-10A or 6-10B

a.

Bank Reconciliation	
Unadjusted Bank Balance	
True Cash Balance	
Unadjusted Book Balance	
True Cash Balance	

b.

Date	Account Titles	Debit	Credit

EXERCISE 6-11A or 6-11B

Unadjusted Bank Balance	
True Cash Balance	

EXERCISE 6-12A or 6-12B

Unadjusted Book Balance,		
True Cash Balance,		

EXERCISE 6-13A or 6-13B

a.

b.

				Statements Model					
Assets		= Liab.	+ S. Equity		Rev.	– Exp.	= Net Inc.		Cash Flow
Cash	Petty Cash								
	+	=	+			–	=		

c.

	General Journal		
Ref.	Account Titles	Debit	Credit
Jan. 1			

EXERCISE 6-14A or 6-14B

a.

		Statements Model							
	Assets		= S. Equity	Rev.	– Exp.	= Net Inc.	Statement of Cash Flows
No.	Cash +	Petty Cash	= Ret. Earn.				
1.	+		=		–	=	
2.	+		=		–	=	
3.	+		=		–	=	

b.

	General Journal Entries		
Event No.	Account Titles	Debit	Credit

EXERCISE 6-15A or 6-15B

a.

b.

c.

EXERCISE 6-16A or 6-16B

PROBLEM 6-17A or 6-17B

a.

b.

c.

PROBLEM 6-18A or 6-18B

a.

Bank Reconciliation	
Unadjusted Bank Balance,	
True Cash Balance,	
Unadjusted Book Balance,	
True Cash Balance,	

b.

General Journal			
Ref.	Account Title	Debit	Credit

PROBLEM 6-19A or 6-19B

Bank Reconciliation		
Unadjusted Bank Balance,		
True Cash Balance,		
Unadjusted Book Balance,		
True Cash Balance,		

PROBLEM 6-20A or 6-20B

	General Journal		
Event No.	Account Titles	Debit	Credit

a.

Bank Reconciliation		
Unadjusted Bank Balance,		
True Cash Balance,		
Unadjusted Book Balance,		
True Cash Balance,		

b.

Account Title	Debit	Credit

PROBLEM 6-22A or 6-22B

Event Number	Type of Event	Assets	=	Liabilities	+	Stockholders' Equity Common Stock	+	Retained Earnings
1.								
2.								
3.								
4.								
5.								

PROBLEM 6-23A

a.

Pizza Express Bank Reconciliation May 31, 2013		
Unadjusted Bank Balance, May 31, 2013		
True Cash Balance, May 31, 2013		
Unadjusted Book Balance, May 31, 2013		
True Cash Balance, May 31, 2013		

b.

c.

PROBLEM 6-23B

a.

Account Title	Debit	Credit

b.

c.

PROBLEM 6-24A or 6-24B

a.

General Journal			
Event	Account Titles	Debit	Credit

b.

c.

Event Number	Type of Event

PROBLEM 6-24A or 6-24B (cont.)

d.

Effect of Transactions on Financial Statements

No.	Assets			Liab.	+	S. Equity	Rev.	–	Exp.	=	Net Inc.	Cash Flow
	Cash	+	Petty Cash	=								
		+	+	=	+					=		
		+	+	=	+					=		
		+	+	=	+					=		
		+	+	=	+					=		

PROBLEM 6-25A or 6-25B

ATC 6-1

Financial Statement Analysis

a.

b.

c.

d.

e.

ATC 6-2

a. (1)

Bank Reconciliation June 30, 2013	Peach Co.	Apple Co.	Pear Co.
Unadjusted Bank Balance, 6/30			
Add: Deposits in Transit			
Less:Outstanding Checks			
True Cash Balance, 6/30			
Unadjusted Book Balance, 6/30			
Add: Credit memo for notes rec.			
Credit memo for interest earned			
Less:NSF Check			
Service Charge			
True Cash Balance, 6/30			

a. (2)

Peach Co. General Journal Entries			
Event	Account Titles	Debit	Credit

a. (2)

Apple Co. General Journal Entries			
Event	Account Titles	Debit	Credit

Pear Co. General Journal Entries			
Event	Account Titles	Debit	Credit

b.

ATC 6-3

ATC 6-3 (cont.)

ATC 6-4

ATC 6-5

ATC 6-6

ATC 6-7

ATC 6-8

a.

Pacilio Security Systems Sales and Service General Journal-2016			
Date	Account Titles	Debit	Credit
1.			
2.			
3.			
4.			
5.			
6.			
7a.			
7b.			
8.			
9.			

Computation of Cost of Goods Sold:

COMPREHENSIVE PROBLEM – CHAPTER 6 a. (cont.)

Pacilio Security Systems Sales and Service General Journal-2016			
Date	Account Titles	Debit	Credit
10.			
11.			
12.			
13.			
14.			
15.			
16.			
17.			
18.			
19			

Computation of expired rent:

Van:

Office

b.

Pacilio Security Services, Inc. General Journal, 2016			
Event	Account Titles	Debit	Credit
	Entries from Bank Reconcilaiation		
20a.			
20b.			

COMPREHENSIVE PROBLEM – CHAPTER 6 (cont.)

c.

Pacilio Security Services, Inc. T-Accounts for 2016

Assets	=	Liabilities	+	Stockholders' Equity

Assets

Cash

Bal. 74,210

Petty Cash

Accounts Receivable

Bal. 13,500

Supplies

Bal. 200

Prepaid Rent

Bal. 3,200

= Liabilities

Accounts Payable

Bal. 1,950

Unearned Revenue

Bal. 900

Salaries Payable

Bal. 1,000

+ Stockholders' Equity

Common Stock

Bal. 50,000

Retained Earnings

Bal. 47,880

Dividends

Alarm Sales

Monitoring Service Rev

Cost of Goods Sold

Advertising Expense

Office Supplies Expense

Maintenance Expense

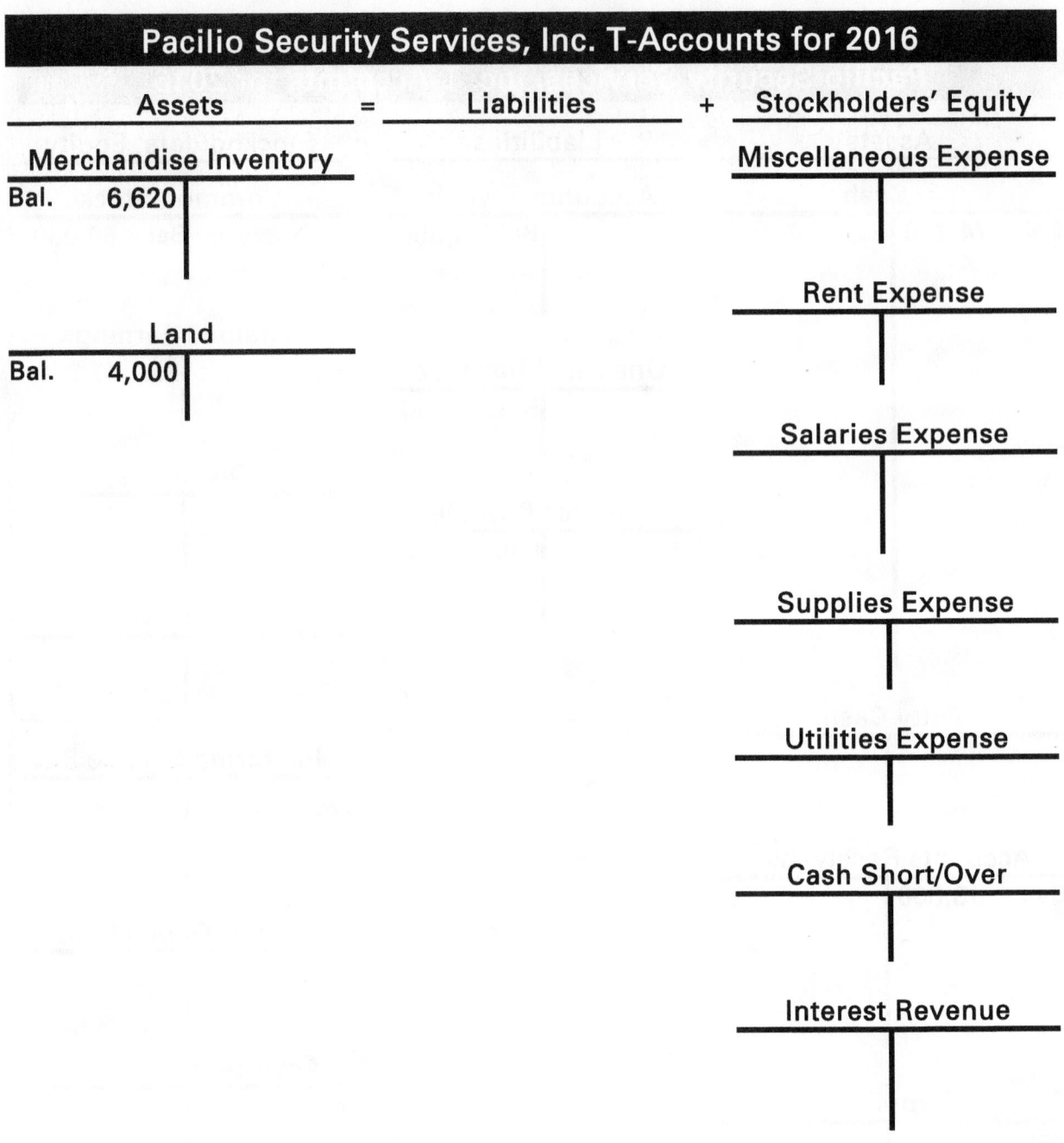

Pacilio Security Services, Inc. T-Accounts for 2016

| Assets | = | Liabilities | + | Stockholders' Equity |

Merchandise Inventory

Bal.   6,620

Land

Bal.   4,000

Miscellaneous Expense

Rent Expense

Salaries Expense

Supplies Expense

Utilities Expense

Cash Short/Over

Interest Revenue

d.

Pacilio Security Services Bank Reconciliation December 31, 2016	
Unadjusted Bank Balance, 12/31/2016	
True Cash Balance, 12/31/2016	
Unadjusted Book Balance, 12/31/2016	
True Cash Balance, 12/31/2016	

e.

Pacilio Security Services, Inc. Trial Balance December 31, 2016		
Cash		
Petty Cash		
Accounts Receivable		
Supplies		
Prepaid Rent		
Merchandise Inventory		
Land		
Accounts Payable		
Salaries Payable		
Common Stock		
Retained Earnings		
Dividends		
Alarms Sales		
Monitoring Service Revenue		
Cost of Goods Sold		
Advertising Expense		
Office Supplies Expense		
Maintenance Expense		
Miscellaneous Expense		
Rent Expense		
Salaries Expense		
Supplies Expense		
Utilities Expense		
Cash Short/Over		
Interest Revenue		
Totals		

f.

Pacilio Security Services, Inc. Income Statement For the Year Ended December 31, 2016		

Pacilio Security Services, Inc. Statement of Changes in Stockholders' Equity For the Year Ended December 31, 2016		
Beginning Common Stock		
Plus: Common Stock Issued		
Ending Common Stock		
Beginning Retained Earnings		
Plus: Net Income		
Less: Dividends		
Ending Retained Earnings		
Total Stockholders' Equity		

Pacilio Security Services, Inc. Balance Sheet As of December 31, 2016		

Pacilio Security Services, Inc. Statement of Cash Flows For the Year Ended December 31, 2016		
Cash Flows From Operating Activities:		
Cash Receipts from Customers[1]		
Cash from Interest Earned		
Cash Payment for Expenses[2]		
Net Cash Flow from Operating Activities		
Cash Flows From Investing Activities:		
Cash Flows From Financing Activities:		
Cash Payments for Dividends		
Net Cash Flow from Financing Activities		
Net Increase in Cash		
Plus: Beginning Cash Balance		
Ending Cash Balance		

Cash Receipts from Customers:	
Total Cash from Customers	

Cash Payment for Expenses:	
Total Cash Payment for Expenses	

COMPREHENSIVE PROBLEM – CHAPTER 6 (cont.)

g.

Date	Account Titles	Debit	Credit
	Closing Entries		

h.

Pacilio Security Services T-Accounts for 2016
T-Accounts with Closing Entries

Assets	=	Liabilities	+	Stockholders' Equity

Assets

Cash
Bal. |

Petty Cash
Bal. |

Accounts Receivable
Bal. |

Supplies
Bal. |

Prepaid Rent
Bal. |

Merchandise Inventory
Bal. |

Land
Bal. |

Liabilities

Accounts Payable
| Bal.

Salaries Payable
| Bal.

Stockholders' Equity

Common Stock
| Bal.

Retained Earnings
| Bal.

Dividends
Bal. |

Alarm Sales
| Bal.

Monit. Service Revenue
| Bal.

Cost of Goods Sold
Bal. |

Advertising Expense
Bal. |

Maintenance Expense
Bal. |

Miscellaneous Expense
Bal. |

Pacilio Security Services T-Accounts for 2016
T-Accounts with Closing Entries

Assets	=	Liabilities	+	Stockholders' Equity

Office Supplies Expense

Bal.

Rent Expense

Bal.

Salaries Expense

Bal.

Supplies Expense

Bal.

Utilities Expense

Bal.

Cash Short/Over

Bal.

Interest Revenue

Bal.

Pacilio Security Systems Sales and Service After-Closing Trial Balance December 31, 2016		
Account Titles	Debit	Credit

WORKING PAPERS – CHAPTER 7

EXERCISE 7-1A or 7-1B

Note 7-1A does not use event 4.

Event	Assets	=	Liab.	+	Equity	Rev.	–	Exp.	=	Net Inc.	Cash Flow
1.		=		+			–		=		
2.		=		+			–		=		
3.		=		+			–		=		
4.		=		+			–		=		

EXERCISE 7-2A or 7-2B

a.

	General Journal		
Date	Account Titles	Debit	Credit
2013			
1.			
2.			
3.			
4.			

b.

	T-Accounts	

Assets = **Liabilities** + **Equity**

Cash

Service Revenue

Accounts Receivable

Salaries Expense

Allow. for Doubt. Accts.

Uncoll. Accts. Expense

c.

Income Statement					
For the Year Ended December 31, 2013					

Balance Sheet					
As of December 31, 2013					

Statement of Cash Flows For the Year Ended December 31, 2013			
Cash Flows From Operating Activities:			
Net Cash Flow from Operating Activities			
Cash Flows From Investing Activities			
Cash Flows From Financing Activities			
Net Change in Cash			
Plus: Beginning Cash Balance			
Ending Cash Balance			

EXERCISE 7-3A or 7-3B

a. Analyze the Accounts Receivable account:

Accounts Receivable	
Beginning Balance	
Plus: Revenue on Account	
Less: Write-off	
Less: Ending Balance	
Collections of Accounts Rec.	

b. Analyze the Allowance for Doubtful Accounts account:

Allowance for Doubtful Accounts	
Beginning Balance	
Less: Write-off	
Less: Ending Balance	
Uncollectible Accounts Expense	

EXERCISE 7-4A

a. and c.

	McCain Dry Cleaning General Journal		
Date	Account Titles	Debit	Credit
2013			
1.			
2.			
3.			
4. cl			
5. cl			
2014			
1.			
2.			
3.			
4.			

EXERCISE 7-4A or 7-4B a. & c. (cont.)

		T-Accounts		
Assets	=	Liabilities	+	Stockholders' Equity

Cash

2013

2014

Accounts Receivable

2013

2014

Allow. For Doubt. Accts.

2013

2014

Retained Earnings

2013

Service Revenue

2013

2014

Uncoll. Accts. Expense

2011

2014

Note: Closing entries for 2014 were not necessary.

EXERCISE 7-4A or 7-4B (cont.)

b.

(1)	Net Income for 2013	
(2)	Net Cash Flow from Operating Activities:	
(3)	Balance of Accounts Receivable, 12/31/2013:	
(4)	Net Realizable Value of Accounts Receivable, 12/31/2013:	
c.		
(1)	Net Income for 2014	
(2)	Net Cash Flow from Operating Activities:	
(3)	Balance of Accounts Receivable, 12/31/2014:	
(4)	Net Realizable Value of Accounts Receivable, 12/31/2014:	

EXERCISE 7-5A or 7-5B

a.

Event	Assets			=	Liab.	+	Equity	Rev.	−	Exp.	=	Net Inc.	Cash Flow
	Cash	A. Rec.	Allow.	=		+	Ret. Earn.						
1.													
2.													
3.													
4.													

b.

General Journal

Event	Account Title	Debit	Credit
1.			
2.			
3.			
4.			

EXERCISE 7-6A or 7-6B

List the transactions:

---

a.

General Journal

Event	Account Title	Debit	Credit
20__			
1.			
2a.			
2b.			
3.			
4.			
5.			

EXERCISE 7-6A or 7-6B a. (cont.)

Selected T-Accounts:

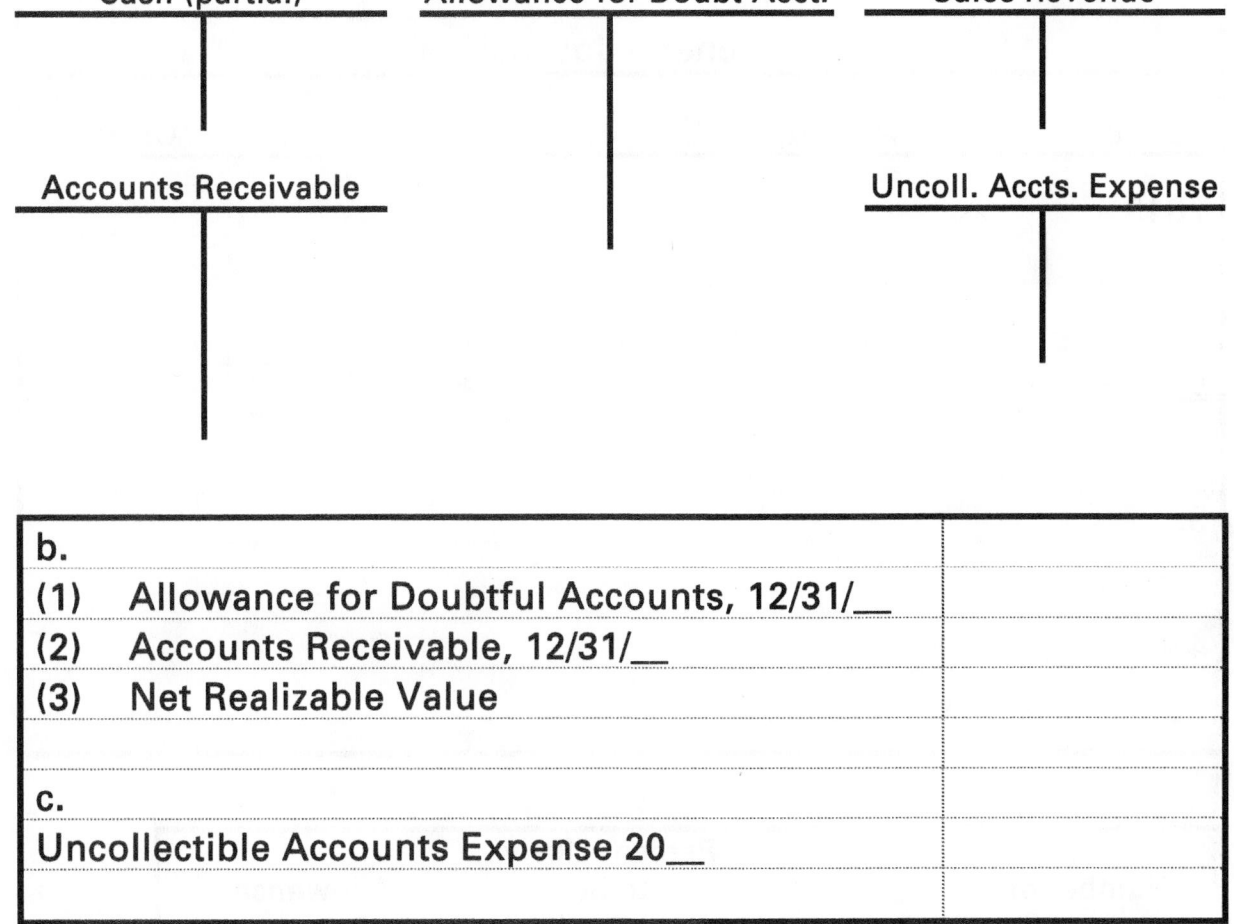

Cash (partial)	Allowance for Doubt Acct.	Sales Revenue

Accounts Receivable		Uncoll. Accts. Expense

b.	
(1) Allowance for Doubtful Accounts, 12/31/__	
(2) Accounts Receivable, 12/31/__	
(3) Net Realizable Value	
c.	
Uncollectible Accounts Expense 20__	

d.

EXERCISE 7-7A or 7-7B

a.

General Journal			
Date	Account Titles	Debit	Credit
2013			
1.			
2.			
3.			
4.			

Number of days Past Due	Amount	Percent Likely to be Uncollectible	Allowance Balance
Current			
0-30			
31-60			
61-90			
Over 90 days			
Total			

EXERCISE 7-7A or 7-7B a. (cont.)

T-Accounts - 2013				
Assets	=	Liabilities	+	Equity

Cash		Service Revenue

Accounts Receivable		Salaries Expense

Allow. For Doubt. Accts.		Uncoll. Accts. Expense

b.

Income Statement
For the Year Ended December 31, 2013

c. Net Realizable Value:

EXERCISE 7-8A or 7-8B

a.

	General Journal		
Date	Account Titles	Debit	Credit
2013			
1.			
2.			
3.			
4.			
5.			
	Closing Entries		

EXERCISE 7-8A or 7-8B a. (cont.)

T-Accounts

Assets	=	Liabilities	+	Stockholders' Equity

Cash

Retained Earnings

Accounts Receivable

Service Revenue

Allow. For Doubt. Accts.

Salaries Expense

Uncoll. Accts. Expense

b.

Income Statement

Statement of Changes in Stockholders' Equity

Beginning Retained Earnings		
Plus: Net Income		
Ending Retained Earnings		
Total Stockholders' Equity		

EXERCISE 7-8A or 7-8B b. (cont.)

	Balance Sheet			

EXERCISE 7-8A or 7-8B b. (cont.)

Statement of Cash Flows		

c.

EXERCISE 7-8Aor 7-8B (cont.)

d.

	General Journal		
Date	Account Titles	Debit	Credit
2014			
1.			
2.			
3.			
4.			
5.			
6.			

EXERCISE 7-8A or 7-8B d. (cont.)

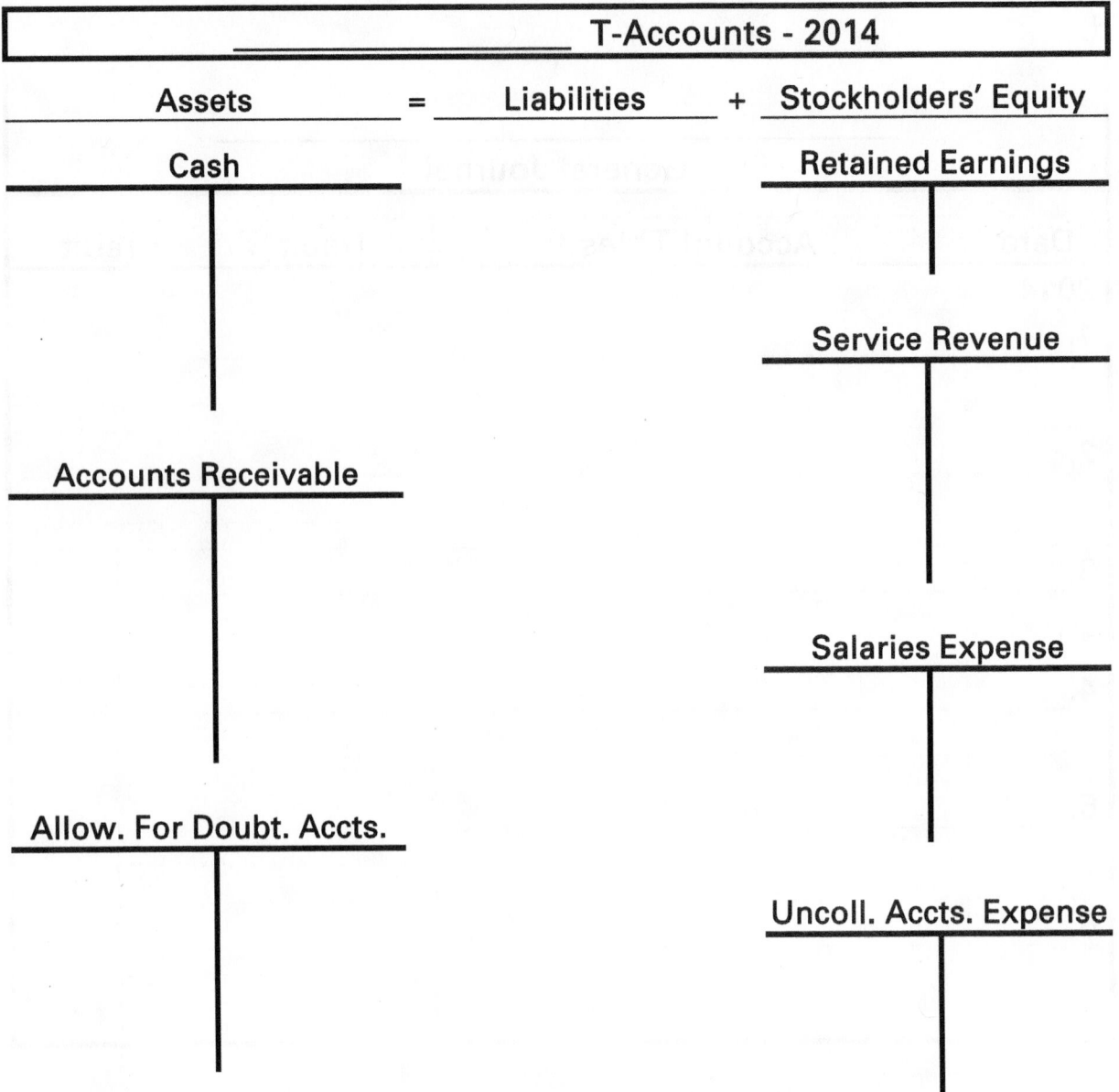

	T-Accounts - 2014
Assets =	**Liabilities** + **Stockholders' Equity**

Assets = **Liabilities** + **Stockholders' Equity**

Cash

Retained Earnings

Service Revenue

Accounts Receivable

Salaries Expense

Allow. For Doubt. Accts.

Uncoll. Accts. Expense

EXERCISE 7-8A or 7-8B d. (cont.)

	Income Statement For the Year Ended December 31, 2014		

	Statement of Changes in Stockholders' Equity For the Year Ended December 31, 2014		
Beginning Retained Earnings			
Plus: Net Income			
Ending Retained Earnings			
Total Stockholders' Equity			

	Balance Sheet As of December 31, 2014		

EXERCISE 7-8A or 7-8B d. (cont.)

	Statement of Cash Flows For the Year Ended December 31, 2014				

Net Realizable Value:

EXERCISE 7-9A or 7-9B

a.

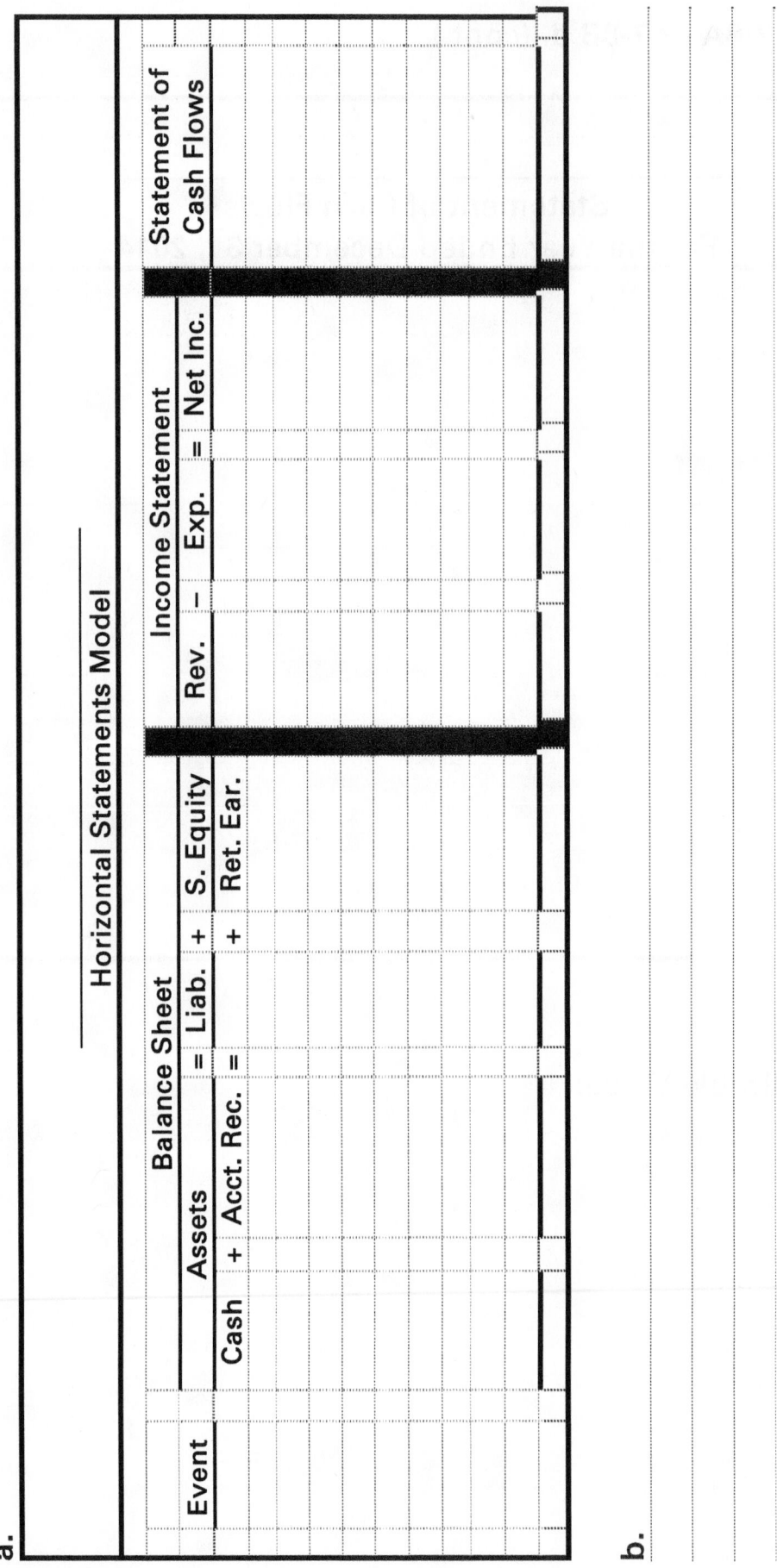

Horizontal Statements Model

Event	Balance Sheet						Income Statement				Statement of Cash Flows
	Assets			=	Liab.	+	S. Equity	Rev.	–	Exp.	=	Net Inc.	
	Cash	+	Acct. Rec.	=		+	Ret. Ear.					

b.

EXERCISE 7-9A or 7-9B (cont.)

c.

	General Journal		
Date	Account Titles	Debit	Credit

EXERCISE 7-10A or 7-10B

Accounts Receivable	Allowance for Doubt. Accts.

a. 1.

a. 2.

a. 3.

a. 4.

b. 1.

b. 2.

b. 3.

EXERCISE 7-11A or 7-11B

a.

General Journal

Date	Account Titles	Debit	Credit

b.

	Balance Sheet						Income Statement			Statement of
	Assets			=	Equity		Rev. −	Exp. =	Net Inc.	Cash Flows
Date	Cash +	Note Rec. +	Int. Rec.	=	Ret. Ear.					

EXERCISE 7-12A or 7-12B

a.

b.

c.

d.

e.

f.

g.

EXERCISE 7-13A or 7-13B

a.

Horizontal Statements Model

	Balance Sheet					Income Statement				Statement of
	Assets			= Liab. +	S. Equity	Rev.	−	Exp.	= Net Inc.	Cash Flows
Event	Cash	+	Acc. Rec.	=	+ Ret. Ear					
1.										
2.										

b. 1.

2.

3.

4.

EXERCISE 7-14A or 7-14B

a. & b.

Event	Account Title	Debit	Credit
a.			
b.			

c.

Net Income	

EXERCISE 7-15A or 7-15B

a.

	Journal Entries for 2013		
Event	Account Titles	Debit	Credit
1.			
2.			
3a.			
3b.			
4.			
5. 9/1			
6.			
7.			
8.			
9.			
10a.			
10b.			

EXERCISE 7-15A or 7-15B a. (cont.)

	Journal Entries for 2013		
Event	Account Titles	Debit	Credit
11.			
12.			

b.

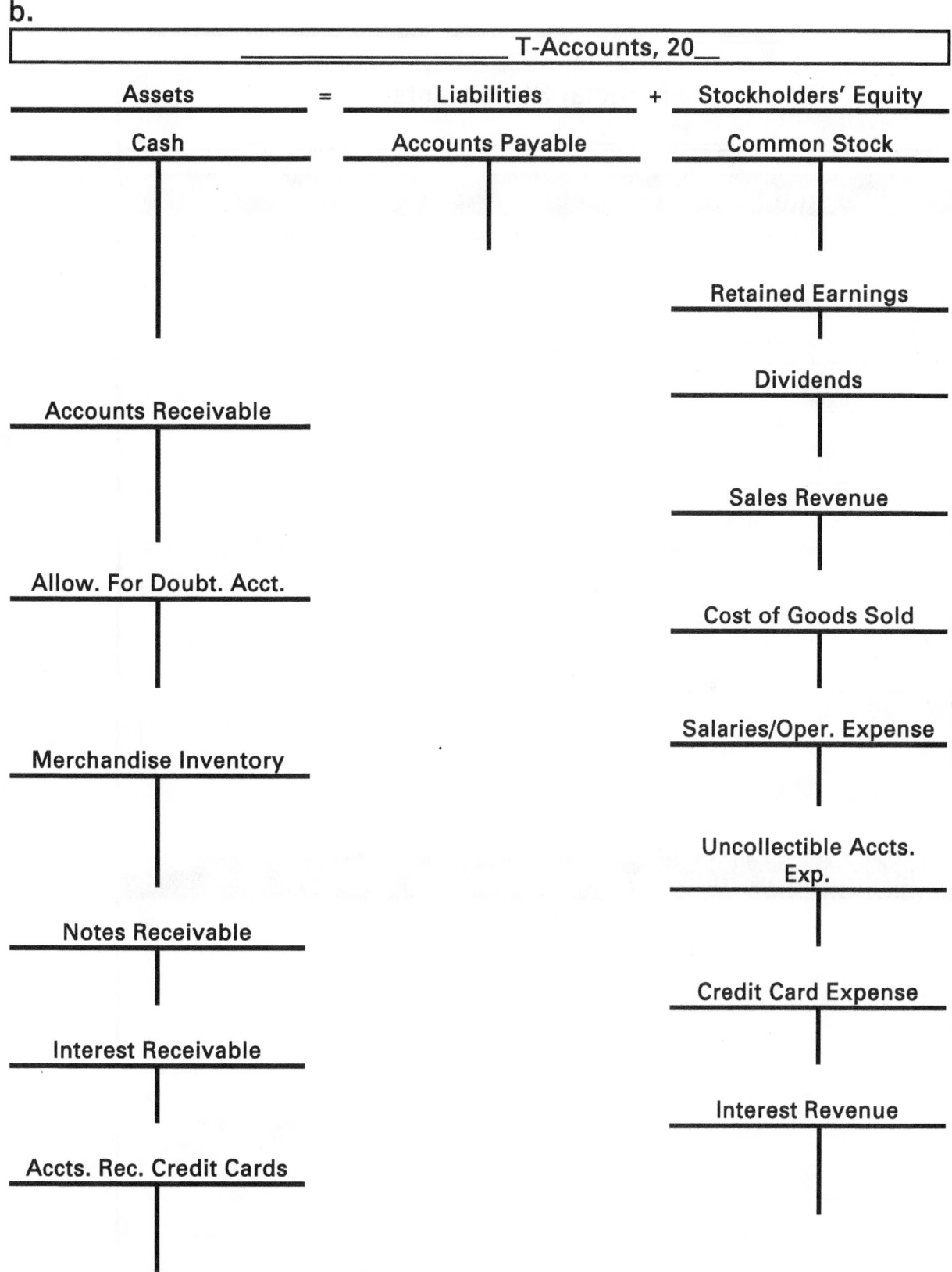

	T-Accounts, 20__	

Assets = **Liabilities** + **Stockholders' Equity**

Cash   Accounts Payable   Common Stock

Retained Earnings

Dividends

Accounts Receivable   Sales Revenue

Allow. For Doubt. Acct.   Cost of Goods Sold

Merchandise Inventory   Salaries/Oper. Expense

Uncollectible Accts. Exp.

Notes Receivable

Credit Card Expense

Interest Receivable

Interest Revenue

Accts. Rec. Credit Cards

c.

	Financial Statements		

Income Statement

Statement of Changes in Stockholders' Equity

EXERCISE 7-15A or 7-15B c. (cont.)

	Balance Sheet			

Statement of Cash Flows			

EXERCISE 7-16A

a. Accounts Receivable Turnover:

Company	Credit Sales	÷	Accts. Rec. Bal.	=	Accts Rec. Turnover
L'Cole		÷		=	
Woodward		÷		=	

b. Average Days to Collect:

Company	365	÷	Turnover	=	Avg. Days to Collect
L'Cole		÷		=	
Woodward		÷		=	

c. Estimated Percentage of Uncollectible Accounts:

Company	Allow. For DA	÷	Accts. Rec. Bal.	=	Estimated Uncoll. %
L'Cole		÷		=	
Woodward		÷		=	

EXERCISE 7-16B

a. Accounts Receivable Turnover:
   Calculate net accounts receivable:

Company	Credit Sales	÷	Accts. Rec. Bal.	=	Accts Rec. Turnover
Adele		÷		=	
Chinstrap		÷		=	

b. Average Days to Collect:

Company	365	÷	Turnover	=	Avg. Days to Collect
Adele		÷		=	
Chinstrap		÷		=	

c. Estimated Percentage of Uncollectible Accounts:

Company	Allow. For DA	÷	Accts. Rec. Bal.	=	Estimated Uncoll. %
Adele		÷		=	
Chinstrap		÷		=	

PROBLEM 7-17A or 7-17B

a.

Event Number	Type of Transaction
20__	
1.	
2.	
3.	
4.*	
20__	
1.	
2.	
3.	
4a.**	
4b.**	
5.	
6.	

*For 7-17B

**4a. is reinstatement of the previously charged off receivable; 4b is the collection of the account.

b. 20__ and 20__

		Effect of Transactions on Financial Statements							
No.	Assets	=	Liab.	+ Equity	Rev.	–	Exp.	= Net Inc.	Cash Flows
2013									
1.									
2.									
3.									
4.									
2014									
1.									
2.									
3.									
4a.*									
4b.*									
5.									
6.									

PROBLEM 7-17A (cont.)

c. (2013)

Date	Account Titles	Debit	Credit
2013			
1.			
2.			
3.			

T-Accounts 2013

Assets   =   Stockholders' Equity

Cash   Accounts Receivable   Service Revenue

Allow. For Doubtful Accounts   Uncoll. Accounts Exp.

c. (2013)

Date	Account Titles	Debit	Credit
2013			
1.			
2.			
3.			
4.			

T-Accounts 2013

Assets = Stockholders' Equity

Cash   Accounts Receivable   Service Revenue

Allow. For Doubtful Accounts   Uncoll. Accts. Expense

Operating Expenses

PROBLEM 7-17A or 7-17B (cont.)

d. (20__)

Financial Statements For the Year Ended 20____		
Income Statement		
Statement of Changes in Stockholders' Equity		
Beginning Common Stock		
Plus: Stock Issued		
Ending Common Stock		
Beginning Retained Earnings		
Plus: Net Income		
Ending Retained Earnings		
Total Stockholders' Equity		

PROBLEM 7-17A or 7-17B d. (cont.)

(20__)

<table>
<tr><td colspan="4" align="center">_____
Financial Statements</td></tr>
<tr><td colspan="4" align="center">**Balance Sheet**
As of December 31, 20___</td></tr>
<tr><td></td><td></td><td></td><td></td></tr>
<tr><td></td><td></td><td></td><td></td></tr>
<tr><td></td><td></td><td></td><td></td></tr>
<tr><td></td><td></td><td></td><td></td></tr>
<tr><td></td><td></td><td></td><td></td></tr>
<tr><td></td><td></td><td></td><td></td></tr>
<tr><td></td><td></td><td></td><td></td></tr>
<tr><td></td><td></td><td></td><td></td></tr>
<tr><td></td><td></td><td></td><td></td></tr>
<tr><td></td><td></td><td></td><td></td></tr>
<tr><td></td><td></td><td></td><td></td></tr>
<tr><td></td><td></td><td></td><td></td></tr>
<tr><td colspan="4" align="center">**Statement of Cash Flows**
For the Year Ended 20___</td></tr>
<tr><td></td><td></td><td></td><td></td></tr>
<tr><td></td><td></td><td></td><td></td></tr>
<tr><td></td><td></td><td></td><td></td></tr>
<tr><td></td><td></td><td></td><td></td></tr>
<tr><td></td><td></td><td></td><td></td></tr>
<tr><td></td><td></td><td></td><td></td></tr>
<tr><td></td><td></td><td></td><td></td></tr>
<tr><td></td><td></td><td></td><td></td></tr>
<tr><td></td><td></td><td></td><td></td></tr>
<tr><td></td><td></td><td></td><td></td></tr>
</table>

PROBLEM 7-17A or 7-17B (cont.)

e. (20___)

Date	Account Titles	Debit	Credit
	Closing Entries		

T-Accounts 20__ Closing Entries

Assets	=	Stockholders' Equity

Cash

Accounts Receivable

Retained Earnings

Allowance for Doubtful Accounts

Service Revenue

Uncoll. Accounts Exp.

Operating Exp. (7-17B)

PROBLEM 7-17A or 7-17B e. (cont.)

After-Closing Trial Balance
December 31, 20__

Account Title	Debit	Credit

PROBLEM 7-17A or 7-17B (cont.)

c. (2014)

Date	Account Titles	Debit	Credit
2014			
1.			
2.			
3.			
4a.			
4b.			
5.			
6.			

(2014)

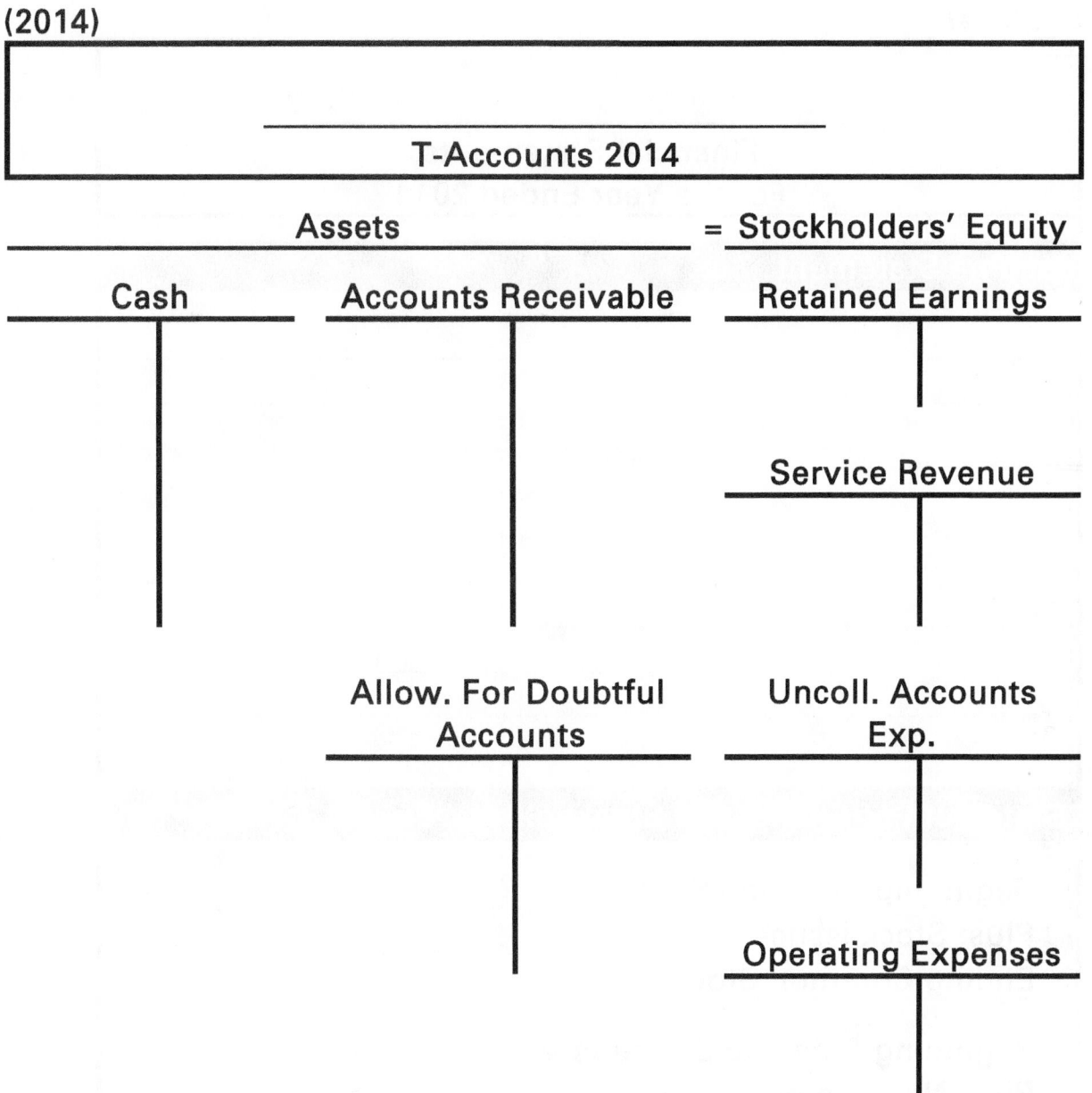

T-Accounts 2014

| Assets | = Stockholders' Equity |

| Cash | Accounts Receivable | Retained Earnings |

Service Revenue

| Allow. For Doubtful Accounts | Uncoll. Accounts Exp. |

Operating Expenses

d. (2014)

Financial Statements **For the Year Ended 2014**			
Income Statement			
Statement of Changes in Stockholders' Equity			
Beginning Common Stock			
Plus: Stock Issued			
Ending Common Stock			
Beginning Retained Earnings			
Plus: Net Income			
Ending Retained Earnings			
Total Stockholders' Equity			

PROBLEM 7-17A or 7-17B d. (cont.)

(2014)

Financial Statements		
Balance Sheet **As December 31, 2014**		
Statement of Cash Flows **For the Year Ended 2014**		

e. (2014)

Date	Account Titles	Debit	Credit
2014	Closing Entries		

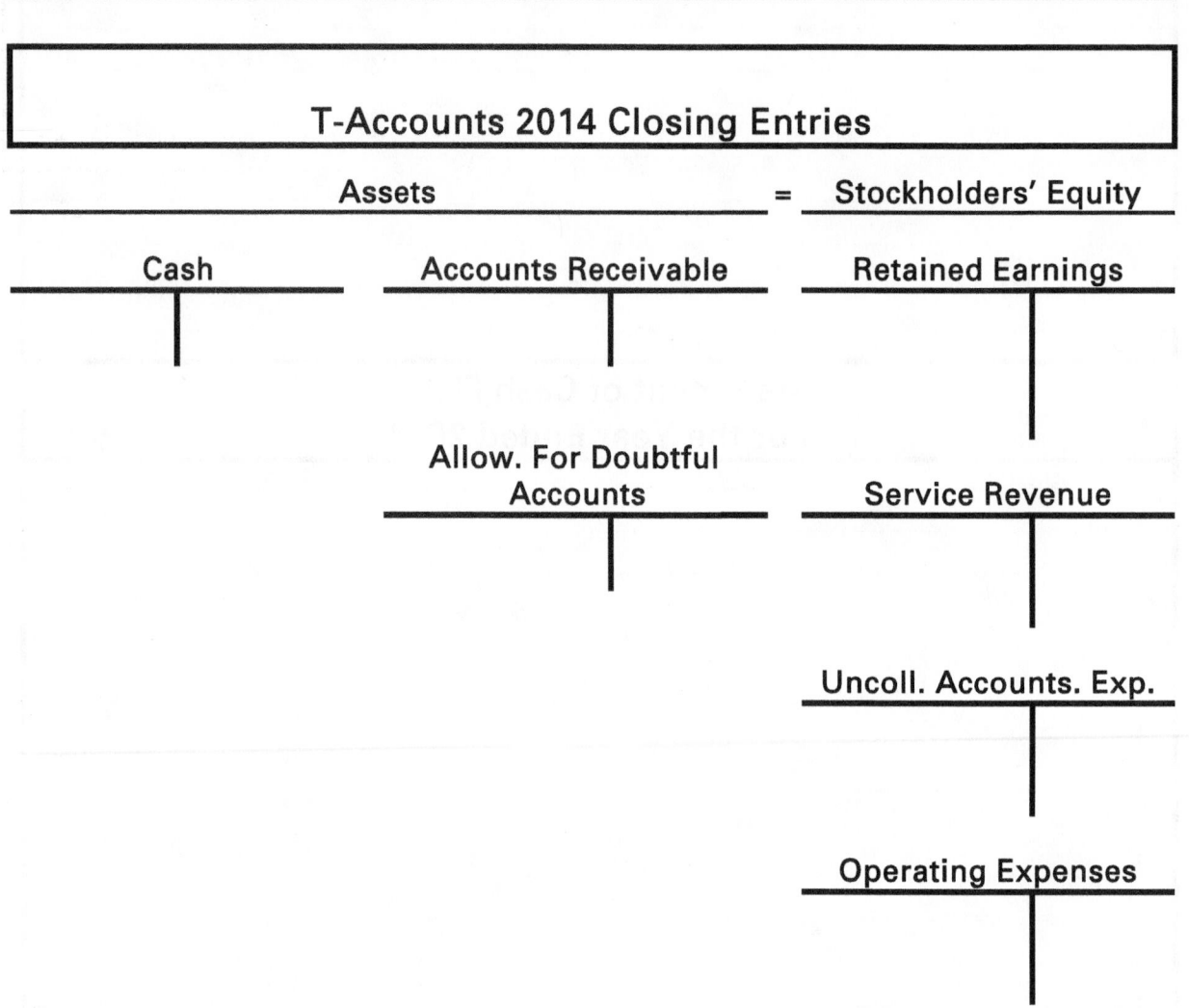

T-Accounts 2014 Closing Entries

| Assets | = | Stockholders' Equity |

Cash   Accounts Receivable   Retained Earnings

Allow. For Doubtful Accounts   Service Revenue

Uncoll. Accounts. Exp.

Operating Expenses

PROBLEM 7-17A or 7-17B e. (cont.)

(2014)

| | Post-Closing Trial Balance December 31, 2014 | | |
Account Title	Debit	Credit

PROBLEM 7-18A

a.

	General Journal		
Event	Account Title	Debit	Credit
1a.			
1b.			
2.			
3.			
4.			

b.

Accounts Receivable	Allowance for Doubtful Accounts

b. (1).

b. (2)

c.

PROBLEM 7-18B

a. ....

....

b. ....

....

c.

Event	Account Title	Debit	Credit
1.			
2.			
3.			

d. ....

....

....

....

PROBLEM 7-18B (cont.)

e.

Event	Assets				= Liab. +	Equity	Rev.	−	Exp.	=	Net Inc.	Cash Flow
	Cash	+	Acc. Rec.	− Allow.	=							
1.												
2.												
3.												
Tot.												

PROBLEM 7-19A

a.

Sales on Account	
Less: Ending Balance of Accounts Receivable	
Collections of Accounts Receivable	

b.

....

....

....

c.

General Journal, 20__			
Event	Account Title	Debit	Credit
1.			
2.			
3.			

d. Accounts Receivable Ending Balance	
Less: Allowance for Doubtful Accounts	
Net Realizable Value of Accounts Receivable	

PROBLEM 7-19A (cont.)

e.

Wells Appliance Co.
Effect of Events on Financial Statements

Event	Assets				=	Liab.	+	Equity		Rev.	−	Exp.	=	Net Inc.	Cash Flows
	Cash	+	Acct. Rec.	−	Allow.	=		+	Ret. Earn.						
1.			+		−	=		+	+			−	=		
2.			+		−	=		+	+			−	=		
3.			+		−	=		+	+			−	=		
Totals			+		−	=		+	+			−	=		

PROBLEM 7-19B

Accounts Receivable	Allowance for Doubtful Accounts

a.(1) ....

a.(2) ....
....

b.

	General Journal, 20__		
Event	Account Title	Debit	Credit
1.			
2.			
3.			
4.			

c. ....
....
....
....

PROBLEM 7-20A or 7-20B

a.

	General Journal, 2013		
Event	Account Titles	Debit	Credit
1.			
2.			
3a.			
3b.			
4.			
5.			
6.			
7.			
8.			

Number of Days Past Due	Amount	Percent Likely to Be Uncollectible	Allowance Balance
Current			
0-30			
31-60			
61-90			
Over 90 days			
Total			

PROBLEM 7-20A or 7-20B a. (cont.)

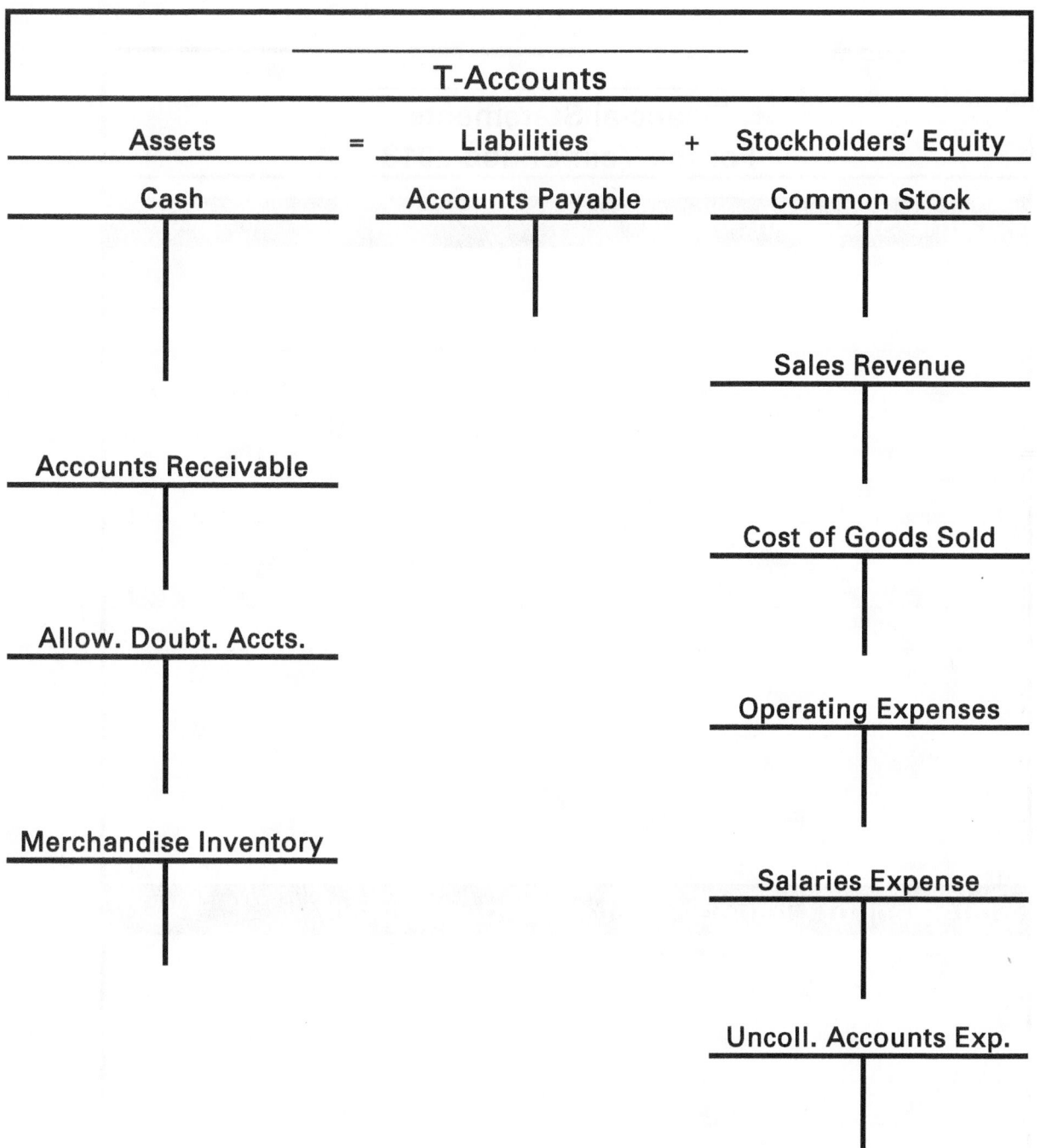

T-Accounts		
Assets =	**Liabilities** +	**Stockholders' Equity**
Cash	Accounts Payable	Common Stock
Accounts Receivable		Sales Revenue
Allow. Doubt. Accts.		Cost of Goods Sold
Merchandise Inventory		Operating Expenses
		Salaries Expense
		Uncoll. Accounts Exp.

b.

	Financial Statements For the Year Ended 2013		
Income Statement			
Statement of Changes in Stockholders' Equity			

	Balance Sheet		
	As of the December 31, 2013		

PROBLEM 7-20A or 7-20B b. (cont.)

	Statement of Cash Flows For the Year Ended 2013		

c. Net Realizable Value:

PROBLEM 7-21A or 7-21B

a.

	Effect of Transactions on Financial Statements								
No.	Assets	=	Liab.	+ Equity	Rev.	– Exp.	= Net Inc.	Cash Flows
20___								
1.								
2.								
3a.								
3b.								
3c.								
3d.								
4.								
5.								
6.								
7.								

Legend:
3a. Cash Sales
3b. Credit Card Sales (remember that credit card expense is recorded).
3c. Sales on Account
3d. Cost of Goods Sold

b.

	General Journal, 20__		
Date	Account Titles	Debit	Credit
1.			
2.			
3a.			
3b.			
3c.			
3d.			
4.			
5.			
6.			
7.			

PROBLEM 7-21A or 7-21B b. (cont.)

T-Accounts

Assets	=	Liabilities	+	Stockholders' Equity

Cash

Common Stock

Accounts Receivable

Sales Revenue

Accounts Receivable - CC

Cost of Goods Sold

Allow. for Doubt. Accts

Credit Card Expense

Merchandise Inventory

Selling & Adm. Expense

Uncoll. Accts. Expense

c.

	Financial Statements		
	For the Year Ended 20__		

Income Statement

Statement of Changes in Stockholders' Equity

	Balance Sheet		
	As of the End of the Year 20__		

PROBLEM 7-21A or 7-21B c. (cont.)

	Statement of Cash Flows For the Year Ended 20____		

Inflow from Customers:	

PROBLEM 7-22A or 7-22B

a.

	General Journal, 20__			
Date	Account Titles		Debit	Credit
1.				
2.				
3.				
4.				
5.				
6.				
7.				
8.				

b.

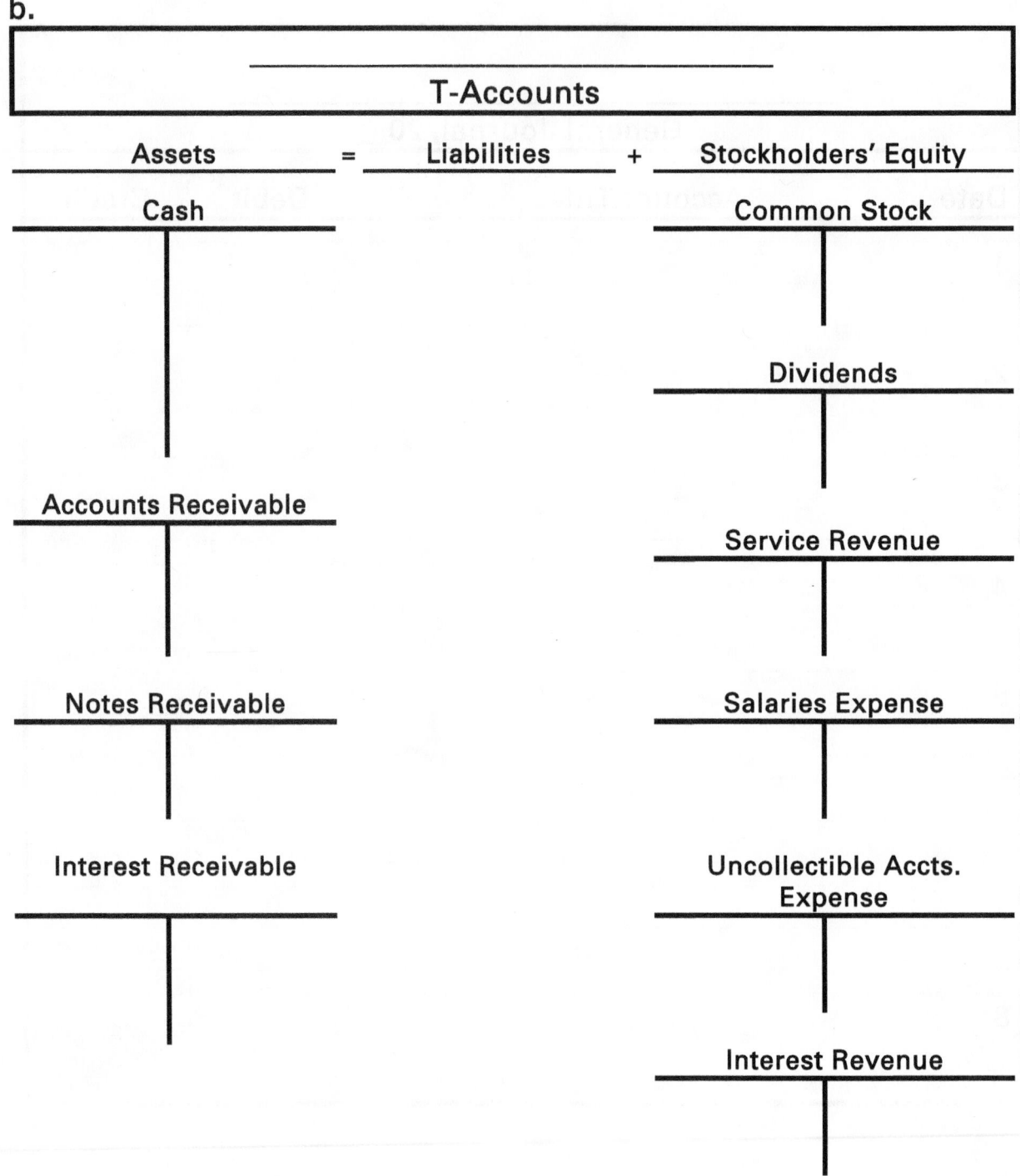

c.

	Income Statement For the Year Ended 20___		

	Balance Sheet As of the End of the Year 20___		

Statement of Cash Flows			
For the Year Ended 20___			

PROBLEM 7-22A or 7-22B (cont.)

d.

Horizontal Statement Model

Event	Assets					=	Equity			Income Statement				Statement of
	Cash	+	Accts. Rec.	+	Notes Rec.	+	Int. Rec.	=	Com. Stock	+	Ret. Earn.	Rev.	−	Exp.	=	Net Inc.	Cash Flows
1.															
2.															
3.															
4.															
5.															
6.															
7.															
8.															
Tot.		+		+		+		=		+			−		=	

PROBLEM 7-23A

Event	Type of Event	Assets	Liabilities	Common Stock	Retained Earnings	Net Income	Cash Flow
a1.*							
a2.*							
b.							
c.							
d.							
e.							
f.							
g.							
h.							
i.							
j.							
k.							
l.							
m.							
n.							
o.							

*a1 recognizes sales revenue, a2 recognizes cost of goods sold.

PROBLEM 7-23B

Event	Type of Event	Assets	Liabilities	Common Stock	Retained Earnings	Net Income	Cash Flow
a.							
b.							
c.							
d.							
e.							
f.							
g.							
h.							
i.							
j.							
l.							
l1.*							
l2.*							
m.							
n.							

*l1. recognizes sales revenue; l2. recognizes cost of goods sold.

PROBLEM 7-24A or 7-24B

Income Statement			
For the Year Ended December 31, 20__			

Balance Sheet **As of December 31, 20__**		
Assets		
Liabilities and Stockholders' Equity		

*Ending Retained Earnings must be computed.

PROBLEM 7-25A or 7-25B

T-Accounts are not required.

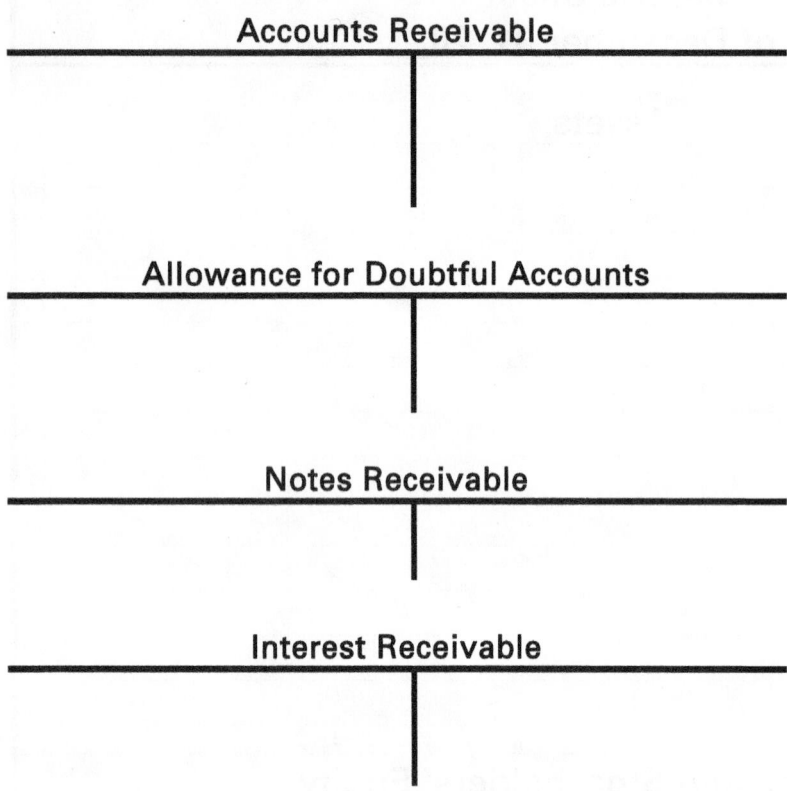

Accounts Receivable

Allowance for Doubtful Accounts

Notes Receivable

Interest Receivable

a. Cash collected:

b. Interest revenue recognized for the period:

PROBLEM 7-26A or 7-26B

General Journal

Date	Account Titles	Debit	Credit

	General Journal		
Date	Account Titles	Debit	Credit

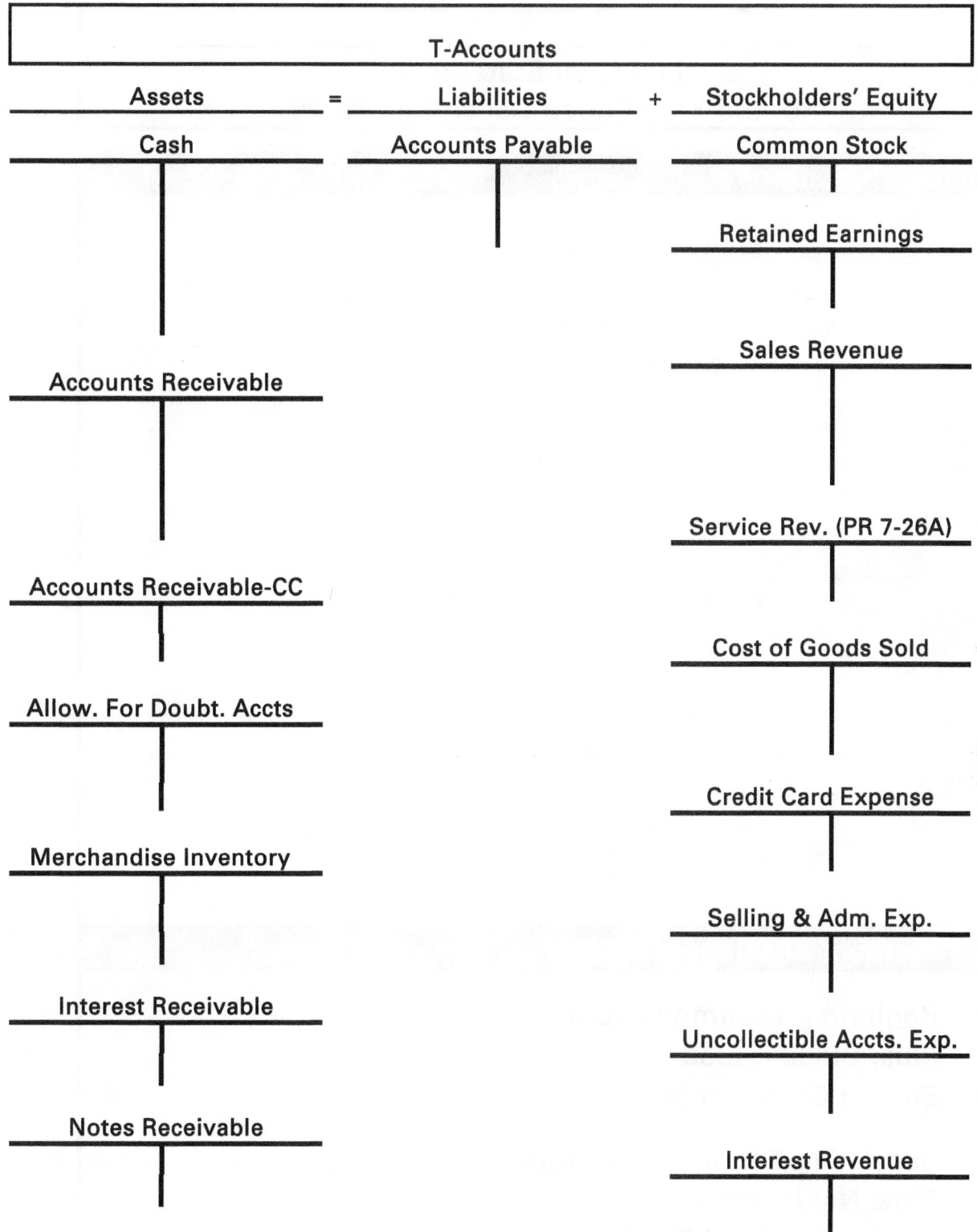

Financial Statements
For the Year Ended December 31, 20___

Income Statement

Statement of Changes in Stockholders' Equity

Beginning Common Stock		
Plus: Stock Issued		
Ending Common Stock		
Beginning Retained Earnings		
Plus: Net Income		
Ending Retained Earnings		
Total Stockholders' Equity		

| Balance Sheet |
| As of December 31, 20___ |

PROBLEM 7-26A or 7-26B (cont.)

Statement of Cash Flows For the Year Ended December 31, 20____			
Cash Flows From Operating Activities:			
Cash Receipts from Revenue*			
Cash Payment for Accounts Pay. (Inv.)			
Cash Payments for Expenses			
Net Cash Flow from Operating Activities			
Cash Flows From Investing Activities:			
Cash Outflow for Notes Receivable			
Net Cash Flow from Investing Activities			
Cash Flows From Financing Activities			
Net Change in Cash			
Plus: Beginning Cash Balance			
Ending Cash Balance			

*

Cash Receipts from Revenue/Customers:	

b. (7-26B)_____

c. (7-26B)_____

ATC 7-1

a. Accounts Receivable Turnover:

Average Days to Collect Accounts Recievable:

b. Uncollectible Percentage:

c.

ATC 7-2

a. 1.

	Expo	White	Zina
Total Sales			
Cash Sales			
Credit Sales			
Accounts Receivable, 1/1/13			
Accounts Receivable, 12/31/13			
Allowance for Doubtful Acct, 1/1/13			
Allowance for Doubtful Acct, 12/31/13			
Bad Debts Expense, 2013			
Uncollectible accounts charged off, 2013			
Collections of accounts receivable, 2013			

2. Uncollectible Accounts
   Expo - 2012:
   Expo - 2013:

   White - 2012:
   White - 2013:

   Zina - 2012:
   Zina - 2013:

3. Sales on Account
   Expo: $
   White:
   Zina:

4. Accounts Receivable Turnover
   Expo:
   White:
   Zina:

c.

d.

ATC 7-3

ATC 7-4

a. Accounts Receivable Turnover:

	Company	Sales ÷ Accounts Receivable
2010		
2009		

b. Average Days to Collect Accounts Receivable:

	Company	365 ÷ Acct. Rec. Turnover
2010		
2009		

c.

d.

ATC 7-5

ATC 7-6

ATC 7-7

ATC 7-8

SOLUTION TO COMPREHENSIVE PROBLEM – CHAPTER 7

a.

Event	Account title	Debit	Credit
\multicolumn{4}{c}{**Pacilio Security Services, Inc.** **General Journal, 2017**}
1.			
2. 3/1			
3. 5/1			
4.			
5.			
6.			
7.			
8a.			
8b.			
9.			
10.			

Compute cost of goods sold:

Event	Account Titles	Debit	Credit
	Pacilio Security Services, Inc. **General Journal, 2017**		
11.			
12.			
13.			
14.			
15.			
16.			
17.			
18.			
19.			

Compute rent expense:

	Pacilio Security Services, Inc. General Journal, 2017			
Event	Account Titles		Debit	Credit
20.				
21.				

Compute uncollectible accounts expense:

b.

Pacilio Security Services, Inc. T-Accounts for 2017

Assets	=	Liabilities	+	Stockholders' Equity

Cash

Bal. 78,972

Petty Cash

Bal. 100

Accounts Receivable

Bal. 33,440

Accounts Rec. Credit Cards

Allow. for Doubt. Accounts

Supplies

Bal. 160

Accounts Payable

Bal. 250

Salaries Payable

Bal. 1,400

Common Stock

Bal. 50,000

Retained Earnings

Bal. 74,662

Dividends

Alarm Sales

Monitoring Service Rev

Cost of Goods Sold

Advertising Expense

Credit Card Expense

Maintenance Expense

Miscellaneous Expense

b.

| Pacilio Security Services, Inc. T-Accounts for 2017 | | | | | |

| Assets | = | Liabilities | + | Stockholders' Equity |

Prepaid Rent

| Bal. | 3,200 | |

Office Supplies Expense

Rent Expense

Merchandise Inventory

| Bal. | 6,440 | |

Salaries Expense

Land

| Bal. | 4,000 | |

Supplies Expense

Uncollectible Accts. Exp.

Utilities Expense

Cash Short/Over

c.

Pacilio Security Services, Inc. Trial Balance December 31, 2017		
Cash		
Petty Cash		
Accounts Receivable		
Allowance for Doubtful Accounts		
Supplies		
Prepaid Rent		
Merchandise Inventory		
Land		
Salaries Payable		
Common Stock		
Retained Earnings		
Dividends		
Alarms Sales		
Monitoring Service Revenue		
Cost of Goods Sold		
Advertising Expense		
Credit Card Expense		
Maintenance Expense		
Miscellaneous Expense		
Office Supplies Expense		
Rent Expense		
Salaries Expense		
Supplies Expense		
Uncollectible Accounts Expense		
Utilities Expense		
Cash Short/Over		
Totals		

d.

Pacilio Security Services, Inc. Income Statement For the Year Ended December 31, 2017			

Pacilio Security Services, Inc. Statement of Changes in Stockholders' Equity For the Year Ended December 31, 2017			

COMPREHENSIVE PROBLEM – CHAPTER 7 d. (cont.)

Pacilio Security Services, Inc. Balance Sheet As of December 31, 2017			

Pacilio Security Services, Inc. Statement of Cash Flows For the Year Ended December 31, 2017		
Cash Flows From Operating Activities:		
Cash Receipts from Customers[1]		
Cash Payment for Expenses[2]		
Net Cash Flow from Operating Activities		
Cash Flows From Investing Activities:		
Cash Flows From Financing Activities:		
Cash Payments for Dividends		
Net Cash Flow from Financing Activities		
Net Increase in Cash		
Plus: Beginning Cash Balance		
Ending Cash Balance		

Cash Reciepts from Customers:	

Cash Payment for Expenses:	

e.

Date	Account Titles	Debit	Credit
	Closing Entries		

Pacilio Security Services T-Accounts for 2017
T-Accounts with Closing Entries

Assets	=	Liabilities	+	Stockholders' Equity

Cash

Bal.

Petty Cash

Bal.

Accounts Receivable

Bal.

Allow. for Doubt. Accts.

Bal.

Supplies

Bal.

Prepaid Rent

Bal.

Merchandise Inventory

Bal.

Land

Bal.

Salaries Payable

Bal.

Common Stock

Bal.

Retained Earnings

Bal.

Dividends

Bal.

Alarm Sales Revenue

Bal.

Monit. Service Revenue

Bal.

Cost of Goods Sold

Bal.

Advertising Expense

Bal.

Credit Card Expense

Bal.

Maintenance Expense

Bal.

COMPREHENSIVE PROBLEM - CHAPTER 7 e. (cont.)

Pacilio Security Services T-Accounts for 2017
T-Accounts with Closing Entries

Assets	=	Liabilities	+	Stockholders' Equity

Miscellaneous Expense
Bal.

Office Supplies Expense
Bal.

Rent Expense
Bal.

Salaries Expense
Bal.

Supplies Expense
Bal.

Uncoll. Accts. Expense
Bal.

Utilities Expense
Bal.

Cash Short/Over
Bal.

Pacilio Security Services, Inc. Post-Closing Trial Balance December 31, 2017		
Account Titles	Debit	Credit
Cash		
Petty Cash		
Accounts Receivable		
Allowance for Doubtful Accounts		
Supplies		
Prepaid Rent		
Merchandise Inventory		
Land		
Salaries Payable		
Common Stock		
Retained Earnings		
Totals		

WORKING PAPERS – CHAPTER 8

EXERCISE 8-1A or 8-1B

a.

b.

c.

d.

EXERCISE 8-2A or 8-2B

	Long-Term Operational Assets:
a.	
b.	
c.	
d.	
e.	
f.	
g.	
h.	
i.	
j.	
k.	
l.	

EXERCISE 8-3A or 8-3B

No.		Tangible (T), Intangible (I)
a.		
b.		
c.		
d.		
e.		
f.		
g.		
h.		
i.		
j.		
k		
l.		

EXERCISE 8-4A or 8-4B

Costs that are to be capitalized:	

b.

Event	Account Titles	Debit	Credit
Purchase			
Freight			
Platform/			
Training			

EXERCISE 8-5A or 8-5B

a. (Exercise 8-5A only)

a. or b.

Total Appraised Value	% of* App. Val.		Purchase Price		Allocated Cost
Land		X		=	
Building		X		=	
Total					

b. or c.

c. or d.

Balance Sheet						Income Statement			Statemt. of Cash Flows
Assets			= Liab. +	S. Equity		Rev. –	Exp. =	Net Inc.	
Cash +	Land +	Bldg. =	+						
+	+	=	+			–	=		

d. or e.

Event	Account Titles	Debit	Credit
Purchase			

EXERCISE 8-6A or 8-6B

a.

Asset	Appraised Value	% of App. Value		Purchase Price		Allocated Cost
Land			x		=	
Building			x		=	
Equip./ Furn.			x		=	
Total						

b.

Assets					=	Liab.	Rev.	–	Exp.	=	Net. Inc.	Cash Flow
Cash	+	Land	+	Building	+	Eq./Fur.	=	N. Pay.				
	+		+		+		=		–		=	

c.

Account Titles	Debit	Credit

EXERCISE 8-7A or 8-7B

a.

	General Journal		
Event	Account Titles	Debit	Credit

EXERCISE 8-7A or 8-7B a. (cont.)

T-Accounts for 2013		
Assets	**=**	**Stockholders' Equity**
Cash	Common Stock	Service Revenue
Equipment -		Operating Exp. (Ex. 8-7A)
Accumulated Depr.		Salaries Expense
		Depreciation Expense

EXERCISE 8-7A

b. ....

c. ....

d. ....

b.

	Sam's Seafood Balance Sheet		

EXERCISE 8-7B b. (cont.)

Sam's Seafood Statement of Cash Flows		

c. Computation of Net Income:

d.

e.

f.

EXERCISE 8-8A or 8-8B

Depreciation Calculation: (Cost − Accumulated Depr.) x (2 x SL Rate)

Year 1

....

Year 2

T-Accounts		

Assets	=	Stockholders' Equity

Cash	Common Stock	Retained Earnings

Equipment

Accumulated Depr.

Service/Sales Revenue

Depreciation Expense

EXERCISE 8-8A or 8-8B (cont.)

Financial Statements	2013	2014
Income Statements		
Service/Sales Revenue		
Depreciation Expense		
Net Income		
Balance Sheets		
Assets		
Cash		
Equipment		
Accumulated Depreciation		
Total Assets		
Stockholders' Equity		
Common Stock		
Retained Earnings		
Total Stockholders' Equity		
Statements of Cash Flows		
Cash Flows From Operating Activities:		
Inflow from Customers		
Cash Flows From Investing Activities:		
Outflow to Purchase Asset		
Cash Flows From Financing Activities:		
Inflow from Stock Issue		
Net Change in Cash		
Plus: Beginning Cash Balance		
Ending Cash Balance		

EXERCISE 8-9A or 8-9B

a. Calculation of Depreciation:

1. Determine Total Cost of the Asset:	
Total Cost	

2. Compute Depreciation Expense per Year

2013 Depreciation:	
2014 Depreciation:	

b.

Date	Account Title	Debit	Credit
2013			

c.

Compute Book Value:	
Compute Gain/Loss on Sale:	

Date	Account Titles	Debit	Credit

EXERCISE 8-10A or 8-10B

a.

1. Straight-Line Calculation:

2. Double-Declining Balance Calculation:

Cost – Accumulated Depreciation x (2 x Straight-Line Rate)

Year	Calculation	Depr. Expense
Year 1		
Year 2		
Year 3		
Year 4		
Year 5		
	Total Depreciation Expense	

b.

Statements Model									
Balance Sheet					Income Statement				Stmt. of
Assets			=	S. Equity	Rev	–	Exp.	= Net Inc.	Cash Flows
Cash	+	Book Value of Equip	=	Ret. Ear.					
Purchase									
	+		=			–		=	
Straight-Line									
	+		=			–		=	
DDB									
	+		=			–		=	

8-13

c. 1.

	General Journal		
Date	Account Title	Debit	Credit
Yr. 1			

EXERCISE 8-10A or 8-10B (cont.)

c. 2.

	General Journal		
Date	Account Title	Debit	Credit
Yr. 1			
Yr. 2			
Yr. 3			
Yr. 4			
Yr. 5			

EXERCISE 8-11A or 8-11B

a. Compute Book Value:

b. Compute Gain on Sale:

c.

d.

e.

EXERCISE 8-12A or 8-12B

	20__ Accounting Equation						
		Assets		=	Stockholders' Equity		
Event		Cash	Land	=	Common Stock	+	Retained Earnings
a.1				=			
b.1				=			

a. (1)

(2)

(3)

b. (1)

(2)

(3)

EXERCISE 8-13A or 8-13B

a. Double-Declining Balance

(Cost – Accum. Depr.) x (2 x SL Rate) = Depr. Exp. Per Year

Year	Computation	Depr. Expense
20__		
20__		
20__		
20__		
20__		
	Total Accumulated Depreciation	

b. Units-of-Production

(Cost – Salvage) ÷ Estimated Production = Depr. Cost per Unit
1. Compute Cost Per Unit:

2.
Annual Depreciation = Depr. Cost per Unit x Actual Annual Units

Year	Computation of annual depreciation:	Depr. Expense
20__		
20__		
20__		
20__		
20__		
	Total Accumulated Depreciation	

EXERCISE 8-13A or 8-13B (cont.)

c. Calculation of Book Value

Double-Declining Balance:	

Units of Production:	

Computation of Gain	Double-Declining Bal.	Units of Production
Sales Price		
Less, Book Value		
Gain/(Loss)		

EXERCISE 8-14A or 8-14B

a. & b. MACRS depreciation = Cost x Table %

	Computation	Depreciation Expense
7-year property		
2013		
2014		
5-year property		
2013		
2014		

EXERCISE 8-15A or 8-15B

Year	Computation	Depreciation Expense
2013		
2014		
2015		
2016		

EXERCISE 8-16A or 8-16B

EXERCISE 8-17A or 8-17B

a.

Assets			=	Stockholders' Equity				Rev.	−	Exp.	=	Net Inc.		Cash Flow
Cash	+	Book Value	=	C. Stock	+	Ret. Ear.								
	+		=		+				−		=			
	+		=		+				−		=			

b.

Assets			=	Stockholders' Equity				Rev.	−	Exp.	=	Net Inc.		Cash Flow
Cash	+	Book Value	=	C. Stock	+	Ret. Ear.								
	+		=		+				−		=			
	+		=		+				−		=			

c.

Assets			=	Stockholders' Equity				Rev.	−	Exp.	=	Net Inc.		Cash Flow
Cash	+	Book Value	=	C. Stock	+	Ret. Ear.								
	+		=		+				−		=			
	+		=		+				−		=			

EXERCISE 8-18A or 8-18B

a.

b.

c.

d.

EXERCISE 8-19A or 8-19B

a. Compute depletion charge per unit:

b.
Depletion Calculation:

Year	Computation	Depreciation Expense

Statements Model									
Assets		=	Stockholders' Equity		Rev.	−	Exp.	= Net Inc.	Cash Flow
Cash	+	. =	C. Stock	+ Ret. Ear.					
	+	=	+			−		=	
	+	=	+			−		=	
Depletion for Year 1									
	+	=	+			−		=	
Depletion for Year 2									
	+	=	+			−		=	

c.

Date	Account Titles	Debit	Credit
Year 1			
Year 2			

EXERCISE 8-20A or 8-20B

a. Compute Amortization per Unit:

	Computation	Amortization Exp.
Patent		

b.

											Net Inc.	Cash Flow
		Assets				= S. Equity		Rev.	–	Exp.	=	
	Cash	+	Patent	+	G. Will	=						
Bal.		+		+		=				–	=	
Pur.		+		+		=				–	=	
amortz.		+		+		=				–	=	

c.

Date	Account Title	Debit	Credit

EXERCISE 8-21A or 8-21B

a. Computation of Goodwill:

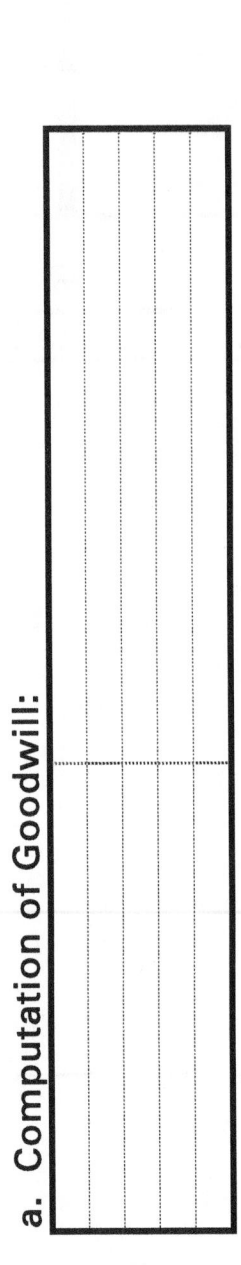

b.

Statements Model

Cash	+	Assets	+	Goodwill	=	Liab.	+	Equity		Rev.	–	Exp.	=	Net Inc.		Cash Flow
		Assets			=	Liab.	+	Equity								
Bal.																
Acq.																

c. (8-21B)

c. or d.

Event	Account Titles	Debit	Credit
Acquisition			

8-26

EXERCISE 8-22A or 8-22B

EXERCISE 8-23A or 8-23B

Determine Book Value:		
	2013	2014
Original Cost		
Less, Salvage Value		
Cost to be depreciated		
Divided by useful life		
Depreciation Expense per year		
Multiply by years the building has been used		
Accumulated Depreciation		
Original Cost		
Less, Accumulated Depreciation		
Book Value of Building		

b.

EXERCISE 8-23A or 8-23B (cont.)

c.

Compute revised book-value for 2014	
Revised fair value	
Less, salvage	
Revised cost to be depreciated	
Divided by remaining life	
Depreciation expense per year	
Multiply by the years the building has been used since revaluation	
Revaluated fair value	
Less, accumulated depreciation	
Book-value of building, 12/31/2014	

d.

PROBLEM 8-24A or 8-24B

Compute Total Cost of Equipment:

Basket Purchase:

Allocation is based on relative market values:

Asset	Fair Market Value	Percent of FMV	Purchase Price	=	Allocated Costs
			x		
			x		
			x		
			x		
Total					

Land and Building:

	Land
Total Cost of Land	
	Building
Total Cost Building	

PROBLEM 8-25A or 8-25B

	Financial Statements				
Income Statements					
	2013	**2014**	**2015**	**2016**	**2017**
Revenue	$	$	$	$	$
Depr. Expense*					
Operating Income					
Gain/(Loss)					
Net Income	$	$	$	$	$
Statements of Changes in Stockholders' Equity					
Beg. Com. Stock	$	$	$	$	$
Plus: Stk. Issued					
End. Com. Stock					
Beg. Ret. Earn.					
Plus: Net Income					
End. Ret. Earn.					
Total Stk. Equity	$	$	$	$	$

Computations:

Depreciation Expense:

Gain/Loss on Sale of Asset:

PROBLEM 8-25A or 8-25B (cont.)

Financial Statements

Balance Sheets

	2013	2014	2015	2016	2017
Assets					
Cash	$	$	$	$	$
Equipment					
Less, Acc. Dep.					
Total Assets	$	$	$	$	$
Stockholders' Equity					
Common Stock	$	$	$	$	$
Retained Earnings					
Total Stk. Equity	$	$	$	$	$

Statements of Cash Flows

	2013	2014	2015	2016	2017
Operating Act.:					
Inflow from Cust.	$	$	$	$	$ -0-
Net Cash Op. Act.					
Investing Act.:					
Inflow from Sale					
Outflow for Equip.					
Net Cash Inv. Act.					
Financing Act.					
Inflow from Stock					
Net Cash Fin. Act.					
Net Change in Cash					
Plus: Beg. Cash Bal.					
Ending Cash Bal.	$	$	$	$	$

PROBLEM 8-26A or 8-26B

a.

		Horizontal Statements Model				
Event	Assets =	Liab. +	S. Equity	Net Income		Cash Flow
2013						
1.						
2.						
3.						
4.						
5.						
6.						
7.						
2014						
1.						
2.						
3.						
4.						
5.						
6.						
2015						
1.						
2.						
3.						
4.						
5.						

PROBLEM 8-26A or 8-26B (cont.)

b.

	General Journal		
Event	Account Titles	Debit	Credit

PROBLEM 8-26A or 8-26B b. (cont.)

	General Journal		
Event	Account Titles	Debit	Credit

PROBLEM 8-26A or 8-26B b. (cont.)

T-Accounts

Assets = Stockholders' Equity

Cash   Common Stock   Retained Earnings

Service Revenue

(Asset)

Maintenance Expense

Accumulated Depr.

T-Accounts

Assets	=	Stockholders' Equity

_____Expense

Depreciation Expense

PROBLEM 8-26A or 8-26B (cont.)

c.

Financial Statements			
Income Statements			
	2013	2014	2015
Service Revenue			
Expenses			
Total Expenses			
Net Income			
Statements of Changes in Stockholders' Equity			
Beginning Common Stock Plus:			
Ending Common Stock			
Beginning Retained Earnings Plus:			
Ending Retained Earnings			
Total Stockholders' Equity			

PROBLEM 8-26A or 8-26B c. (cont.)

Financial Statements

Balance Sheets

	2013	2014	2015
Assets			
Total Assets			
Liabilities			
Stockholders' Equity			
Total Stockholders' Equity			
Total Liab. and Stkholders' Equity			

Statements of Cash Flows

Cash Flows From Oper. Act.:			
Net Cash Flow from Oper. Act.			
Cash Flows From Inv. Act.:			
Net Cash Flow from Inv. Act.			
Cash Flows From Fin. Act.:			
Net Cash Flow from Fin. Act.			
Net Change in Cash			
Plus: Beginning Cash Balance			
Ending Cash Balance			

PROBLEM 8-27A or 8-27B

Compute Asset Cost:

a. Straight-line:

Year	Computation:	Depr. Expense
2013		
2014		

b. Units of Production/Double-Declining Balance or Units-of-Production:

Year	Computation:	Depr. Expense
2013		
2014		

PROBLEM 8-27A or 8-27B (cont.)

c. Double-Declining Balance or Units-of-Production:

Year	Computation:	Depr. Expense
2013		
2014		

d. MACRS

Year	Computation:	Depr. Expense
2013		
2014		

PROBLEM 8-28A or 8-28B

a. <u>Straight-Line</u>

(Cost − Salvage Value) ÷ Useful Life = Annual Depreciation

Year	Computations:	Depreciation Exp.
1.		
2.		
3.		
4.		
5.		

b. <u>Double-Declining Balance</u>

Accum. Depreciation — Annual
Cost − at Beginning of Period x (2 x SL Rate) = Depreciation

Year	Computations:	Depreciation Exp.
1.		
2.		
3.		
4.		
5.		

c. ....

....

....

....

....

PROBLEM 8-28A or 8-28B (cont.)

d. <u>Straight-Line</u>

Calculate Book Value:

Calculate Gain or Loss:

<u>Double-Declining-Balance</u>

Calculate Book Value:

Calculate Gain or Loss:

e. (8-28B)

PROBLEM 8-29A or 8-29B

Units-of-Production

Total Estimated
(Cost − Salvage Value) ÷ Units of Production = Cost per Unit

Annual
Cost per Unit x Current Units of Production = Depreciation

a. Cost per Unit:

Year	Computation	Depreciation Exp.

PROBLEM 8-29A or 8-29B (cont.)

b.

Horizontal Statements Model

Event		Balance Sheet							Income Statement					Statement of
		Assets			Stockholders' Equity				Rev.	−	Exp.	=	Net Inc.	Cash Flows
	Cash	+	Book Value of Van	=	=	C. Stock	+	Ret. Ear.						
Bal.		+		=	=		+					=		
Rev.		+		=	=		+					=		
Depr.		+		=	=		+					=		
Bal.		+		=	=		+					=		

c.

Compute Gain/Loss on Sale:	
Sales Price	
Less, Book Value	
Gain/Loss	

Account Title	Debit	Credit

PROBLEM 8-30A or 8-30B

Company A: Straight Line:

Depreciation Per Year:

Company B: Double-Declining Balance:

Company B

Year	Computation	Depreciation Exp.

Company C: Units-of-Production:

Per Unit Cost:

Year	Computation	Depreciation Exp.

PROBLEM 8-30A or 8-30B (cont.)

a. Company A - 20__
    Revenue $ _____
    Depreciation Expense   (_____)
    Net Income $ _____

   Company B - 20__
    Revenue $ _____
    Depreciation Expense   (_____)
    Net Income $ _____

   Company C - 20__
    Revenue $ _____
    Depreciation Expense   (_____)
    Net Income $ _____

Highest net income in 20__: _____

b. Company A - 20__
    Revenue $ _____
    Depreciation Expense   (_____)
    Net Income $ _____

   Company B - 20__
    Revenue $ _____
    Depreciation Expense   (_____)
    Net Income $ _____

   Company C - 20__
    Revenue $ _____
    Depreciation Expense   (_____)
    Net Income $ _____

Lowest net income for 20__ _____

PROBLEM 8-30A or 8-30B (cont.)

c. Company A   Accumulated Depreciation

Year	Depreciation expense
20__	
20__	
20__	
Total Depr.	

Cost	
Accumulated Depreciation	
Book Value	

Company B   Accumulated Depreciation

Year	Depreciation expense
20__	
20__	
20__	
Total Depr.	

Cost	
Accumulated Depreciation	
Book Value	

Company C   Accumulated Depreciation

Year	Depreciation expense
20__	
20__	
20__	
Total Depr.	

Cost	
Accumulated Depreciation	
Book Value	

Highest Book Value:_____

PROBLEM 8-30A or 8-30B (cont.)

d.   Company A:

Sales (four years)	
Depreciation (four years)	
Retained Earnings – 20__	

Company B:

Sales (four years)	
Depreciation (four years)	
Retained Earnings – 20__	

Company C:

Sales (four years)	
Depreciation (four years)	
Retained Earnings – 20__	

e.

PROBLEM 8-31A or 8-31b

Computations of depletion for journal entries:

PROBLEM 8-31A or 8-31B (cont.)

a.

	General Journal		
Date	Account Titles	Debit	Credit

PROBLEM 8-31A or 8-31B (cont.)

b.

Natural Resources	
Total	

Computation of Natural Resources:

c.

Account Titles	Debit	Credit

PROBLEM 8-32A or 8-32B

a.

Horizontal Statements Model								
Date	Assets	=	Liab.	+	S. Equity	Net Income		Cash Flows
1/1/13								
12/31/13								
/14								
12/31/14								
/15								
12/31/15								
/16								
12/31/16								
/17								
12/31/17								
/18*								
/18**								

*record depreciation.
** record sale of asset.

b.

Year	Computation	Depr. Exp.
2013		
2014		
2015		
2016		
2017		
2018*		

*8-32B

PROBLEM 8-32A or 8-32B (cont.)

c.

Computation of Book Value						
Year	Cost	–	Acc. Depr.	=	Book Value	
2013		–		=		
2014		–		=		
2015		–		=		
2016		–		=		
2017		–		=		

d. Computation of Depreciation Expense for 2018:

Book Value at Date of Sale:

Computation of Gain on Sale:

e.

Account Titles	Debit	Credit

PROBLEM 8-33A or 8-33B

a.

Statements Model

	Assets			=	Stockholders' Equity				Rev.	−	Exp.	=	Net Inc.		Cash Flow
Date	Cash	+	Book Value of___	=	C. Stock	+	Ret. Ear.								
Bal.		+	+	=		+	+			−		=			
		+	+	=		+	+			−		=			
		+	+	=		+	+			−		=			
		+	+	=		+	+			−		=			
		+	+	=		+	+			−		=			
Bal.		+	+	=		+	+			−		=			

*Depreciation Calculation:

PROBLEM 8-33A or 8-33B (cont.)

b.

	General Journal		
Date	Account Titles	Debit	Credit

PROBLEM 8-34A or 8-34B

a.

Computation of Goodwill Acquired:		

b.

Account Title	Debit	Credit

PROBLEM 8-35A or 8-35B

a. (8-35A)

....

....

....

....

b.

Date	Account Title	Debit	Credit

ATC 8-1

a.

b.

c.

d.

e.

ATC 8-2

Computation of depreciation expense:

Straight-line:
(Cost − Salvage Value) ÷ useful life = depreciation per year

Double-declining balance:
(Cost − Accumulated depreciation) x (2 x SL rate)

MACRS:
Cost x MACRS table factor

ATC 8-2 (cont.)

Note: It is useful to prepare a horizontal statements model before preparing the financial statements.

Horizontal Statement Model
Using Straight-line Depreciation

	Balance Sheet							Income Statement					Statement of Cash Flows
	Assets					Stockholders' Equity							
Event	Cash	+	Equip.	−	A. Dep.	=	C. Stock	+	Ret. Ear.	Rev.	−	Exp.	=	Net Inc.	
1.	+			−		=		+	+	−			=		
2.	+			−		=		+	+	−			=		
3.	+			−		=		+	+	−			=		
4.	+			−		=		+	+	−			=		
5.	+			−		=		+	+	−			=		
6.	+			−		=		+	+	−			=		
7.	+			−		=		+	+	−			=		
Bal.														

ATC 8-2 (cont.)

Horizontal Statement Model
Using Double-Declining Balance Depreciation

Event			Balance Sheet							Income Statement					Statement of Cash Flows
			Assets			=	Stockholders' Equity								
	Cash	+	Equip.	−	A. Dep.	=	C. Stock	+	Ret. Ear.	Rev.	−	Exp.	=	Net Inc.	
1.	+			−		=		+			−		=		
2.	+			−		=		+			−		=		
3.	+			−		=		+			−		=		
4.	+			−		=		+			−		=		
5.	+			−		=		+			−		=		
6.	+			−		=		+			−		=		
7.	+			−		=		+			−		=		
Bal.	+			−		=		+			−		=		

ATC 8-2 (cont.)

Horizontal Statement Model
Using MACRS Depreciation

	Balance Sheet										Income Statement							Statement of Cash Flows
	Assets						=	Stockholders' Equity				Rev.	−	Exp.	=	Net Inc.		
Event	Cash	+	Equip.	−	A. Dep.	=		C. Stock	+	Ret. Ear.								
1.	+					=			+				−		=			
2.	+					=			+				−		=			
3.	+					=			+				−		=			
4.	+					=			+				−		=			
5.	+					=			+				−		=			
6.	+					=			+				−		=			
7.	+					=			+				−		=			
Bal.	+					=			+				−		=			

ATC 8-2 (cont.)

a.

Sweet's Bakery Financial Statements			
Income Statements			
	SL	DDB	MACRS
Sales Revenue			
Expenses			
Supplies Expense			
Operating Expenses			
Depreciation Expense			
Income Tax Expense			
Total Expenses			
Net Income			
Balance Sheets			
Assets			
Cash			
Equipment			
Less: Accumulated Depreciation			
Total Assets			
Liabilities			
Stockholders' Equity			
Common Stock			
Ending Retained Earnings			
Total Stockholders' Equity			
Total Liab. and Stkholders' Equity			

b.

ATC 8-3

ATC 8-4

a.

Depreciation Expense as a Percentage of Sales:				
Company	Depreciation Expense	÷	Sales	Percent of Sales

b.

Property, Plant and Equipment as a Percentage of Sales:				
Company	Property, Plant and Equipment	÷	Sales	Percent of Sales

c.

d.

Return on Assets				
Company	Net Income	÷	Total Assets	ROA

ATC 8-5

a.

Depreciation Expense as a Percentage of Sales:				
Company	Depreciation Expense	÷	Sales	Percent of Sales

b.

Property, Plant and Equipment as a Percentage of Sales:				
Company	Property, Plant and Equipment	÷	Sales	Percent of Sales

c.

d.

ATC 8-6

ATC 8-7

ATC 8-8

a.

	Current Assets	Property, Plant and Equipment	Total Assets
Microsoft:			
Dollar Amount:			
% of Total Assets:			
Intel:			
Dollar Amount:			
% of Total Assets:			

b.

a.

Pacilio Security Services, Inc. General Journal, 2018			
Event	Account title	Debit	Credit
1.			
2.			
3. 5/1			
4.			
5.			
6.			
7a.			
7b.			
8.			

*Compute Cost of Goods Sold:

Event	Account Titles	Debit	Credit
9.			
10.			
11.			
12.			
13.			
14.			
15.			
16.			
17.			
18.			

Pacilio Security Services, Inc.
General Journal, 2018

COMPREHENSIVE PROBLEM – CHAPTER 8 a. (cont.)

	Pacilio Security Services, Inc. General Journal, 2018		
Event	Account Titles	Debit	Credit
19.			
20.			
21.			
22.			

[1]Van: Expired lease paid in 2017:

Office: Expired rent paid in 2017:
              Expired rent paid in 2018:
              Total rent expense for 2018

[2]Alarm sales on account
 Monitoring Service Revenue on account
 Total Credit Sales
 Estimated Uncollectible Percent
 Uncollectible Account Expense

[3]Equipment cost: $9,000 – Salvage $2,000 = $7,000; $7,000 ÷ 5 =
    Van cost: $27,000 x (2 x .25) =
    Total depreciation expense

b.

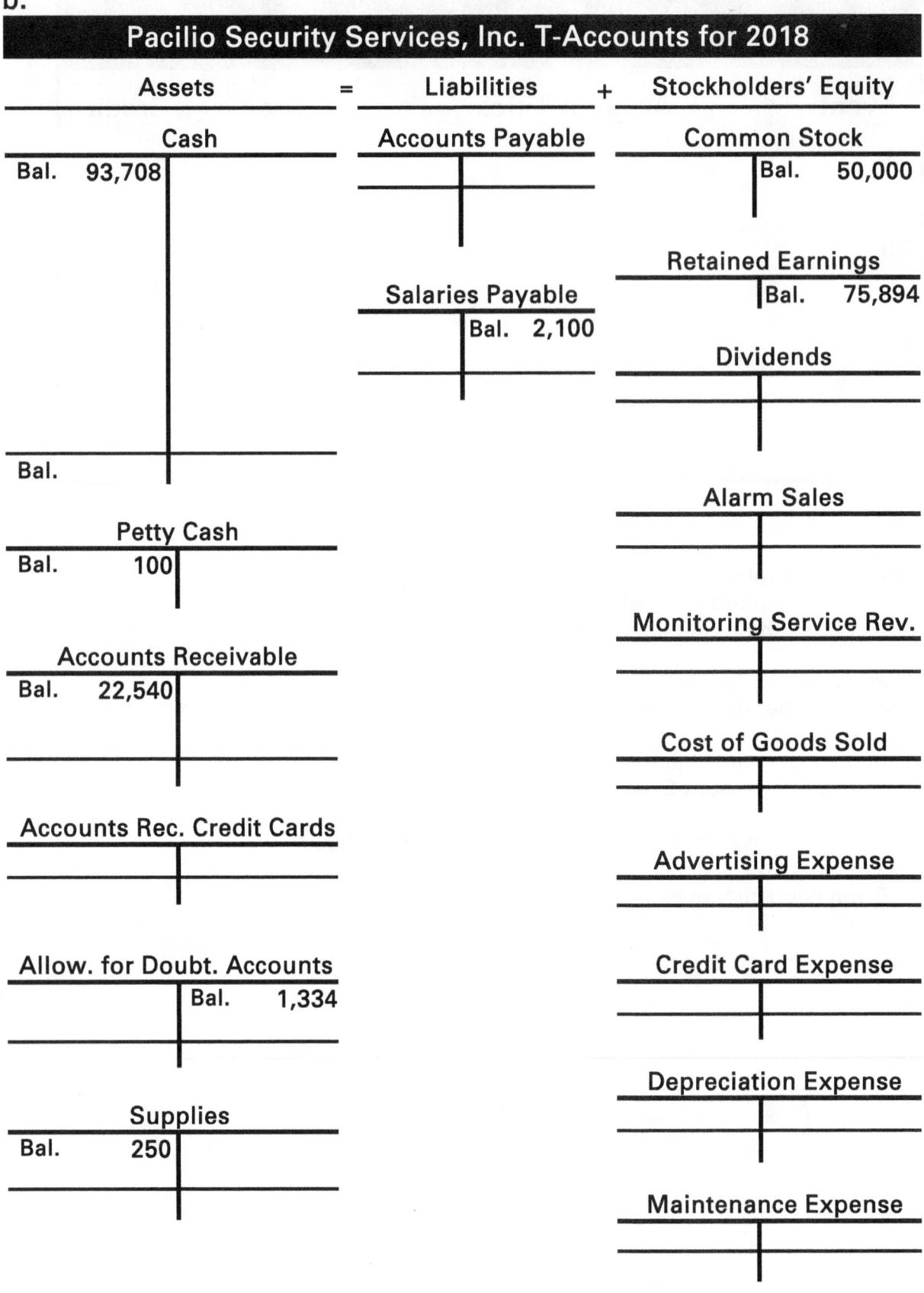

Pacilio Security Services, Inc. T-Accounts for 2018

Assets = Liabilities + Stockholders' Equity

Cash
Bal. 93,708

Bal.

Petty Cash
Bal. 100

Accounts Receivable
Bal. 22,540

Accounts Rec. Credit Cards

Allow. for Doubt. Accounts
Bal. 1,334

Supplies
Bal. 250

Accounts Payable

Salaries Payable
Bal. 2,100

Common Stock
Bal. 50,000

Retained Earnings
Bal. 75,894

Dividends

Alarm Sales

Monitoring Service Rev.

Cost of Goods Sold

Advertising Expense

Credit Card Expense

Depreciation Expense

Maintenance Expense

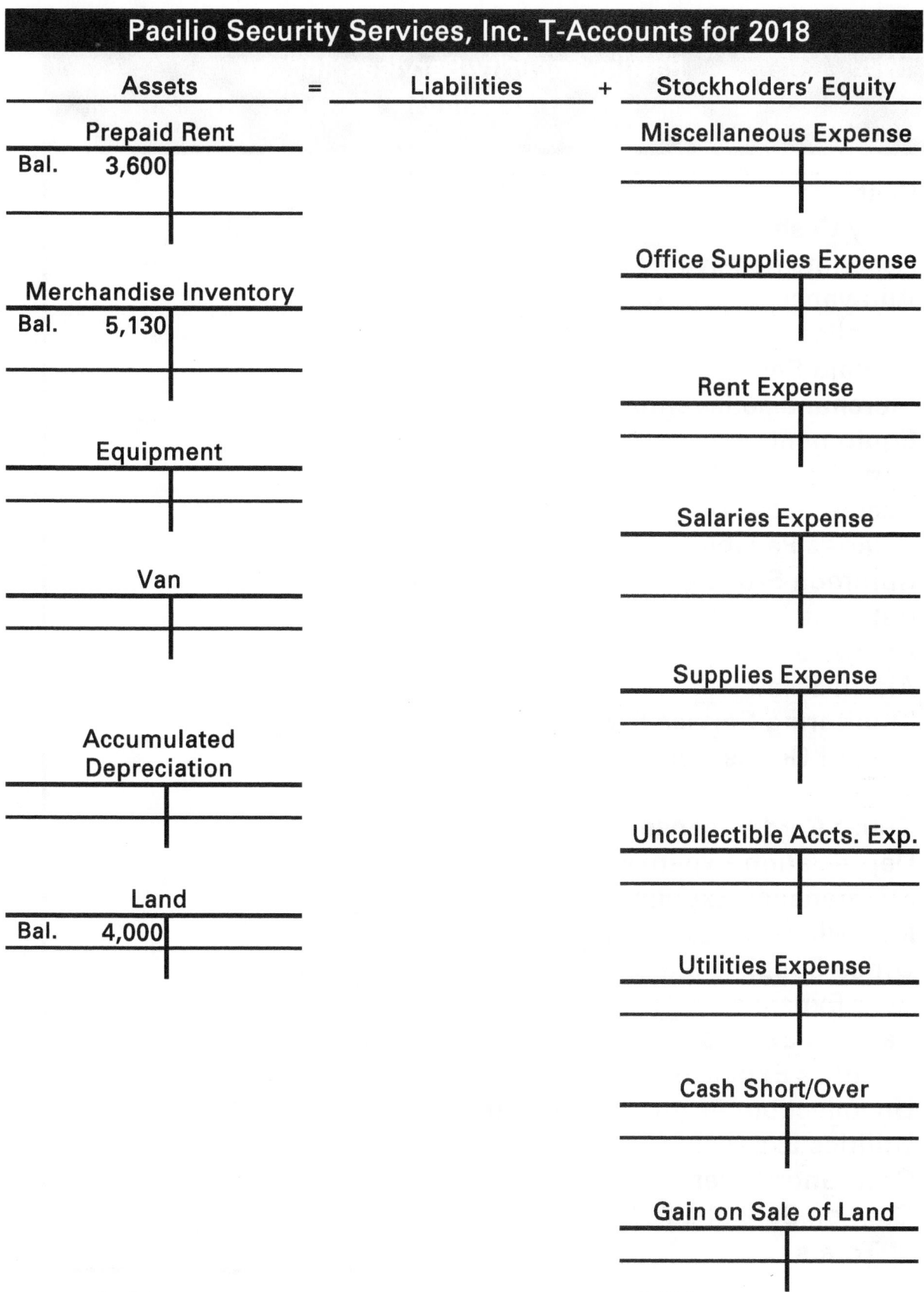

Pacilio Security Services, Inc. T-Accounts for 2018

Assets	=	Liabilities	+	Stockholders' Equity

Prepaid Rent
Bal. 3,600

Merchandise Inventory
Bal. 5,130

Equipment

Van

Accumulated Depreciation

Land
Bal. 4,000

Miscellaneous Expense

Office Supplies Expense

Rent Expense

Salaries Expense

Supplies Expense

Uncollectible Accts. Exp.

Utilities Expense

Cash Short/Over

Gain on Sale of Land

c.

Pacilio Security Services, Inc. Trial Balance December 31, 2018		
Cash		
Petty Cash		
Accounts Receivable		
Allowance for Doubtful Accounts		
Supplies		
Prepaid Rent		
Merchandise Inventory		
Equipment		
Van		
Accumulated Depreciation		
Salaries Payable		
Common Stock		
Retained Earnings		
Dividends		
Alarm Sales		
Monitoring Service Revenue		
Cost of Goods Sold		
Advertising Expense		
Credit Card Expense		
Depreciation Expense		
Maintenance Expense		
Miscellaneous Expense		
Office Supplies Expense		
Rent Expense		
Salaries Expense		
Supplies Expense		
Uncollectible Accounts Expense		
Utilities Expense		
Cash Short/Over		
Gain on Sale of Land		
Totals		

d.

Pacilio Security Services, Inc. Income Statement For the Year Ended December 31, 2018		
Revenues		
Monitoring Service Revenue		
Alarm Sales		
Total Revenues		
Cost of Goods Sold		
Gross Margin		
Expenses		
Advertising Expense		
Credit Card Expense		
Depreciation Expense		
Maintenance Expense		
Miscellaneous Expense		
Office Supplies Expense		
Rent Expense		
Salaries Expense		
Supplies Expense		
Uncollectible Accounts Expense		
Utilities Expense		
Cash Short and Over		
Total Operating Expenses		
Net Operating Income		
Non-Operating Income		
Gain on Sale of Land		
Net Income		

Pacilio Security Services, Inc. Statement of Changes in Stockholders' Equity For the Year Ended December 31, 2018		
Beginning Common Stock		
Plus: Common Stock Issued		
Ending Common Stock		
Beginning Retained Earnings		
Plus: Net Income		
Less: Dividends		
Ending Retained Earnings		
Total Stockholders' Equity		

Pacilio Security Services, Inc. Balance Sheet As of December 31, 2018		
Assets		
Cash		
Petty Cash		
Accounts Receivable		
Allowance for Doubtful Accounts		
Supplies		
Prepaid Rent		
Merchandise Inventory		
Equipment		
Van		
Accumulated Depreciation		
Total Assets		
Liabilities		
Salaries Payable		
Total Liabilities		
Stockholders' Equity		
Common Stock		
Retained Earnings		
Total Stockholders' Equity		
Total Liabilities and Stockholders' Equity		

Pacilio Security Services, Inc. Statement of Cash Flows For the Year Ended December 31, 2018		
Cash Flows From Operating Activities:		
Cash Receipts from Customers[1]		
Cash Payment for Expenses[2]		
Net Cash Flow from Operating Activities		
Cash Flows From Investing Activities:		
Inflow from Sale of Land		
Outflow to Purchase Equip. and Van		
Net Cash Flow from Investing Activities		
Cash Flows From Financing Activities:		
Cash Payments for Dividends		
Net Cash Flow from Financing Activities		
Net Increase in Cash		
Plus: Beginning Cash Balance		
Ending Cash Balance		

[1]Cash Receipts from Customers:
    Collection of Accounts Receivable
    Collection of Credit Cards
    Total Cash from Customers

[2]Cash Payment for Expenses
    Payment of Prepaid Rent
    Payment of Salaries
    Payment of Inventory
    Payment of Accounts Payable
    Payment of Advertising
    Payment of Utilities Expense
    Payment of Expense from Petty Cash
    Total Cash Payment for Expenses

COMPREHENSIVE PROBLEM – CHAPTER 8 (cont.)

e.

Date	Account Titles	Debit	Credit
	Closing Entries		

COMPREHENSIVE PROBLEM – CHAPTER 8 e. (cont.)

Pacilio Security Services T-Accounts for 2018
T-Accounts with Closing Entries

Assets	=	Liabilities	+	Stockholders' Equity

Cash

Petty Cash

Accounts Receivable

Allow. for Doubt. Accts.

Supplies

Prepaid Rent

Merchandise Inventory

Equipment

Van

Accumulated Depr.

Salaries Payable

Common Stock

Retained Earnings

Dividends

Alarm Sales

Monit. Service Revenue

Cost of Goods Sold

Advertising Expense

Credit Card Expense

Depreciation Expense

Pacilio Security Services T-Accounts for 2018
T-Accounts with Closing Entries

Assets	=	Liabilities	+	Stockholders' Equity

Maintenance Expense

Miscellaneous Expense

Office Supplies Expense

Rent Expense

Salaries Expense

Supplies Expense

Uncoll. Accts. Expense

Utilities Expense

Cash Short/Over

Gain on Sale of Land

Pacilio Security Services, Inc. After-Closing Trial Balance December 31, 2018		
Account Titles	Debit	Credit
Cash		
Petty Cash		
Accounts Receivable		
Allowance for Doubtful Accounts		
Supplies		
Prepaid Rent		
Merchandise Inventory		
Equipment		
Van		
Accumulated Depreciation		
Salaries Payable		
Common Stock		
Retained Earnings		
Totals		

WORKING PAPERS – CHAPTER 9

EXERCISE 9-1A or 9-1B

a.

b.

c.

d.

e.

EXERCISE 9-2A or 9-2B

a. ....

b. ....

c. (Ex 9-2B) ....

c. or d. ....

Statements Model for 2013

Event	Assets =	Liabilities		+ Stockholders' Equity			Income Statement			Statement of Cash Flows
		Notes	Int.	Common	Ret.					
No.	Cash =	Payable +	Payable +	Stock +	Earn.		Rev. −	Exp. =	Net Inc.	
1.										
2.										
3.										

EXERCISE 9-3A or 9-3B

a.

Calculate Sales Tax Collected:	

b.

General Journal

Event	Account Title	Debit	Credit
1.			
2.			
3.			
4.			
5.			

c.

Total Sales	
Less: Cost of Goods Sold	
Gross Margin	
Less: Operating Expenses	
Net Income	

EXERCISE 9-4A or 9-4B

a.

General Journal

Event	Account Titles	Debit	Credit
1. Nov.			
2. Dec. 10			
3. Dec.			

b.

	Assets	=	Liabilities +	Stockholder's Equity		Income Statement				Statement of
Event	Cash	=	Sales Tax Pay.	Com. Stock +	Ret. Earn.	Rev.	–	Exp.	= Net Inc.	Cash Flow
1. Nov.										
2. Dec.										
3. Dec.										

c.

d.

e.

f. (9-4A)

9-4

EXERCISE 9-5A

1.

Account Title	Debit	Credit

2.

Account Title	Debit	Credit

3.

EXERCISE 9-5B

a.

b. 1.

Account Title	Debit	Credit

2.

3.

EXERCISE 9-6A

a.

Event	Account Titles	Debit	Credit
1.			
2a.			
2b.			
3.			
4.			

b.

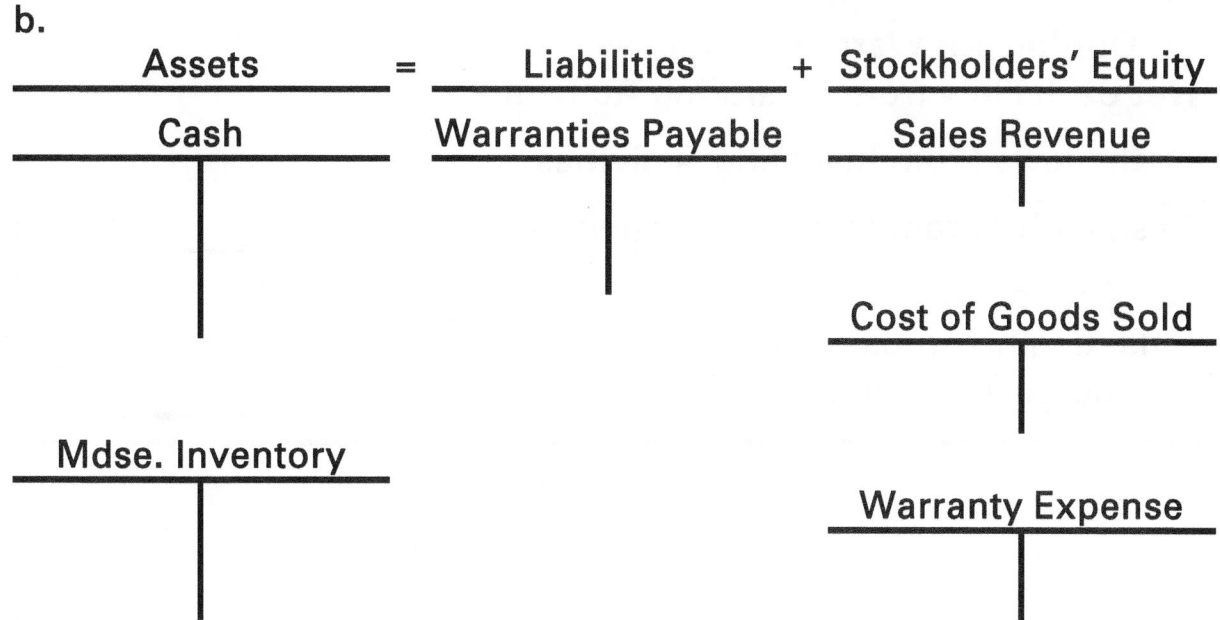

Assets	=	Liabilities	+	Stockholders' Equity
Cash		Warranties Payable		Sales Revenue
				Cost of Goods Sold
Mdse. Inventory				Warranty Expense

EXERCISE 9-6A (cont.)

c.

Devon's Computers Financial Statements		
Income Statement		
Sales Revenue		
Cost of Goods Sold		
Gross Margin		
Warranty Expense		
Net Income		
Statement of Cash Flows		
Cash Flows From Operating Activities:		
Inflow from Customers		
Outflow for Inventory		
Outflow for Warranty Expense		
Net Cash Flow from Operating Activities		
Cash Flows From Investing Activities		
Cash Flows From Financing Activities		
Net Change in Cash		
Plus: Beginning Cash Balance		
Ending Cash Balance		

d.

EXERCISE 9-6B

Note: T-Accounts are not required

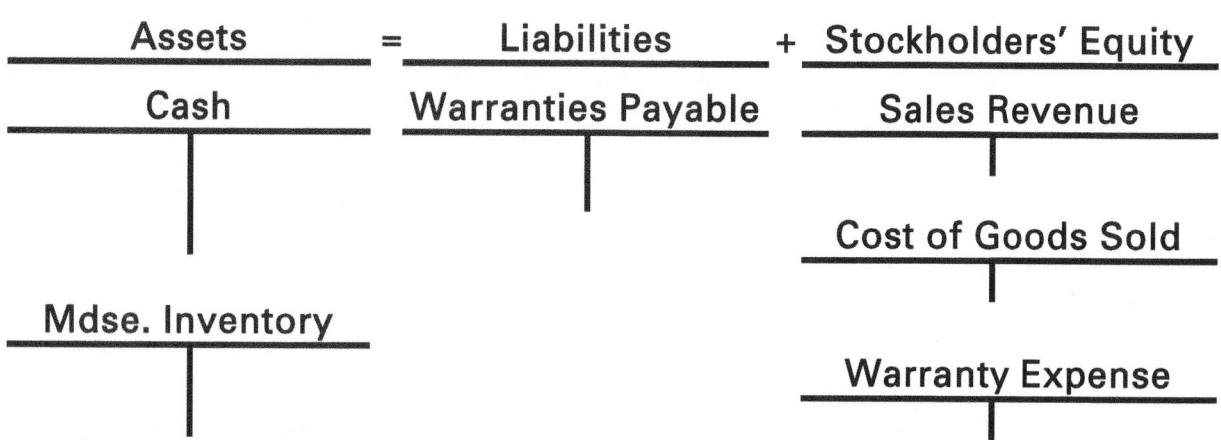

Assets	=	Liabilities	+	Stockholders' Equity
Cash		Warranties Payable		Sales Revenue
				Cost of Goods Sold
Mdse. Inventory				Warranty Expense

Shen's Stereos Financial Statements		
Income Statement		
Sales Revenue		
Cost of Goods Sold		
Gross Margin		
Warranty Expense		
Net Income		
Statement of Cash Flows		
Cash Flows From Operating Activities:		
Inflow from Customers		
Outflow for Inventory		
Outflow for Warranty Expense		
Net Cash Flow from Operating Activities		
Cash Flows From Investing Activities		
Cash Flows From Financing Activities		
Net Change in Cash		
Plus: Beginning Cash Balance		
Ending Cash Balance		

EXERCISE 9-6B (cont.)

EXERCISE 9-7A or 9-7B

a.

Event	Assets	=	Liab.	+	Equity	Rev.	−	Exp.	=	Net Inc.	Cash Flow
Est.											
Pd.											

Event	Account Titles	Debit	Credit
b. Est.			
c. Payment			

d.

EXERCISE 9-8A or 9-8B

a.

Event	Assets	=	Liab.	+	Equity	Rev.	–	Exp.	=	Net Inc.	Cash Flow
1.											
2.											
3a.											
3b.											
4.											
5.											
6.											
7.											
8.											
9.											
10.											

EXERCISE 9-8A or 9-8B (cont.)

b.

	General Journal		
Event	**Account Title**	**Debit**	**Credit**
1.			
2.			
3a.			
3b.			
4.			
5.			
6.			
7.			
8.			
9.			
10.			

EXERCISE 9-8A or 9-8B b. (cont.)

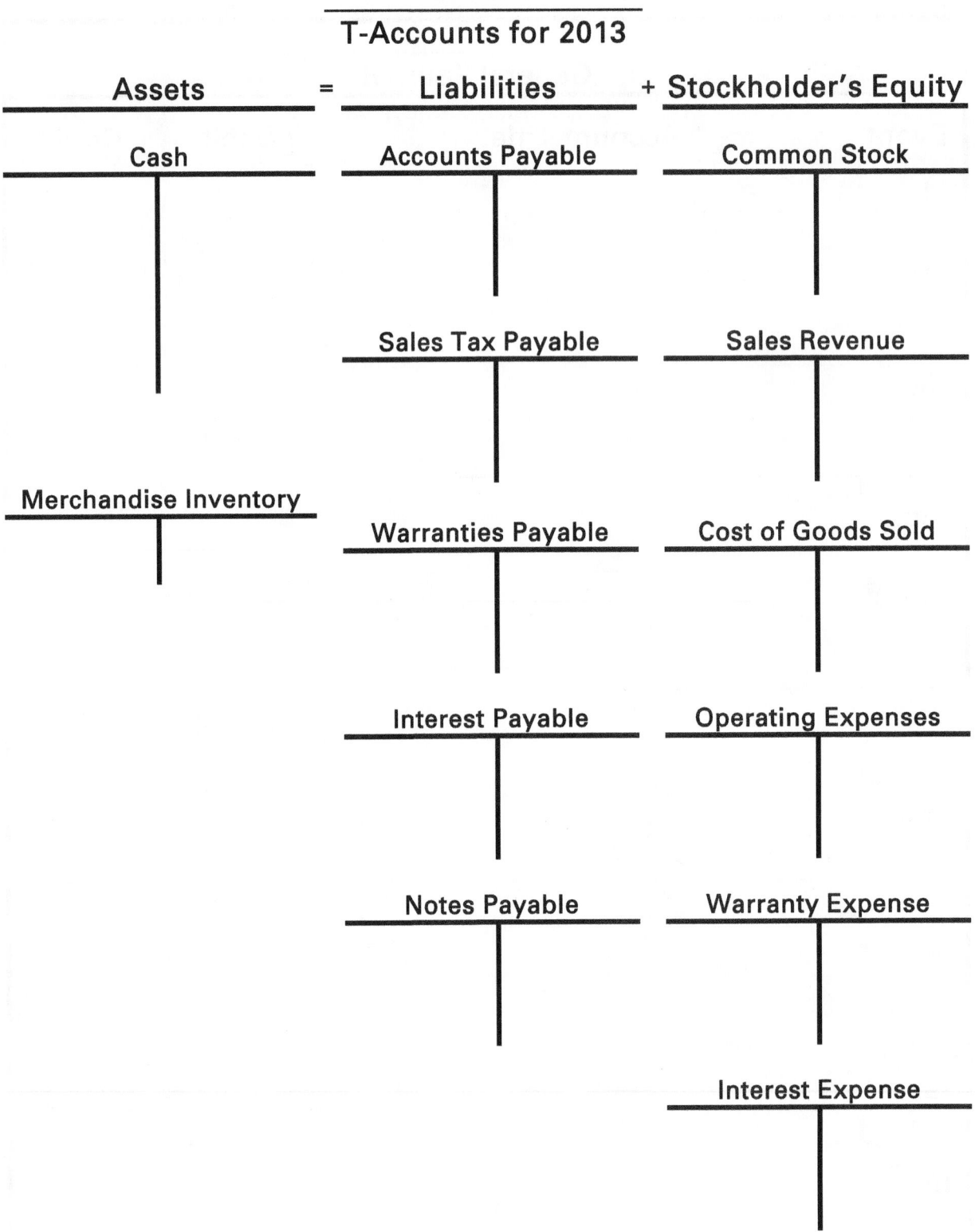

T-Accounts for 2013

Assets = Liabilities + Stockholder's Equity

Cash | Accounts Payable | Common Stock

Sales Tax Payable | Sales Revenue

Merchandise Inventory | Warranties Payable | Cost of Goods Sold

Interest Payable | Operating Expenses

Notes Payable | Warranty Expense

Interest Expense

EXERCISE 9-8A or 9-8B (cont.)

c.

_____ -			
Income Statement			
For the Year Ended December 31, 2013			

	Balance Sheet As of December 31, 2013			

EXERCISE 9-8A or 9-8B c. (cont.)

	Statement of Cash Flows For the Year Ended December 31, 2013			

d. Current Liabilities:

EXERCISE 9-9A or 9-9B

a.

Computation of Gross Earnings					
Employee	Hours Worked	x	Wage Rate per Hour	=	Gross Pay

b.

Name:		
Gross Earnings		
Deductions:		
Federal Income Taxes		
FICA Tax – SS		
FICA Tax – Medicare		
Total Deductions		
Net Pay		

Name:		
Gross Earnings		
Deductions:		
Federal Income Taxes		
FICA Tax – SS		
FICA Tax – Medicare		
Total Deductions		
Net Pay		

EXERCISE 9-9A or 9-9B (cont.)

c.

	General Journal Entries		
Date	Account Titles	Debit	Credit

EXERCISE 9-10A or 9-10B

a.

Employee_____ - March		
Gross Earnings		
Deductions:		
Federal Income Taxes		
FICA Tax - SS		
FICA Tax - Medicare		
Total Deductions		
Net Pay		
Employee_____ - March		
Gross Earnings		
Deductions:		
Federal Income Taxes		
FICA Tax - SS		
FICA Tax - Medicare		
Total Deductions		
Net Pay		

EXERCISE 9-10A or 9-10B (cont.)

b.

Employee_____ - December		
Gross Earnings		
Deductions:		
Federal Income Taxes		
FICA Tax - SS		
FICA Tax - Medicare		
Total Deductions		
Net Pay		
Employee_____ - December		
Gross Earnings		
Deductions:		
Federal Income Taxes		
FICA Tax - Medicare		
Total Deductions		
Net Pay		

c.

d.

Amount appearing on W-2 for 2013		
Employee_____	computation	Totals
Box 1 Wages, tips, and other compensation		
Box 2 Federal Income tax withheld		
Box 3 Social Security wages		
Box 4 Social security tax withheld		
Box 5 Medicare wages and tips		
Box 6 Medicare tax withheld		

EXERCISE 9-10A or 9-10B d. (cont.)

Amount appearing on W-2 for 2013		
Employee_____	computation	Total
Box 1 Wages, tips, and other compensation		
Box 2 Federal Income tax withheld		
Box 3 Social Security wages		
Box 4 Social security tax withheld		
Box 5 Medicare wages and tips		
Box 6 Medicare tax withheld		

EXERCISE 9-11A or 9-11B

a. (1)

Employee:		
Gross Earnings		
Deductions:		
Federal Income Taxes		
FICA Tax – SS		
FICA Tax – Medicare		
Total Deductions		
Net Pay		

(2). _____ monthly FICA tax:	
Social security tax	
Medicare tax	
Total monthly FICA tax	

(3). _____ payroll tax expense - January	
Employer FICA social security tax	
Employer FICA Medicare tax	
Employer unemployment tax	
Total employer payroll tax	

_____ payroll tax expense - February:	
Employer FICA social security tax	
Employer FICA Medicare tax	
Employer unemployment tax	
Total employer payroll tax	

_____ payroll tax expense - March	
Employer FICA social security tax	
Employer FICA Medicare tax	
Total employer payroll tax	

_____ payroll tax expense - December	
Employer FICA social security tax	
Employer FICA Medicare tax	
Total employer payroll tax	

EXERCISE 9-11A or 9-11B (cont.)

b. (1) January - November

Employee:		
Gross Earnings		
Deductions:		
Federal Income Taxes		
FICA Tax – SS		
FICA Tax – Medicare		
Total Deductions		
Net Pay		

b. (1) December

Employee:		
Gross Earnings		
Deductions:		
Federal Income Taxes		
FICA Tax – SS		
FICA Tax – Medicare		
Total Deductions		
Net Pay		

(2) Monthly FICA tax (Jan - Nov):	
Social security tax	
Medicare tax	
Total monthly FICA tax	

(2) Monthly FICA tax (Dec):	
Social security tax	
Medicare tax	
Total monthly FICA tax	

EXERCISE 9-11A or 9-11B b. (cont.)

b. (3)

_____ payroll tax expense - January	
Employer FICA social security tax	
Employer FICA Medicare tax	
Employer unemployment tax	
Total employer payroll tax	

_____ payroll tax expense - February	
Employer FICA social security tax	
Employer FICA Medicare tax	
Total employer payroll tax	

_____ payroll tax expense - March	
Employer FICA social security tax	
Employer FICA Medicare tax	
Total employer payroll tax	

_____ payroll tax expense - December	
Employer FICA social security tax	
Employer FICA Medicare tax	
Total employer payroll tax	

EXERCISE 9-12A or 9-12B

a.

Computation of Accrued Fringe Benefits per month	
Vacation Pay Expense	
Employee Medical Insurance Expense	
Employee Pension Expense	
Total Monthly Fringe Benefits Expense	

Account Titles	Debit	Credit

b.

Assets	=	Liabilities	+	Equity			Income Statement				Statement
Cash	=	Various Payables	+	Com. Stock	+	Ret. Earn.	Rev.	− Exp.	=	Net Inc.	of Cash Flow

c.

Schedule of Payroll Costs		
	computations	Totals
Salary Costs:		
FICA social security tax expense		
FICA Medicare tax expense		
Unemployment tax expense		
Vacation Pay Expense		
Employee Medical Insurance Expense		
Employee Pension Expense		
Total Payroll Cost		

EXERCISE 9-13A or 9-13B

a.

	General Journal		
Event	**Account Titles**	**Debit**	**Credit**
1.			
2.			
3a.			
3b.			
4.			
5.			
6.			
7.			
8.			
9.			
10.			

EXERCISE 9-13A or 9-13B a. (cont.)

	General Journal		
Event	Account Titles	Debit	Credit
11.			
12.			
13.			

EXERCISE 9-13A or 9-13B (cont.)

b.

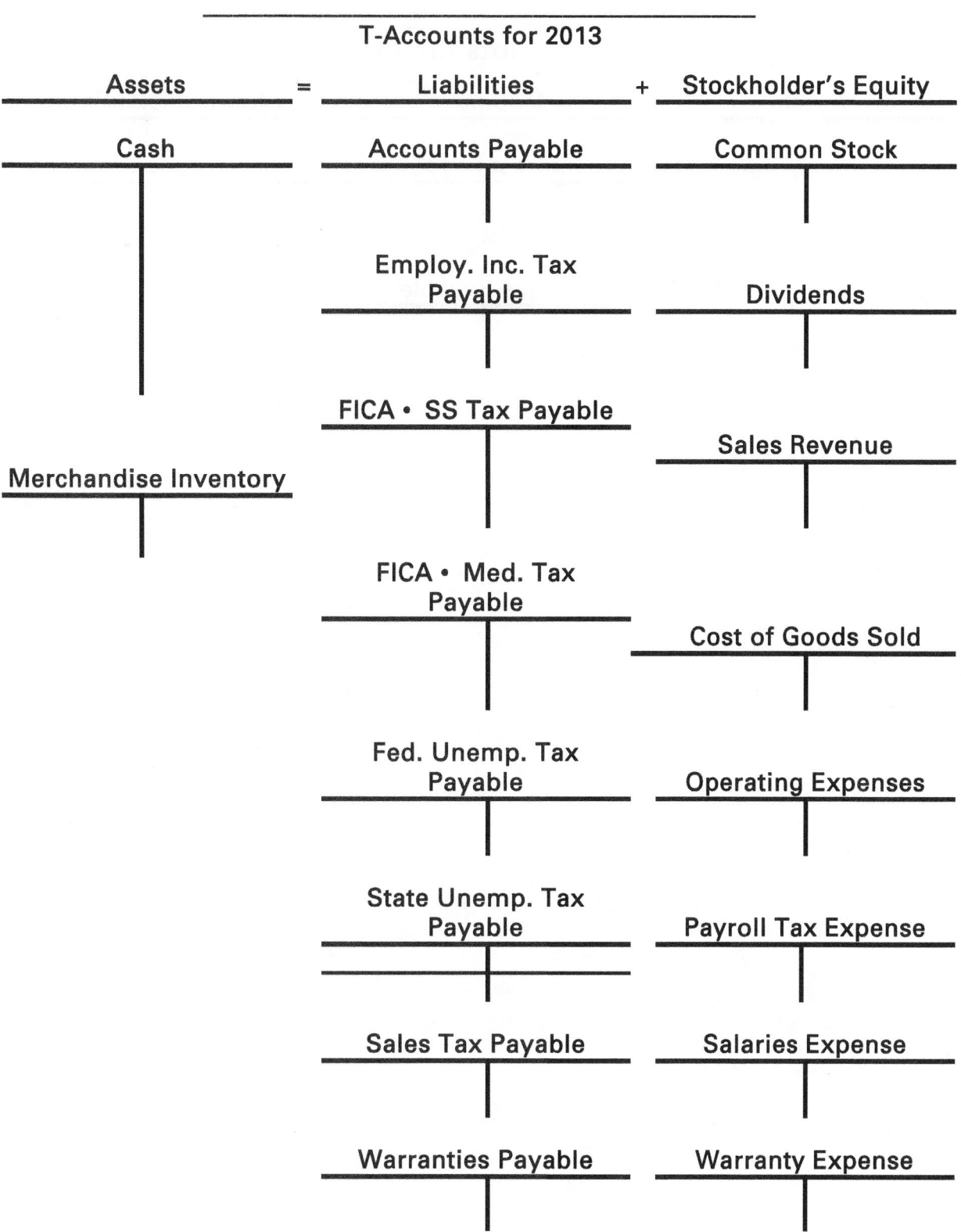

T-Accounts for 2013

Assets = Liabilities + Stockholder's Equity

Cash	Accounts Payable	Common Stock

	Employ. Inc. Tax Payable	Dividends

	FICA • SS Tax Payable	

Merchandise Inventory		Sales Revenue

	FICA • Med. Tax Payable	

		Cost of Goods Sold

	Fed. Unemp. Tax Payable	Operating Expenses

	State Unemp. Tax Payable	Payroll Tax Expense

	Sales Tax Payable	Salaries Expense

	Warranties Payable	Warranty Expense

EXERCISE 9-13A or 9-13B b. (cont.)

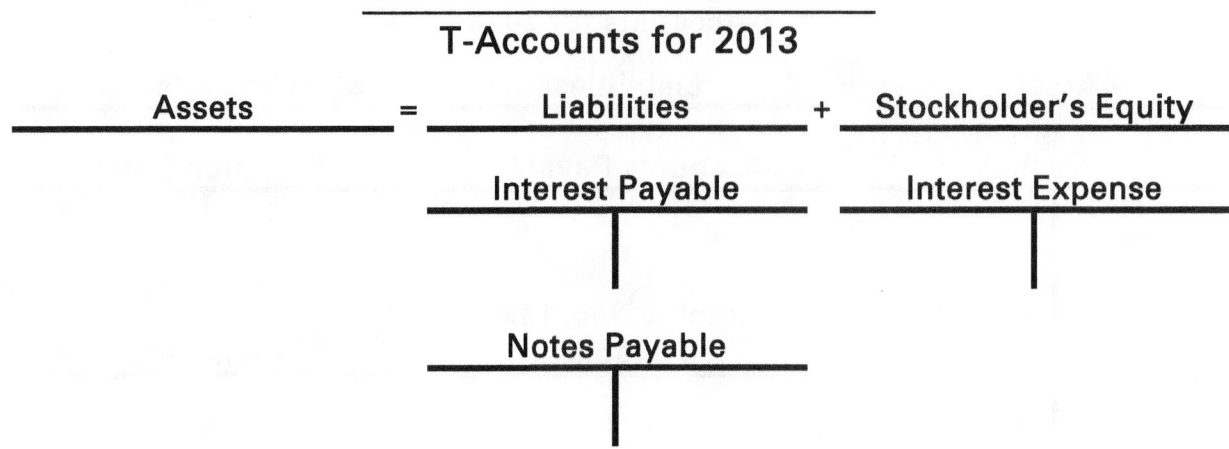

T-Accounts for 2013

Assets = Liabilities + Stockholder's Equity

Interest Payable   Interest Expense

Notes Payable

c.

Income Statement			
For the Year Ended December 31, 2013			

	Statement of Changes in Stockholders' Equity For the Year Ended December 31, 2013	
Beginning Common Stock		
Add: Common Stock Issued		
Ending Common Stock		
Beginning Retained Earnings		
Add: Net Income		
Less: Dividends		
Ending Retained Earnings		
Total Stockholders' Equity		

Balance Sheet		
As of December 31, 2013		

Statement of Cash Flows
For the Year Ended December 31, 2013

EXERCISE 9-14A or 9-14B

Classified Balance Sheet		
As of December 31, 2013		

EXERCISE 9-15A or 9-15B

a.

	Co.		Co.
Current Assets:			
Total Current Assets			
Current Liabilities:			
Total Current Liab.			

Company	Current Assets	÷	Current Liabilities	=	Current Ratio
		÷		=	
		÷		=	

b.

c.

EXERCISE 9-16A or 9-16B (Appendix)

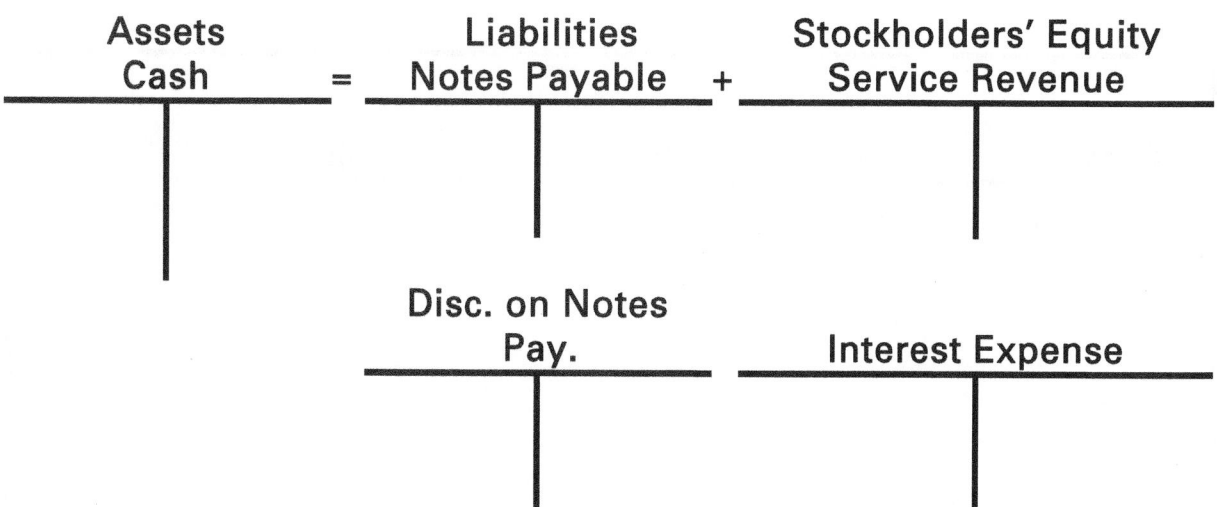

a. Total Liabilities:

Notes Payable	
Less: Discount on Notes Payable	
Total Liabilities	

b. Income Reported on the Income Statement:

Service Revenue	
Less: Interest Expense	
Net Income	

c.

Cash Flows From Operating Activities	

EXERCISE 9-16A or 9-16B (Appendix) (cont.)

d.

Date	Account Titles	Debit	Credit

EXERCISE 9-17A or 9-17B (Appendix)

a.

Event	Balance Sheet							Income Statement					Statement of Cash Flows
	Assets	=	Liabilities			+	Equity	Rev.	−	Exp.	=	Net Inc.	
	Cash	=	Notes Pay.	−	Disc. on NP	+	Ret. Ear.						
1.		=		−		+			−		=		

Event	Balance Sheet							Income Statement					Statement of Cash Flows
	Assets	=	Liabilities			+	Equity	Rev.	−	Exp.	=	Net Inc.	
	Cash	=	Notes Pay.	+	Int. Pay.	+	Ret. Ear.						
2.		=		+		+			−		=		

b.

c.

d.

EXERCISE 9-18A or 9-18B (Appendix)

	General Journal		
Date	Account Titles	Debit	Credit
a.			
b.			
c.			

PROBLEM 9-19A or 9-19B

Note: The accounting equation is not required.

								Effect of Events on the General Ledger 2013 and 2014	
		Assets	=	Liabilities		+	Stockholders' Equity		
Event	Cash	Accts. Rec.	=	Notes Pay.	Int. Pay.	+	Com. Stock	Retained Earnings	Acct. Title/RE
2013									
1.									
2.									
3.									
4.									
5.									
Bal.			=			+			
2014									
B. Bal.			=			+			
1.									
2.									
3.									
4.									
5.									
Bal.			=			+			

a.	f.
b.	g.
c.	h.
d.	i. *
e.	j. *

*9-19B

PROBLEM 9-20A or 9-20B

a.

	General Journal for 2013		
Event	Account Title	Debit	Credit
1.			
2.			
3.			
4.			
5.			

b.

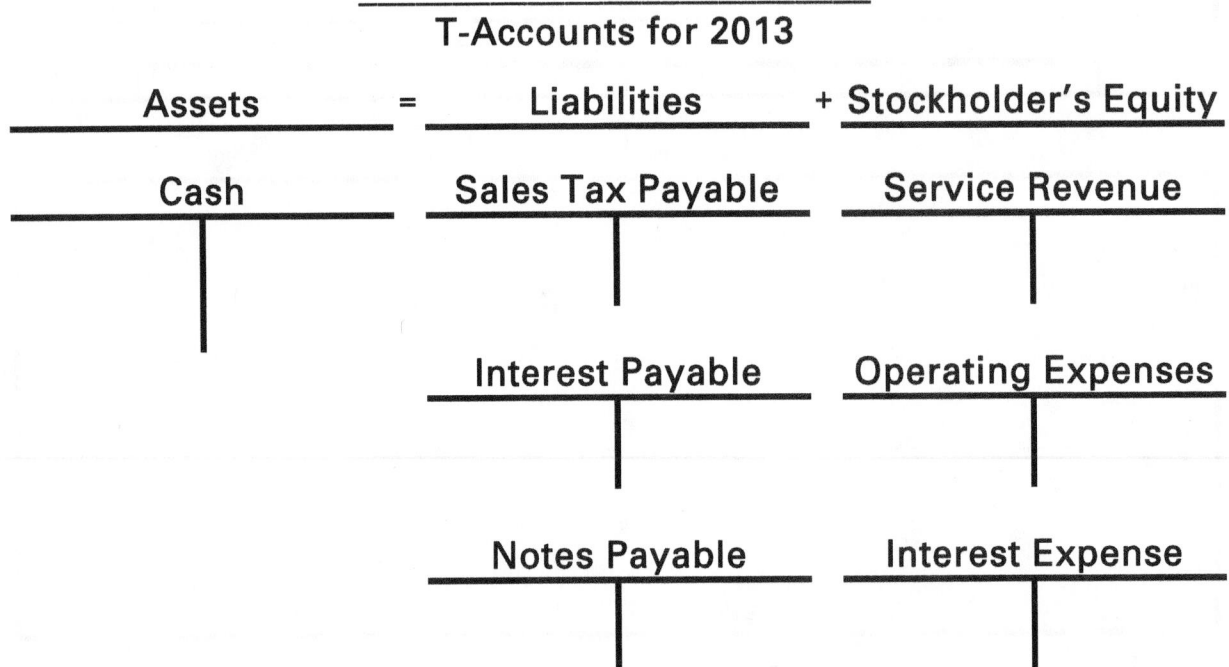

T-Accounts for 2013

| Assets | = | Liabilities | + Stockholder's Equity |

Cash   Sales Tax Payable   Service Revenue

Interest Payable   Operating Expenses

Notes Payable   Interest Expense

PROBLEM 9-20A or 9-20B (cont.)

c.

Income Statement
For the Year Ended December 31, 2013

Statement of Changes of Stockholders' Equity
For the Year Ended December 31, 2013

	Balance Sheet As of December 31, 2013		

	Statement of Cash Flows		
	For the Year Ended December 31, 2013		

d.

	General Journal for 2013		
Event	Account Title	Debit	Credit
	Closing Entries		

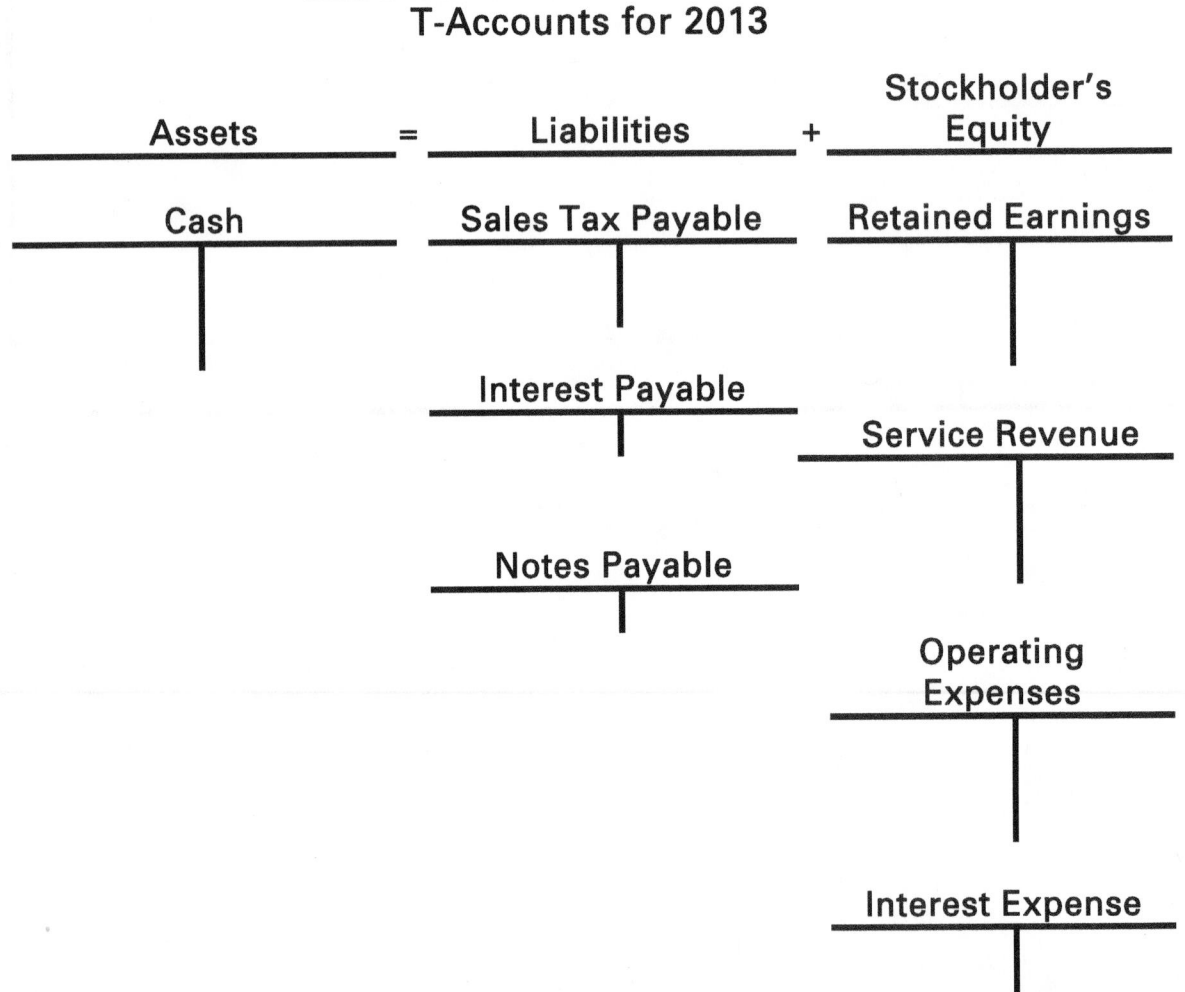

T-Accounts for 2013

| Assets | = | Liabilities | + | Stockholder's Equity |

Cash   Sales Tax Payable   Retained Earnings

Interest Payable   Service Revenue

Notes Payable

Operating Expenses

Interest Expense

e.

	Post Closing Trial Balance As of Ended December 31, 2013		
Totals			

f.

	General Journal for 2014		
Event	Account Title	Debit	Credit
1.			
2.			
3a.			
3b.			
4.			
5.			

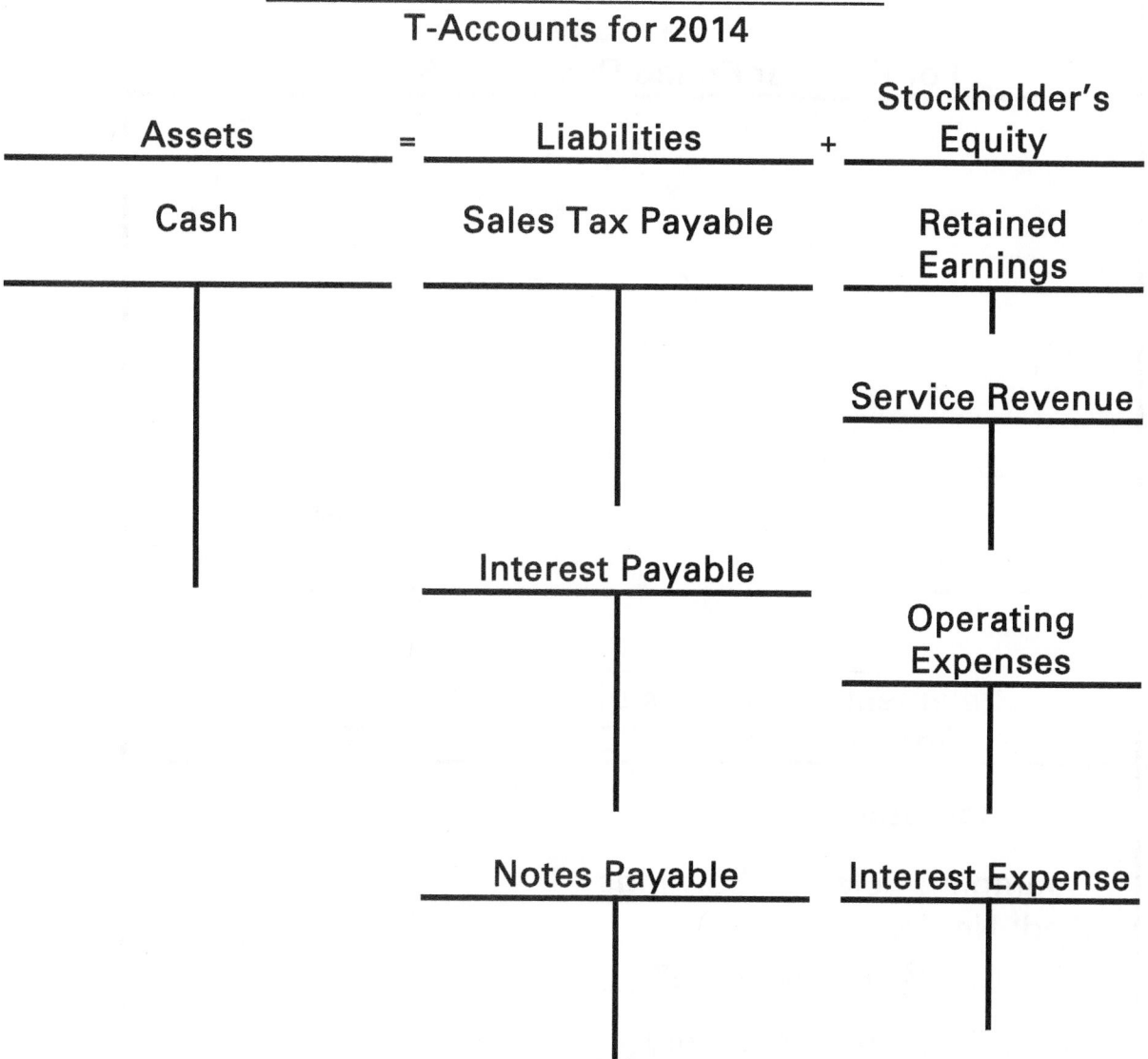

T-Accounts for 2014

Assets = Liabilities + Stockholder's Equity

Cash

Sales Tax Payable

Retained Earnings

Service Revenue

Interest Payable

Operating Expenses

Notes Payable

Interest Expense

Income Statement
For the Year Ended December 31, 2014

Statement of Changes of Stockholders' Equity
For the Year Ended December 31, 2014

Common Stock			
Beginning Retained Earnings			
Add: Net Income			
Ending Retained Earnings			
Total Stockholders' Equity			

Balance Sheet			
As of December 31, 2014			

PROBLEM 9-20A or 9-20B f. (cont.)

Statement of Cash Flows **For the Year Ended December 31, 2014**		

	General Journal for 2014		
Event	Account Title	Debit	Credit
	Closing Entries		

T-Accounts for 2014

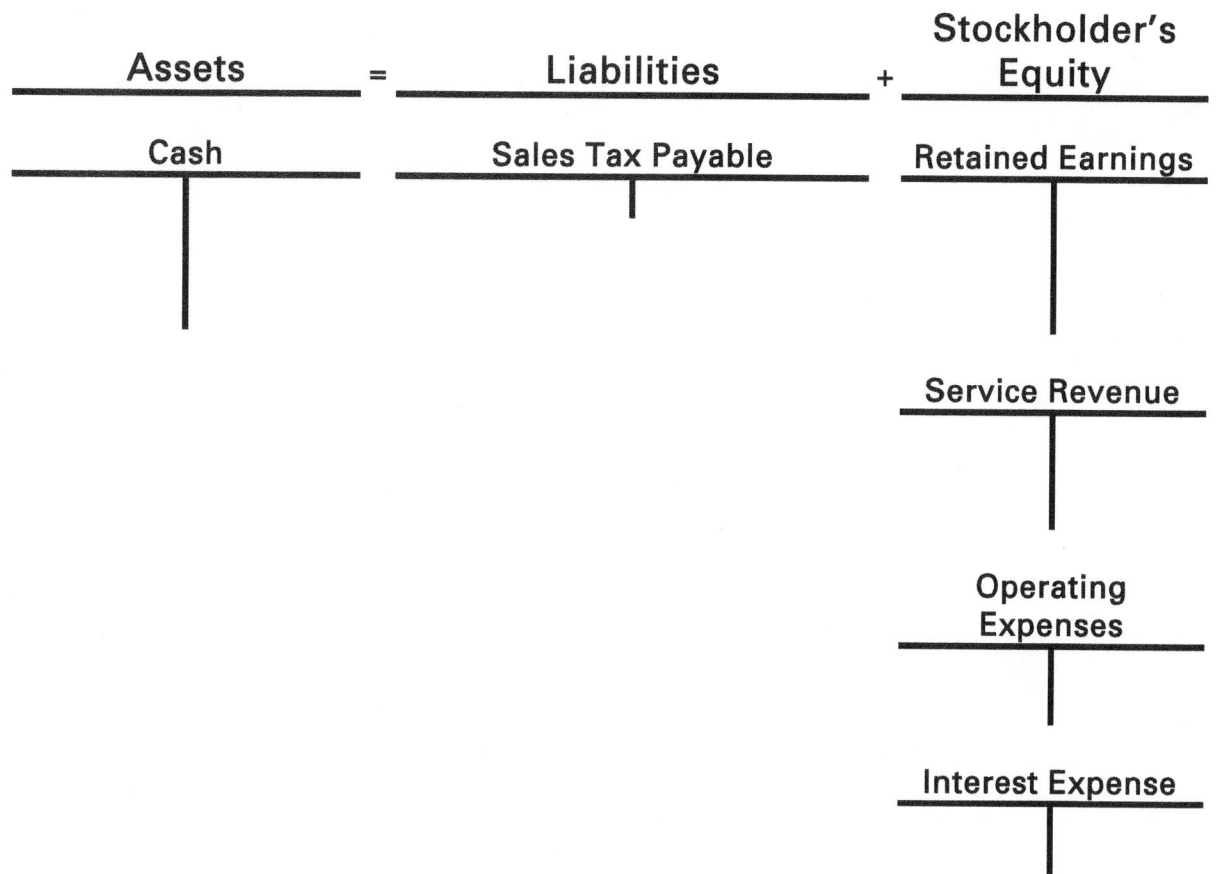

Assets = Liabilities + Stockholder's Equity

Cash | Sales Tax Payable | Retained Earnings

Service Revenue

Operating Expenses

Interest Expense

PROBLEM 9-20A or 9-20B f. (cont.)

After Closing Trial Balance As of Ended December 31, 2014		
Totals		

PROBLEM 9-21A or 9-21B

PROBLEM 9-22A or 9-22B

a. (1) Cash paid for interest:

(2) Interest Expense:

(3) Warranty Expense:

b.

Interest Payable	Sales Tax Payable

Warranty Payable	Notes Payable

_____ Company	
Current Liabilities	

PROBLEM 9-22A or 9-22B (cont.)

c.

Event	Assets	=	Liab.	+	Equity	Rev.	−	Exp.	=	Net Inc.	Cash Flow
1.											
2.											
3.											
4.											
5.											
6.											
7.											
8.											

PROBLEM 9-23A or 9-23B

	General Journal		
Date	Account Title	Debit	Credit

PROBLEM 9-24A or 9-24B

a.

Computation of Gross Earnings					
Employee	Hours Worked	x	Wage Rate per Hour	=	Gross Pay
	Reg.				
	OT				
Total					

b.

Employee_____		
Gross Earnings		
Deductions:		
Federal Income Taxes		
FICA Tax – SS		
FICA Tax – Medicare		
Total Deductions		
Net Pay		

Employee_____		
Gross Earnings		
Deductions:		
Federal Income Taxes		
FICA Tax – SS		
FICA Tax – Medicare		
Total Deductions		
Net Pay		

c.

General Journal Entries			
Date	Account Titles	Debit	Credit

d.

General Journal Entries			
Date	Account Titles	Debit	Credit

e.

Total Compensation Costs	

PROBLEM 9-25A or 9-25B

	Income Statement For the Year Ended December 31, 2013				
Sales Revenue					
Cost of Goods Sold					
Gross Margin					
Operating Expenses					
Salaries Expense					
Operating Expenses					
Warranty Expense					
Uncollectible Accounts Expense					
Depreciation Expense (9-25B)					
Total Operating Expenses					
Operating Income					
Non-Operating Items					
Interest Revenue					
Interest Expense					
Gain on Sale of Equipment					
Total Non-Operating Items					
Net Income					

Balance Sheet As of December 31, 2013			
Assets			
Current Assets			
Total Current Assets			
Property, Plant and Equipment			
Total Property, Plant and Equipment			
Total Assets			
Liabilities and Stockholders' Equity			
Current Liabilities			
Total Current Liabilities			
Long-Term Liabilities			
Total Long-Term Liabilities			
Total Liabilities			
Stockholders' Equity			
Total Stockholders' Equity			
Total Liabilities and Stockholders' Equity			

*Retained Earnings must be computed:

PROBLEM 9-26A or 9-26B

a.

Current Assets		
Totals		

Current Liabilities		
Totals		

Current ratios:

Company	Current Assets	÷	Current Liab.	=	Current Ratio

b.

Current Assets (see above)	
Building	
Land	
Total Assets	
Current Liabilities (see above)	
Long-term Notes Payable	
Total Liabilities	

Debt to assets ratios:

Company	Total Liab.	÷	Total Assets	=	Debt to Assets Ratio

c.

PROBLEM 9-27A or 9-27B (Appendix)

a.

										Net		Cash
No.	Assets	=	Liab.	+	Equity		Rev.	–	Exp.	=	Inc.	Flows
2013												
1.												
2.												
3.												
4.												
2014												
1.												
2.												
3a.												
3b.												

_____.
Effect of Transactions on Financial Statements

b.

	General Journal 2013 and 2014		
Date	Account Titles	Debit	Credit

PROBLEM 9-27A or 9-27B (Appendix) b. (cont.)

General Journal, 2013 and 2014		
Closing Entries		

T-Accounts		
Assets	= Liabilities	+ Stockholders' Equity

Cash

Notes Payable

Retained Earnings

Discount on Notes Pay.

Service Revenue

Selling/Operating Exp.

Interest Expense

c.

Financial Statements

Income Statements

	2013	2014
Service Revenue		
Expenses		
Selling and Adm./Oper. Expenses		
Interest Expense		
Total Expenses		
Net Income		

Statements of Changes in Stockholders' Equity

	2013	2014
Beginning Common Stock		
Plus: Stock Issued		
Ending Common Stock		
Beginning Retained Earnings		
Plus: Net Income		
Ending Retained Earnings		
Total Stockholders' Equity		

PROBLEM 9-27A or 9-27B (Appendix) c. (cont.)

Financial Statements Balance Sheets	2013	2014
Assets		
Cash		
Total Assets		
Liabilities		
Notes Payable		
Less: Discount on Notes Payable		
Total Liabilities		
Stockholders' Equity		
Common Stock		
Retained Earnings		
Total Stockholders' Equity		
Total Liabilities and Stockholders' Equity		

Statements of Cash Flows		
	2013	2014
Cash Flows From Operating Activities:		
Inflow from Customers		
Outflow for Expenses		
Ouflow for Interest		
Net Cash Flow from Operating Activities		
Cash Flows From Investing Activities		
Cash Flows From Financing Activities:		
Cash Inflow from Loan		
Cash Ouflow to Repay Loan		
Net Cash Flow From Financing Activities		
Net Change in Cash		
Plus: Beginning Cash Balance		
Ending Cash Balance		

ATC 9-1

a.

b.

c.

ATC 9-2

a. (1) Brooks Company

Brooks Company Computation of Gross Earnings				
Employee	Hours Worked	× Wage Rate per Hour	=	Gross Pay
No. 1	Reg.			
	OT			
Total				
No. 2	Reg.			
	OT			
Total				

Employee No. 1		
Gross Earnings		
Deductions:		
Federal Income Taxes		
FICA Tax – SS		
FICA Tax – Medicare		
Total Deductions		
Net Pay		

Employee No. 2		
Gross Earnings		
Deductions:		
Federal Income Taxes		
FICA Tax – SS		
FICA Tax – Medicare		
Total Deductions		
Net Pay		

ATC 9-2 (cont.)

a. (2) Brooks Company

Schedule of Compensation Costs		
	computations	Totals
Salary Costs:		
FICA soc. sec. tax expense		
FICA Medicare tax expense		
Fed. Unemp. tax expense		
State Unemp. tax expense		
Employee Med. Ins. Expense		
Employee Pension Expense		
Total Payroll Cost		

a. (1) Hill Company:

Hill Company Computation of Gross Earnings					
Employee	Hours/Weeks Worked	x	Wage Rate per Hour/ Week	=	Gross Pay
No. 1					
Total					
No. 2	Reg.				
	OT				
Total					

ATC 9-2 a. (1) (cont.)

Hill Company

Employee No. 1		
Gross Earnings		
Deductions:		
Federal Income Taxes		
FICA Tax – SS		
FICA Tax – Medicare		
Total Deductions		
Net Pay		

Employee No. 2		
Gross Earnings		
Deductions:		
Federal Income Taxes		
FICA Tax – SS		
FICA Tax – Medicare		
Total Deductions		
Net Pay		

a. (2) Hill Company

Schedule of Compensation Costs		
	Computations	Totals
Salary Costs:		
FICA soc. sec. tax expense		
FICA Medicare tax expense		
Fed. Unemp. tax expense		
State Unemp. tax expense		
Employee Med. Ins. Expense		
Employee Pension Expense		
Total Payroll Cost		

ATC 9-2 (cont.)

a. (1) Valley Company

	Valley Company Computation of Gross Earnings				
Employee	Hours/Months Worked	x	Wage Rate per Hour/Month	=	Gross Pay
No. 1 Total	Reg.				
No. 2 Total	Reg.				

Employee No. 1		
Gross Earnings		
Deductions:		
Federal Income Taxes		
FICA Tax – SS		
FICA Tax – Medicare		
Total Deductions		
Net Pay		

Employee No. 2		
Gross Earnings		
Deductions:		
Federal Income Taxes		
FICA Tax – SS		
FICA Tax – Medicare		
Total Deductions		
Net Pay		

ATC 9-2 (cont.)

a. (2) Valley Company

Schedule of Compensation Costs		
	Computations	Totals
Salary Costs:		
FICA soc. sec. tax expense		
FICA Medicare tax expense		
Fed. Unemp. tax expense		
State Unemp. tax expense		
Employee Med. Ins. Expense		
Employee Pension Expense		
Total Payroll Cost		

a (3) & b.

Company	Total Compensation Costs	Total Salary Costs	% Salary of Compensation
Brooks Company			
Hill Company			
Valley Company			

ATC 9-3

ATC 9-4

a.

Current Ratios:					
Year	Current Assets	÷	Current Liab.	=	Current Ratio
2010					
2009					

b.

Debt to Assets Ratio:					
Year	Total Debt	÷	Total Assets	=	Debt to Assets Ratio
2010					
2009					

c.

d.

ATC 9-5

a.

Current Assets	National Semiconductor	Texas Instruments
Total Current Assets		
Current Liabilities		
Total Current Liabilities		

Current Ratios:

Company	Current Assets	÷	Current Liab.	=	Current Ratio
National					
Texas Inst.					

b.

	National	Texas Inst.
Current Assets (see above)		
Building		
Land		
Total Assets		
Current Liabilities (see above)		
Long-term Notes Payable		
Total Liabilities		

Debt to Assets Ratio:

Company	Total Debt	÷	Total Assets	=	Debt to Assets Ratio
National					
Texas Inst.					

ATC 9-5 (cont.)

c.

d.

ATC 9-6

ATC 9-7

ATC 9-8

a.

Pacilio Security Services, Inc. General Journal, 2019			
Event	Account title	Debit	Credit
1.			
2.			
3.			
4.			
5.			
6a.			
6b.			
7.			

Compute Cost of Goods Sold:

COMPREHENSIVE PROBLEM – CHAPTER 9 a. (cont.)

Event	Account Titles	Debit	Credit
8.			
9.			
10.			
11.			
12.			
13.			
14.			
15.			
16.			

Pacilio Security Services, Inc.
General Journal, 2019

Event	Account Titles	Debit	Credit
	Pacilio Security Services, Inc. **General Journal, 2019**		
17.			
18.			
19.			
20.			
21.			
22.			

Compute expired rent:

Compute uncollectible accounts expense:

	Pacilio Security Services, Inc. General Journal, 2019		
Event	Account Titles	Debit	Credit
23.			
24.			
25.			
26.			
27.			

Compute depreciation expense:

Compute warranty expense:

Compute payroll tax expense:

COMPREHENSIVE PROBLEM – CHAPTER 9 (cont.)

b.

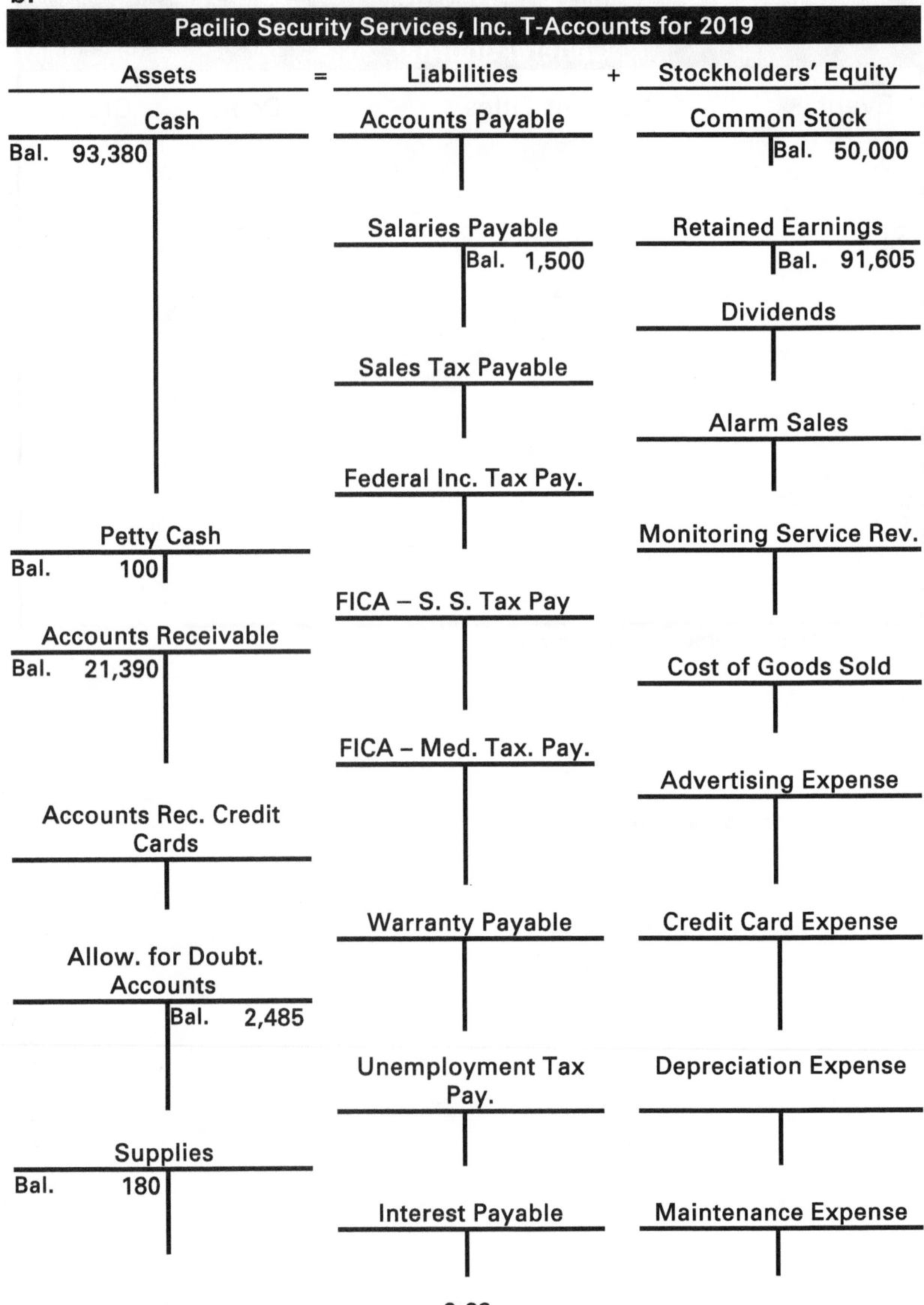

Pacilio Security Services, Inc. T-Accounts for 2019		
Assets =	**Liabilities** +	**Stockholders' Equity**

Assets

Cash
Bal. 93,380

Petty Cash
Bal. 100

Accounts Receivable
Bal. 21,390

Accounts Rec. Credit Cards

Allow. for Doubt. Accounts
Bal. 2,485

Supplies
Bal. 180

Liabilities

Accounts Payable

Salaries Payable
Bal. 1,500

Sales Tax Payable

Federal Inc. Tax Pay.

FICA – S. S. Tax Pay

FICA – Med. Tax. Pay.

Warranty Payable

Unemployment Tax Pay.

Interest Payable

Stockholders' Equity

Common Stock
Bal. 50,000

Retained Earnings
Bal. 91,605

Dividends

Alarm Sales

Monitoring Service Rev.

Cost of Goods Sold

Advertising Expense

Credit Card Expense

Depreciation Expense

Maintenance Expense

COMPREHENSIVE PROBLEM – CHAPTER 9 b. (cont.)

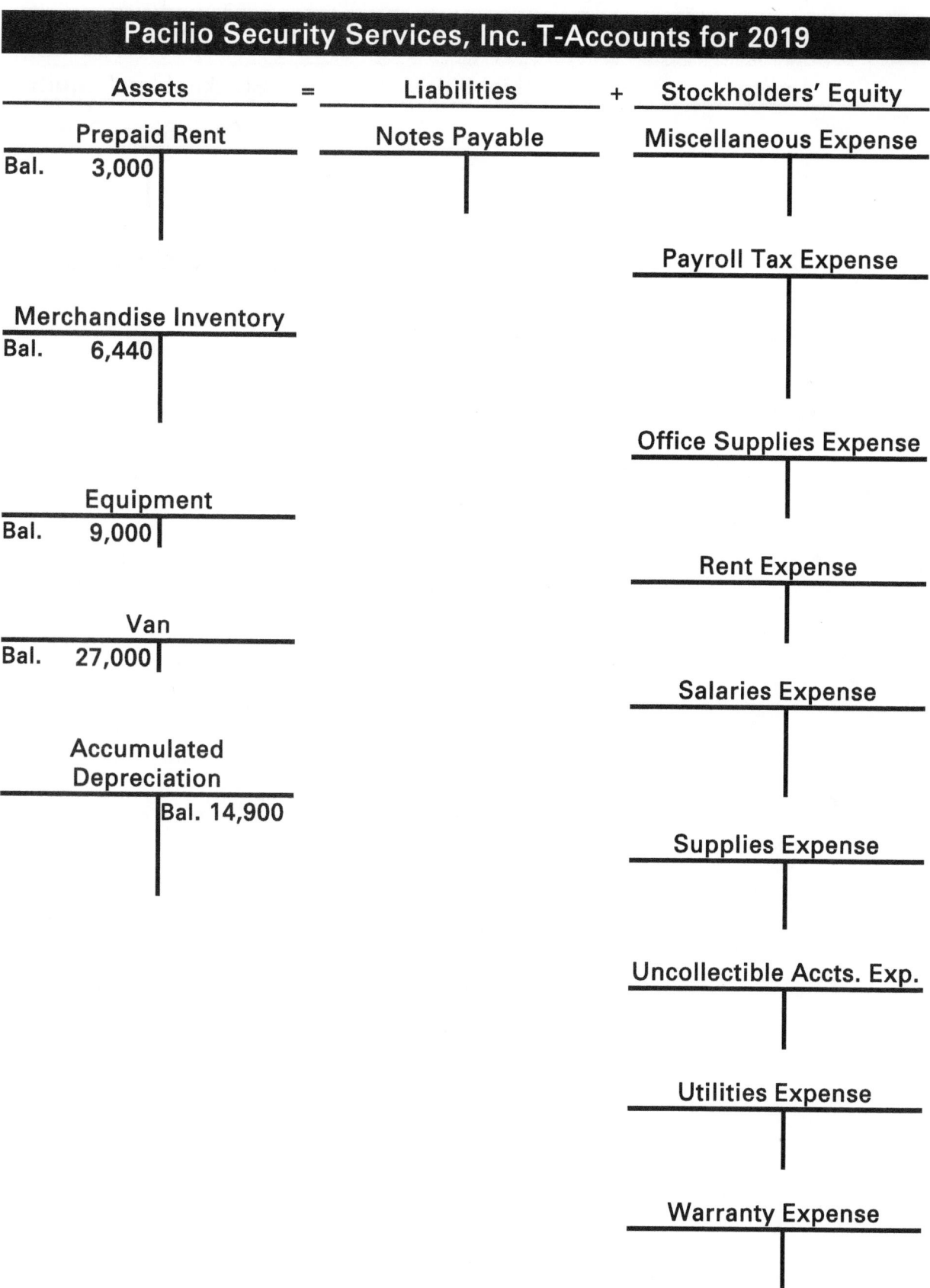

Pacilio Security Services, Inc. T-Accounts for 2019

| Assets | = | Liabilities | + | Stockholders' Equity |

Prepaid Rent

Bal. 3,000

Notes Payable

Miscellaneous Expense

Payroll Tax Expense

Merchandise Inventory

Bal. 6,440

Office Supplies Expense

Equipment

Bal. 9,000

Rent Expense

Van

Bal. 27,000

Salaries Expense

Accumulated Depreciation

Bal. 14,900

Supplies Expense

Uncollectible Accts. Exp.

Utilities Expense

Warranty Expense

Pacilio Security Services, Inc. T-Accounts for 2019

Assets	=	Liabilities	+	Stockholders' Equity

Cash Short/Over

Interest Expense

c.

Pacilio Security Services, Inc. Trial Balance December 31, 2019		
Cash		
Petty Cash		
Accounts Receivable		
Allowance for Doubtful Accounts		
Supplies		
Prepaid Rent		
Merchandise Inventory		
Equipment		
Van		
Accumulated Depreciation		
Sales Tax Payable		
Federal Income Tax Payable		
FICA – Social Security Tax Payable		
FICA – Medicare Tax Payable		
Warranty Payable		
Unemployment Tax Payable		
Interest Payable		
Notes Payable		
Common Stock		
Retained Earnings		
Dividends		
Alarm Sales		
Monitoring Service Revenue		
Cost of Goods Sold		
Advertising Expense		
Credit Card Expense		
Depreciation Expense		
Maintenance Expense		
Miscellaneous Expense		
Payroll Tax Expense		
Office Supplies Expense		
Rent Expense		
Salaries Expense		
Supplies Expense		
Uncollectible Accounts Expense		
Utilities Expense		
Warranty Expense		
Cash Short/Over		
Interest Expense		
Totals		

d.

Pacilio Security Services, Inc. Income Statement For the Year Ended December 31, 2019		

Pacilio Security Services, Inc. Statement of Changes in Stockholders' Equity For the Year Ended December 31, 2019		
Beginning Common Stock		
Plus: Common Stock Issued		
Ending Common Stock		
Beginning Retained Earnings		
Plus: Net Income		
Less: Dividends		
Ending Retained Earnings		
Total Stockholders' Equity		

Pacilio Security Services, Inc. Balance Sheet As of December 31, 2019		

COMPREHENSIVE PROBLEM – CHAPTER 9 d. (cont.)

Pacilio Security Services, Inc. Statement of Cash Flows For the Year Ended December 31, 2019			

Cash Receipts from Customers:	

Cash Payment for Expenses	

e.

Date	Account Titles	Debit	Credit
	Closing Entries		

Pacilio Security Services T-Accounts for 2019
T-Accounts with Closing Entries

Assets	=	Liabilities	+	Stockholders' Equity

Cash

Bal. |

Sales Tax Payable

| Bal.

Common Stock

| Bal.

Petty Cash

Bal. |

Federal Income Tax Pay

| Bal.

Retained Earnings

| Bal.

Accounts Receivable

Bal. |

FICA – SS Tax Pay.

| Bal.

Allow. for Doubt. Accts.

| Bal.

FICA – Med. Tax Pay.

| Bal.

Dividends

Bal. |

Supplies

Bal. |

Warranty Payable

| Bal.

Alarm Sales Revenue

| Bal. 75,400

Monit. Service Revenue

| Bal.

Prepaid Rent

Bal. |

Unempl Tax Payable

| Bal.

Cost of Goods Sold

Bal. |

Merchandise Inventory

Bal. |

Interest Payable

| Bal.

Advertising Expense

Bal. |

Equipment

Bal. |

Notes Payable

| Bal.

Credit Card Expense

Bal. |

Van

Bal. |

Depreciation Expense

Bal. |

Accumulated Depr.

| Bal.

Pacilio Security Services T-Accounts for 2019
T-Accounts with Closing Entries

Assets	=	Liabilities	+	Stockholders' Equity

Maintenance Expense
Bal.

Miscellaneous Expense
Bal.

Office Supplies Expense
Bal.

Payroll Tax Expense
Bal.

Rent Expense
Bal.

Salaries Expense
Bal.

Supplies Expense
Bal.

Uncoll. Accts. Expense
Bal.

Utilities Expense
Bal.

Warranty Expense
Bal.

Pacilio Security Services T-Accounts for 2019
T-Accounts with Closing Entries

Assets	=	Liabilities	+	Stockholders' Equity

Cash Short/Over

Bal.

Interest Expense

Bal.

Pacilio Security Services, Inc. Post-Closing Trial Balance December 31, 2019		
Account Titles	Debit	Credit
Cash		
Petty Cash		
Accounts Receivable		
Allowance for Doubtful Accounts		
Supplies		
Prepaid Rent		
Merchandise Inventory		
Equipment		
Van		
Accumulated Depreciation		
Sales Tax Payable		
Federal Income Tax Payable		
FICA – Social Security Tax Payable		
FICA – Medicare Tax Payable		
Warranty Payable		
Unemployment Tax Payable		
Interest Payable		
Notes Payable		
Common Stock		
Retained Earnings		
Totals		

EXERCISE 10-1A or 10-1B

EXERCISE 10-2A or 10-2B

| | | Amortization Schedule | | | |
| | $\qquad$, __Yr. Term Note, __% Interest Rate | | | | |

Year	Prin. Bal. on Jan 1	Cash Pay. Dec. 31	Applied to Interest	Applied to Principal	Prin. Bal. End of Period

EXERCISE 10-3A or 10-3B

The amortization schedule is not required, but is useful in working the exercise:

		Amortization Schedule $_____$, $\_\_$-Yr. Term Note, $\_\_$% Interest Rate			
Year	Prin. Bal. on Jan 1	Cash Pay. Dec. 31	Applied to Interest	Applied to Principal	Prin Bal. end of Period

a.

(1)

(2)

b.

c.

(1)

(2)

EXERCISE 10-4A or 104B

a. (10-4A)

a/b.

Effect of Transactions on Financial Statements									
	Balance Sheet				Income Statement				Statement of
No.	Assets	=	Liab.	+	S. Equity	Rev.	−	Exp.	=	Net Inc.	Cash Flows
1.		=		+			−		=	
2.		=		+			−		=	

b/c. (1)

Revenue		
Expenses		
Operating Expenses		
Interest Expense		
Total Expenses		
Net Income		

b/c. (2)

Cash Flows From Operating Activities:	
Net Cash Flow from Operating Activities	

b/c. (3)

Cash Flows From Financing Activities:	
Net Cash Flow from Financing Activities	

c/d.

EXERCISE 10-5A or 10-5B

Month	Amount Borrowed (Repaid)	Balance End of Month	Interest Rate	Interest Expense

Date	Account Titles	Debit	Credit

EXERCISE 10-6A or 10-6B

a.

	General Journal		
Date	Account Titles	Debit	Credit

Assets	=	Liabilities	+	Stockholders' Equity
Cash		Bonds Payable		Retained Earnings
Land				Lease Revenue
				Interest Expense

EXERCISE 10-6A or 10-6B (cont.)

b.

	Financial Statements	
Income Statements	20___	20___
Lease Revenue		
Interest Expense		
Net Income		
Balance Sheets		
Assets		
Total Assets		
Liabilities		
Stockholders' Equity		
Total Stockholders' Equity		
Total Liab. and Stockholders' Equity		
Statements of Cash Flows		
Cash Flows From Operating Activities:		
Net Cash Flow from Operating Act.		
Cash Flows From Investing Activities:		
Cash Flows From Financing Activities:		
Net Change in Cash		
Plus: Beginning Cash Balance		
Ending Cash Balance		

EXERCISE 10-7A or 10-7B

<table>
<tr><td colspan="4" align="center">General Journal</td></tr>
<tr><td>Date</td><td>Account Titles</td><td>Debit</td><td>Credit</td></tr>
<tr><td>20___
Jan.1</td><td></td><td></td><td></td></tr>
<tr><td></td><td></td><td></td><td></td></tr>
<tr><td>Dec. 31</td><td></td><td></td><td></td></tr>
<tr><td></td><td></td><td></td><td></td></tr>
<tr><td>20___
Dec. 31</td><td></td><td></td><td></td></tr>
<tr><td></td><td></td><td></td><td></td></tr>
</table>

EXERCISE 10-8A or 10-8B

Date	Account Titles	Debit	Credit

EXERCISE 10-9A or 10-9B

EXERCISE 10-10A or 10-10B

	Face x Selling Price	Cash Proceeds	Discount or Premium
a.			
b.			
c.			
d.			

EXERCISE 10-11A or 10-11B

	Bond will sell for : Premium (P), Discount (D), Face (F)
a.	
b.	
c.	
d.	
e.	

EXERCISE 10-12A or 12-12B

	Bond will sell for : Premium (P), Discount (D), Face (F)
a.	
b.	
c.	

EXERCISE 10-13A or 10-13B

	Computation	Amount	Premium/Discount
a.			
b.			
c.			
d.			

EXERCISE 10-14A

a.

Effect of Transactions on Financial Statements									
	Balance Sheet				Income Statement				Statement of Cash Flows
No.	Assets	=	Liab.	+ S. Equity	Rev.	−	Exp.	= Net Inc.	
1.		=	+			−		=	
2a.*		=	+			−		=	
2b.*		=	+			−		=	

*2a is amortization of discount; 2b is payment of interest

b. Amount of Bond Discount:
   Amortization of bond discount per year:

Interest Expense, 20___:

Stated Interest	
Amortization of Bond Discount	
Interest Expense	

c.

Carrying Value, December 31, 20___:

Bonds Payable	
Less: Discount on Bonds Payable, 12/31/20___	
Carrying Value, December 31, 20___	

d. Interest Expense, 20___:

Stated Interest	
Amortization of Bond Discount	
Interest Expense	

e. Carrying Value, December 31, 20___:

Bonds Payable	
Less: Discount on Bonds Payable, 12/31/20___	
Carrying Value, December 31, 20___	

EXERCISE 10-14B

a.

Effect of Transactions on Financial Statements									
	Balance Sheet				**Income Statement**				**Statement of**
No.	Assets	=	Liab.	+	S. Equity	Rev.	–	Exp.	=	Net Inc.	Cash Flows
1.		=		+			–		=		
2a.		=		+			–		=		
2b.		=		+			–		=		

b. Amount of Bond Discount:
Amortization of bond discount per year:

Carrying Value, December 31, 20___:

Bonds Payable	
Less: Discount on Bonds Payable, 12/31/20___	
Carrying Value, December 31, 20___	

c. Interest Expense, 20___:

Stated Interest	
Amortization of Bond Discount	
Interest Expense	

d. Carrying Value, December 31, 20___:

Bonds Payable	
Less: Discount on Bonds Payable, 12/31/20___	
Carrying Value, December 31, 20___	

e. Interest Expense, 20___:

Stated Interest	
Amortization of Bond Discount	
Interest Expense	

EXERCISE 10-15A or 10-15B

a.

	General Journal		
Date	Account Titles	Debit	Credit

T-accounts

Assets	=	Liabilities	+	Stockholders' Equity

Cash

Bonds Payable

Retained Earnings

Prem./Disc. on Bonds Pay.

Interest Expense

EXERCISE 10-15A or 10-15B (cont.)

b.

Balance Sheet		
Liabilities	20___	20___
Net Carrying Value of Bonds		
Total Liabilities		

c.	20___	20___
Interest Expense		
d.		
Cash Outflow for Interest		

EXERCISE 10-16A or 10-16B

	General Journal		
Date	Account Titles	Debit	Credit
2013			
Jan. 1			
Dec. 31			
2014			
Dec. 31			

EXERCISE 10-17A or 10-17B

a.

	Effect of Transactions on Financial Statements							
	Balance Sheet				**Income Statement**			**Stmt. of**
No.	Assets	= Liab.	+ S. Equity		Rev.	− Exp.	= Net Inc.	Cash Flows
1.		=	+			−	=	
2a.		=	+			−	=	
2b.		=	+			−	=	

b. Amount of Premium:
Amortization of bond premium per year:

Carrying Value, December 31, 2013:

Bonds Payable	
Plus: Premium on Bonds Payable, 12/31/2013	
Carrying Value, December 31, 2013	

c. Interest Expense, 2013:

Stated Interest	
Amortization of Bond Premium	
Interest Expense	

d. Carrying Value, December 31, 2013:

Bonds Payable	
Plus: Premium on Bonds Payable	
Carrying Value, December 31, 2013	

e. Interest Expense, 2013:

Stated Interest	
Amortization of Bond Premium	
Interest Expense	

EXERCISE 10-18A or 10-18B

General Journal

Date	Account Titles	Debit	Credit

EXERCISE 10-19A or 10-19B

a.

	_____ Company	_____ Company	_____ Company
Bonds Payable			
Interest Rate			
Before Tax Interest Cost			

b.

	_____ Company	_____ Company	_____ Company
Before Tax Interest Cost			
x (1 – Tax Rate)			
After Tax Interest Cost			

c.

_____

_____

_____

1.	_____ Company	_____ Company	_____ Company
After Tax Interest Cost			
÷ Bonds Payable			
= After Tax Interest Rate			
OR			
2.			
Interest Rate x (1 – Tax Rate)			
= After Tax Interest Rate			

EXERCISE 10-20A or 10-20B

a.

Face Value	–	Bond Price	=	Discount
	–		=	

b.

Carrying Value	x	Effective Rate	=	Interest Expense
	x		=	

c. Compute the Ending Balance in the Discount Account

Face Value	x	Stated Rate	=	Cash Payment
	x		=	
Interest Expense	–	Cash Payment	=	Amortization
	–		=	
Beginning Discount	–	Amortization	=	Ending Discount
	–		=	

Bond Carrying Value as of December 31, 2013

Bond Payable (Face Value)	
Bond Discount	
Carrying Value	

d.

Account Titles	Debit	Credit
Interest Expense		
Bond Discount on Bonds Payable		
Cash		

EXERCISE 10-21A or 10-21B (Appendix)

a.

Date	Cash Payment	Interest Expense	Discount Amortization	Carrying Value
January 1, 2013				
December 31, 2013				
December 31, 2014				
December 31, 2015				
December 31, 2016				
December 31, 2017				
Totals				

b.

c.

d.

EXERCISE 10-22A or 10-22B

a.

Situation	Current Assets	Total Assets	Current Liabilities	Total Liabilities
Currently	$			
Using bonds				
Using stock				

	Currently	If Bonds Are Issued	If Stock Is Issued
Current ratio			
Debt to assets ratio			

Computations:

b.

	Bonds	Stock
EBIT		
Interest expense		
Pretax earnings		
Tax expense (30%)		
Net earnings		
Dividends		
Additional retained earnings		

EXERCISE 10-23A or 10-23B (Appendix)

a.

Bond Price	−	Face Value	=	Premium
	−		=	

b.

Carrying Value	x	Effective Rate	=	Interest Expense
	x		=	

c. Compute the Ending Balance in the Premium Account

Face Value	x	Stated Rate	=	Cash Payment
	x		=	
Cash Payment	−	Interest Expense	=	Amortization
	−		=	
Beginning Premium	−	Amortization	=	Ending Discount
	−		=	

Bond Carrying Value as of December 31, 2008

Bond Payable (Face Value)	
Premium on Bonds Payable	
Carrying Value	

d.

Account Titles	Debit	Credit

EXERCISE 10-24A or 10-24B

a.

Date	Cash Payment	Interest Expense	Premium Amortization	Carrying Value
January 1, 2013				
December 31, 2013				
December 31, 2014				
December 31, 2015				
December 31, 2016				
December 31, 2017				
Totals				

b.

c.

d.

EXERCISE 10-25A or 10-25B

PROBLEM 10-26A or 10-26B

a.

		Amortization Schedule			
	$	, __-Yr. Term Note, __% Interest Rate			
Year	Prin. Bal. on Jan 1	Cash Pay. Dec. 31	Applied to Interest	Applied to Principal	Prin. Bal. End of Period

PROBLEM 10-26A or 10-26B (cont.)

b. T-accounts are not required, but are helpful in working the problem.

Cash	Notes Payable	Retained Earnings

Land		Lease (Rent) Revenue

Interest Expense

Mixon Company
Financial Statements

Income Statements	2013	2014	2015
Lease Revenue			
Interest Expense			
Net Income			

Balance Sheets			
Assets			
Total Assets			
Liabilities			
Stockholders' Equity			
Retained Earnings			
Total Liab. and Stockholders' Equity			

Statements of Cash Flows			
Cash Flows From Operating Act.:			
Net Cash Flow from Operating Act.			
Cash Flow From Investing Act.:			
Outflow to Purchase _____			
Cash Flow From Financing Act.:			
Inflow from _____			
Outflow for_____			
Net Cash Flow from Financing Act.			
Net Change in Cash			
Plus: Beginning Cash Balance			
Ending Cash Balance			

PROBLEM 10-26B b. (cont.)

Spain Company Financial Statements				
Income Statements	2013	2014	2015	2016
Rent Revenue				
Interest Expense				
Net Income				
Balance Sheets				
Assets				
Total Assets				
Liabilities				
Notes Payable				
Equity				
Retained Earnings				
Total Liabilities and Equity				
Statements of Cash Flows				
Cash Flows From Oper. Act.:				
Net Cash Flow fm. Op. Act.:				
Cash Flows From Inv. Act.:				
Outflow				
Cash Flows From Fin. Act.:				
Inflow				
Outflow				
Net Cash Flow from Fin. Act.				
Net Change in Cash				
Plus: Beginning Cash Balance				
Ending Cash Balance				

PROBLEM 10-26A or 10-26B (cont.)

c.

PROBLEM 10-27A or 10-27B

Computation of Interest Expense

Month	Amount Borrowed (Repaid)	End of Month Balance	x	Interest Rate per Month	=	Interest Expense
January						
February						
March						
April						
May						
June						
July						
August						
September						
October						
November						
December						
Total						

a.

Income Statement		
For the Year Ended December 31, 2013		
Service Revenue		
Expenses		
Interest Expense		
Net Income		

PROBLEM 10-27A or 10-27B a. (cont.)

Financial Statements

Balance Sheet
As of December 31, 2013

Statement of Cash Flows
For the Year Ended December 31, 2013

PROBLEM 10-27A or 10-27B (cont.)

PROBLEM 10-28A or 10-28B

a.

			Effect of Transactions on Financial Statements								
No.	Assets	=	Liab.	+	S. Equity	Rev. Gain	–	Exp./ Loss	=	Net Inc.	Cash Flows
1		=		+			–		=		
2.		=		+			–		=		
3.		=		+			–		=		

b.

Date	Account Titles	Debit	Credit
1.			
2.			
3.			

PROBLEM 10-29A or 10-29B

Event No.	Type of Event	Assets	=	Liabilities	+	Common Stock	+	Retained Earnings	Net Income	Cash Flow
1.			=		+		+			
2.			=		+		+			
3.			=		+		+			
4.			=		+		+			
5a.			=		+		+			
5b.										
6.	Closing									
7.	Closing		=		+		+			
8.			=		+		+			
9a.			=		+		+			
9b.										
10.	Closing		=		+		+			
11.	Closing		=		+		+			
12.			=		+		+			
13.			=		+		+			

PROBLEM 10-30A or 10-30B

a.

b.

	General Journal		
Date	Account Titles	Debit	Credit

PROBLEM 10-30A or 10-30B b. (cont.)

	General Journal		
Date	Account Titles	Debit	Credit

c.

	2013	2014
Liabilities		

PROBLEM 10-30A or 10-309B (cont.)

d.		2013	2014
	Interest Expense Reported on Income Statement		
e.		2013	2014
	Interest Paid in Cash to Bondholders		

PROBLEM 10-31A or 10-31B

Computations and list of transactions:

1.

2.

3.

4.

5.

6.

7.

PROBLEM 10-31A or 10-31B

T-Accounts Are Not Required

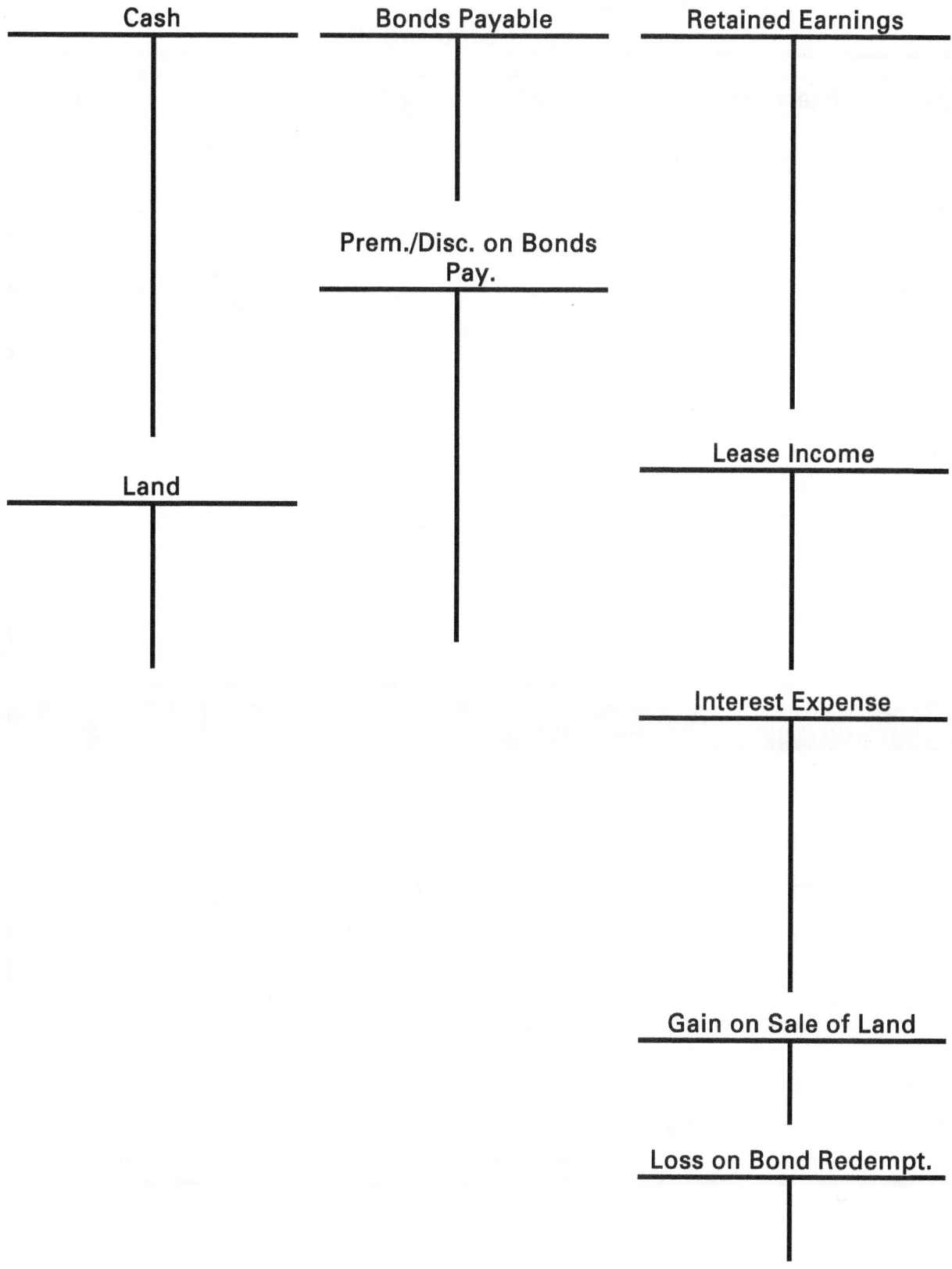

Cash

Bonds Payable

Retained Earnings

Prem./Disc. on Bonds Pay.

Land

Lease Income

Interest Expense

Gain on Sale of Land

Loss on Bond Redempt.

Financial Statements

Income Statements	2013	2014	2015	2016

Statement of Changes in Stockholders' Equity

	Balance Sheet As of December 31			
	2013	2014	2015	2016

	2013	2014	2015	2016
Statements of Cash Flows				
For the Period Ended December 31				

PROBLEM 10-32A

						Effect of Transactions on Financial Statements				
No.	Assets	=	Liab.	+	S. Equity	Rev./ Gain	−	Exp./ Loss	=	Net Inc.	Cash Flows
a.		=		+			−		=		
b.		=		+			−		=		
c.		=		+			−		=		
d.		=		+			−		=		
e.		=		+			−		=		
f.		=		+			−		=		
g.		=		+			−		=		
h.		=		+			−		=		
i.		=		+			−		=		

PROBLEM 10-32B

a.

Effect of Transactions on Financial Statements									
No.	Assets	=	Liab.	+	S. Equity	Rev.	–	Exp.	=	Net Inc.	Cash Flows
1.											
2.											
3.											

b.

Effect of Transactions on Financial Statements									
No.	Assets	=	Liab.	+	Equity	Rev.	–	Exp.	=	Net Inc.	Cash Flows
1.											
2a.											
2b.											
3.											

c.

Effect of Transactions on Financial Statements									
No.	Assets	=	Liab.	+	Equity	Rev.		Exp.	=	Net Inc.	Cash Flows
1.											
2a.											
2b.											
3.											

PROBLEM 10-33A or 10-33B

a.

Date	Account Title	Debit	Credit

b. Calculation of Interest Expense and Premium/Discount Amortization:

Date	Bond Pay.	Unamortz. Premium/ Discount	Bond Carrying Value	Interest Exp. (CV x __%)	Interest Paid (BP x__%)	Premium/ Discount Amortized (Exp - Paid)

Date	Account Title	Debit	Credit

PROBLEM 10-33A or 10-33B

c.

Date	Account Title	Debit	Credit

d.

e.

PROBLEM 10-34A or 10-34B

a. First, compute EBIT for each company:

	Company	Company
Net Income		
Interest Expense		
Tax Expense		
EBIT		

Debt-to-assets ratio:

Company	Total Liabilities	÷	Total Asset	=	Debt-to-assets ratio

Current ratio:

Company	Current Assets	÷	Current Liabilities	=	Current ratio

Times interest earned:

Company	EBIT	÷	Interest Expense	=	Times interest earned

PROBLEM 10-34A or 10-34B (cont.)

b.
Return-on-equity:

Company	Net Income	÷	Stockholders' Equity	=	Return-on-Equity

Return-on-assets:

Company	EBIT	÷	Total Assets	Return-on-assets ratio

ATC 10-1

a.

b.

c.

ATC 10-2

a.

(1)(a) Compute cash proceeds:
Car, Inc.:
Kim, Inc.:
Jay, Inc.:

(1)(b)

    Interest Paid:
    Car, Inc.:
    Kim, Inc.:
    Jay, Inc.:

(1)(c)Interest Expense: Interest paid +/– amortized discount/premium

    Amortization of premium or discount:
    Car, Inc.:
    Kim, Inc.:
    Jay, Inc.:

    Interest Expense:
    Car, Inc.:
    Kim, Inc.:
    Jay, Inc.:

(2)

December 31, 2013			
	Car	Kim	Jay
Liabilities			
Bonds Payable			
Less: Discount on Bonds Payable			
Plus: Premium on Bonds Payable			
Carrying Value of Bonds Payable			

ATC 10-2 (cont.)

c.

d.

e.

ATC 10-4

a. Sonic Corporation, dollar amounts in thousands.

	2010	2009
Net Income		
Interest Expense		
Tax Expense		
EBIT		

b. Times interest earned: (EBIT ÷ Interest Expense)
   2010
   2009

c. Current ratio   (Current Assets ÷ Current Liabilities)
   2010
   2009

   Debt-to-assets ratio: (Total Liabilities ÷ Total Assets)
   2010
   2009

ATC 10-5

a. The EBIT for each company is:

	Jos. A. Banks	Men's Wearhouse
Net Income		
Interest Expense		
Tax Expense		
EBIT		

b. Times interest earned: (EBIT ÷ Interest Expense)
   Jos. A. Banks:
   Men's Warehouse:

c. Current ratio: (Current Assets ÷ Current Liabilities)
   Jos. A. Banks
   Men's Wearhouse

   Debt-to-assets ratio: (Total Liabilities ÷ Total Assets)
   Jos. A. Banks
   Men's Wearhouse

d.
   Return-on-assets: (EBIT ÷ Total Assets)
   Jos. A. Banks
   Men's Wearhouse

   Return-on-equity: (Net Income ÷ Stockholders' Equity)
   Jos. A. Banks
   Men's Wearhouse

ATC 10-6

a.

	Mack Company Selected Financial Statements for 2013		
		Type of Financing	
		Debt	Equity
Income Statement			
Rental Revenue			
Interest Expense			
Net Income Before Tax			
Income Tax Expense (30%)			
Net Income After Tax			
Statement of Cash Flows			
Cash Flows From Operating Activities			
Inflow from Revenue			
Outflow for Interest Expense			
Outflow for Tax Expense			
Net Cash Flow from Operating Activities			
Cash Flows from Investing Activities			
Cash Flows From Financing Activities			
Issue of Bonds			
Issue of Stock			
Payment of Dividends			
Net Cash Flow from Financing Activities			
Net Change in Cash			
Add, Beginning Cash Balance			
Ending Cash Balance			

ATC 10-6 (cont.)

ATC 10-7

a. Forecast Statements

Financial Statements	Forecast 1	Forecast 2	Forecast 3
Income Statements			
Revenue			
Operating Expenses			
Income Before Interest and Taxes			
Interest Expense			
Income Tax Expense (30%)			
Net Income			
Statements of Changes in Stockholders' Equity			
Beginning Retained Earnings			
Plus: Net Income			
Less: Dividend to Watson			
Ending Retained Earnings			
Balance Sheets			
Assets (see Note 1 below)			
Liabilities			
Stockholders' Equity			
Common Stock			
Retained Earnings			
Total Liab. And Stockholders' Equity			

Note 1: The asset balance for the current period must be computed.

ATC 10-7 (cont.)

b.

c.

d.

ATC 10-8

COMPREHENSIVE PROBLEM – CHAPTER 10

a.

	Pacilio Security Services, Inc. General Journal, 2020		
Event	Account title	Debit	Credit
1.			
2.			
3.			
4.			
5.			
6.			
7.			
8a.			
8b.			

Compute Cost of Goods Sold:

COMPREHENSIVE PROBLEM – CHAPTER 10 a. (cont.)

Event	Account Titles	Debit	Credit
9.			
10.			
11.			
12.			
13.			
14.			
15.			
16.			
17.			

Pacilio Security Services, Inc.
General Journal, 2020

Event	Account Titles	Debit	Credit
Pacilio Security Services, Inc. **General Journal, 2020**			
18.			
19.			
20.			
21.			
22.			
23.			
24.			
25.			

Compute rent expense:

Event	Account Titles	Debit	Credit
Pacilio Security Services, Inc.			
General Journal, 2020			
26.			
27.			
28.			
29.			
30.			

Compute uncollectible accounts expense:

Compute depreciation expense:

Compute payroll tax expense:

b.

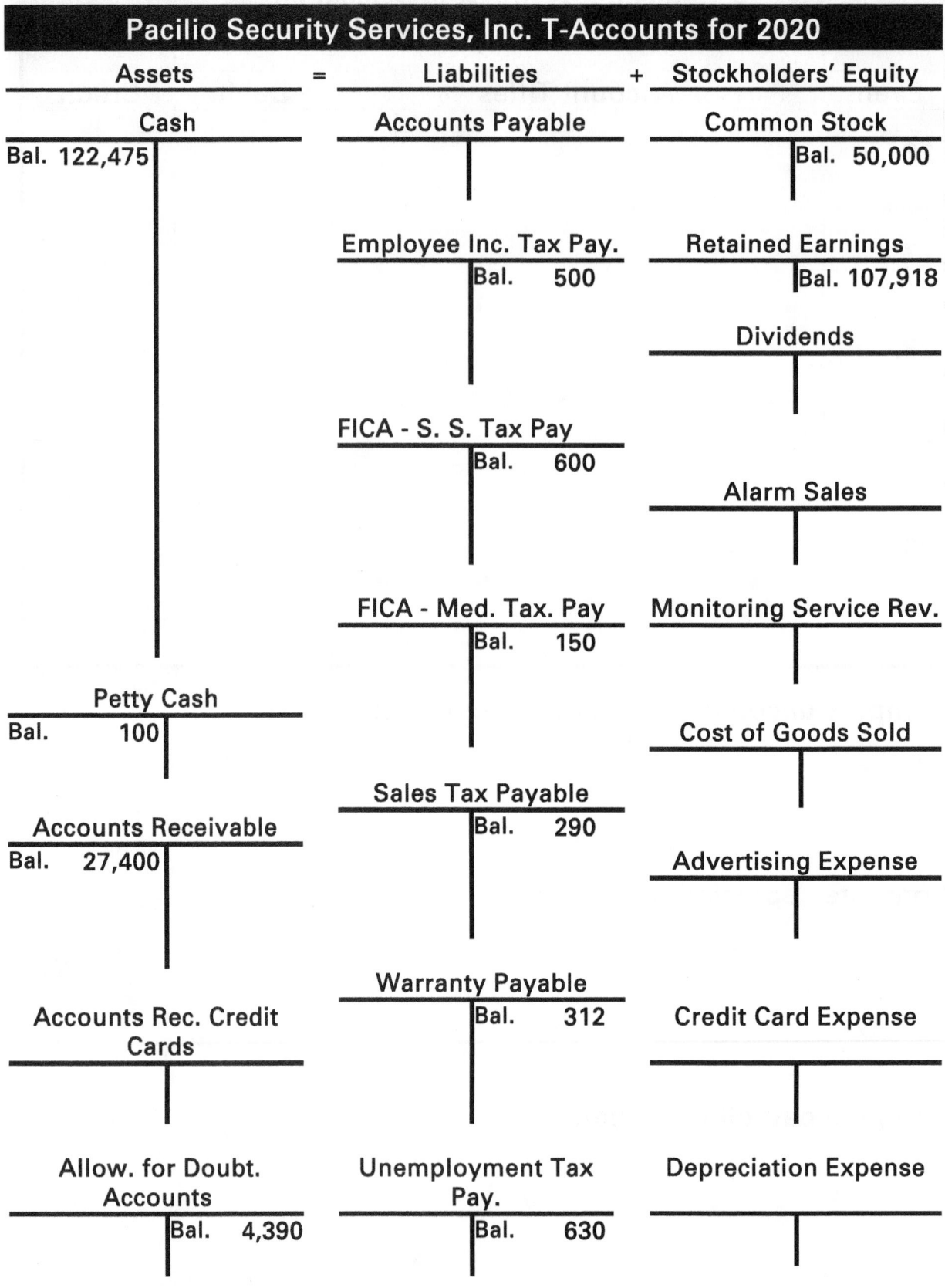

Pacilio Security Services, Inc. T-Accounts for 2020

Assets	=	Liabilities	+	Stockholders' Equity

Cash
Bal. 122,475

Accounts Payable

Common Stock
Bal. 50,000

Employee Inc. Tax Pay.
Bal. 500

Retained Earnings
Bal. 107,918

Dividends

FICA - S. S. Tax Pay
Bal. 600

Alarm Sales

FICA - Med. Tax. Pay
Bal. 150

Monitoring Service Rev.

Petty Cash
Bal. 100

Cost of Goods Sold

Sales Tax Payable
Bal. 290

Accounts Receivable
Bal. 27,400

Advertising Expense

Warranty Payable
Bal. 312

Accounts Rec. Credit Cards

Credit Card Expense

Allow. for Doubt. Accounts
Bal. 4,390

Unemployment Tax Pay.
Bal. 630

Depreciation Expense

Pacilio Security Services, Inc. T-Accounts for 2020

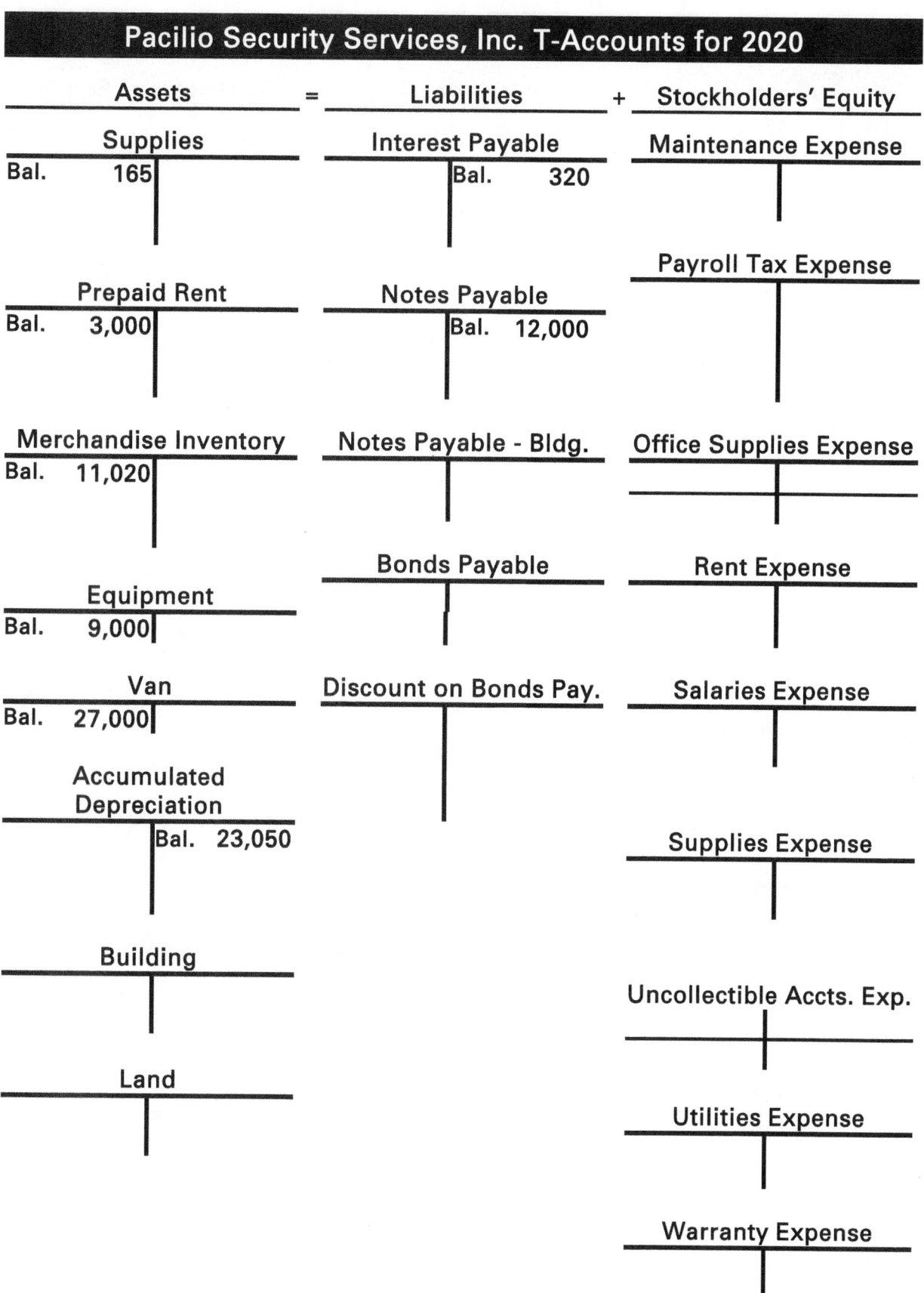

Assets	=	Liabilities	+	Stockholders' Equity

Supplies
Bal. 165

Interest Payable
Bal. 320

Maintenance Expense

Prepaid Rent
Bal. 3,000

Notes Payable
Bal. 12,000

Payroll Tax Expense

Merchandise Inventory
Bal. 11,020

Notes Payable - Bldg.

Office Supplies Expense

Equipment
Bal. 9,000

Bonds Payable

Rent Expense

Van
Bal. 27,000

Discount on Bonds Pay.

Salaries Expense

Accumulated Depreciation
Bal. 23,050

Supplies Expense

Building

Uncollectible Accts. Exp.

Land

Utilities Expense

Warranty Expense

Pacilio Security Services, Inc. T-Accounts for 2020

Assets	=	Liabilities	+	Stockholders' Equity
				Interest Expense

c.

Pacilio Security Services, Inc. Trial Balance December 31, 2020		
Cash		
Petty Cash		
Accounts Receivable		
Allowance for Doubtful Accounts		
Supplies		
Merchandise Inventory		
Equipment		
Van		
Building		
Accumulated Depreciation		
Land		
Sales Tax Payable		
Employee Income Tax Payable		
FICA – Social Security Tax Payable		
FICA – Medicare Tax Payable		
Warranty Payable		
Unemployment Tax Payable		
Notes Payable		
Bonds Payable		
Discount on Bonds		
Common Stock		
Retained Earnings		
Dividends		
Alarms Sales		
Monitoring Service Revenue		
Cost of Goods Sold		
Advertising Expense		
Credit Card Expense		
Depreciation Expense		
Maintenance Expense		
Payroll Tax Expense		
Office Supplies Expense		
Rent Expense		
Salaries Expense		
Supplies Expense		
Uncollectible Accounts Expense		
Utilities Expense		
Warranty Expense		
Interest Expense		
Totals		

d.

Pacilio Security Services, Inc.		
Income Statement		
For the Year Ended December 31, 2020		

Pacilio Security Services, Inc. Statement of Changes in Stockholders' Equity For the Year Ended December 31, 2020		
Beginning Common Stock		
Plus: Common Stock Issued		
Ending Common Stock		
Beginning Retained Earnings		
Plus: Net Income		
Less: Dividends		
Ending Retained Earnings		
Total Stockholders' Equity		

Pacilio Security Services, Inc. Balance Sheet As of December 31, 2020		

COMPREHENSIVE PROBLEM – CHAPTER 10 d. (cont.)

Pacilio Security Services, Inc. Statement of Cash Flows For the Year Ended December 31, 2020			

e.

Date	Account Titles	Debit	Credit
	Closing Entries		

Pacilio Security Services T-Accounts for 2020
T-Accounts with Closing Entries

Assets	=	Liabilities	+	Stockholders' Equity

Cash

Bal.

Employee Inc. Tax Pay

Bal.

Common Stock

Bal.

Petty Cash

Bal.

FICA – SS Tax Pay

Bal.

Retained Earnings

Bal.

Accounts Receivable

Bal.

FICA – Med. Tax Pay.

Bal.

Allow. for Doubt. Accts.

Bal.

Sales Tax Payable

Bal.

Dividends

Bal.

Supplies

Bal.

Unempl Tax Payable

Bal.

Alarm Sales Revenue

Bal.

Merchandise Inventory

Bal.

Warranty Payable

Bal.

Monit. Service Revenue

Bal.

Equipment

Bal.

Notes Payable

Bal.

Cost of Goods Sold

Bal.

Van

Bal.

Bonds Payable

Bal.

Advertising Expense

Bal.

Building

Bal.

Disc. on Bonds Pay.

Bal.

Credit Card Expense

Bal.

Accumulated Depr.

Bal.

Depreciation Expense

Bal.

Pacilio Security Services T-Accounts for 2020
T-Accounts with Closing Entries

Assets	=	Liabilities	+	Stockholders' Equity

Land

Bal.

Maintenance Expense

Bal.

Office Supplies Expense

Bal.

Payroll Tax Expense

Bal.

Rent Expense

Bal.

Salaries Expense

Bal.

Supplies Expense

Bal.

Uncoll. Accts. Expense

Bal.

Utilities Expense

Bal.

Warranty Expense

Bal.

Interest Expense

Bal.

Pacilio Security Systems Sales and Service Post-Closing Trial Balance December 31, 2020		
Account Titles	Debit	Credit

EXERCISE 11-1A or 11-1B

Transactions

Cash Acquired from Owner	
Revenues	
Expenses	
Withdrawals	

Financial Statements
For the Year Ended December 31, 2013

Income Statement

Revenues		
Expenses		
Net Income		

Capital Statement

Beginning Capital Balance		
Plus: Capital Acquired from Owner		
Plus: Net Income		
Less: Withdrawal by Owner		
Ending Capital Balance		

Financial Statements
For the Year Ended December 31, 2013

Balance Sheet

Assets		
Total Assets		
Liabilities		
Equity		
_____, Capital		
Total Liabilities and Equity		

Statement of Cash Flows

Cash Flows From Operating Activities:		
Net Cash Flow from Operating Activities		
Cash Flows From Investing Activities		
Cash Flows From Financing Activities:		
Net Cash Flow from Financing Activities		
Net Change in Cash		
Plus: Beginning Cash Balance		
Ending Cash Balance		

EXERCISE 11-2A or 11-2B

Transactions:

Cash Contributions		%
Partner_____		
Partner_____		
Total		
Revenues		
Expenses		
_____Withdrawal		
_____Withdrawal		

Financial Statements
For the Year Ended December 31, 2013

Income Statement

Revenues		
Expenses		
Net Income		

Capital Statement

Beginning Capital Balance		
Plus: Capital Acquired from Owners		
Plus: Net Income		
Less: Withdrawal by Owners		
Ending Capital Balance		

EXERCISE 11-2A or 11-2B (cont.)

Analysis of capital is not required, but may be helpful in working this exercise.

Analysis of Capital Accounts:			
			Total
Beginning Capital Balance			
Investments			
Net Income			
_____%			
_____%			
Withdrawals			
Ending Capital Balances			

Financial Statements
For the Year Ended December 31, 2013

Balance Sheet

Assets		
Total Assets		
Liabilities		
Equity		
, Capital		
, Capital		
Total Equity		
Total Liabilities and Equity		

Statement of Cash Flows

Cash Flows From Operating Activities:		
Net Cash Flow from Operating Activities		
Cash Flows From Investing Activities		
Cash Flows From Financing Activities:		
Net Cash Flow from Financing Activities		
Net Change in Cash		
Plus: Beginning Cash Balance		
Ending Cash Balance		

EXERCISE 11-3A or 11-3B

Transactions:

Issued _____shares of ___ par stock @ ___	
Revenues	
Expenses	
Dividends Paid	

Financial Statements For the Year Ended December 31, 2013		
Income Statement		
Revenues		
Expenses		
Net Income		
Statement of Changes in Stockholders' Equity		
Beginning Common Stock		
Ending Common Stock		
Beginning Retained Earnings		
Ending Retained Earnings		
Total Stockholders' Equity		

EXERCISE 11-3A or 11-3B (cont.)

	Financial Statements For the Year Ended December 31, 2013			
Balance Sheet				
Assets				
Total Assets				
Liabilities				
Stockholders' Equity				
Common Stock,				
Total Paid-In Capital				
Retained Earnings				
Total Liabilities and Stockholders' Equity				
Statement of Cash Flows				
Cash Flows From Operating Activities:				
Net Cash Flow from Operating Activities				
Cash Flows From Investing Activities				
Cash Flows From Financing Activities:				
Net Cash Flow from Financing Activities				
Net Change in Cash				
Plus: Beginning Cash Balance				
Ending Cash Balance				

EXERCISE 11-4A or 11-4B

a.

	Balance Sheet						Income Statement			Stmt. of
Event	Assets	=	Liab	+	Stkholders' Equity		Rev.	– Exp.	= Net Inc.	Cash Flow
	Cash	=		+	C. Stk.	+ PIC Exc.				

b.

Common Stock:	
_____ shs. x $___ =	
_____ shs. x $___ =	
Total	

c.

Paid-In Capital in Excess of Par	
Total	

d.

Total Paid-In Capital	
Total	

e.

....

f.

General Journal			
Date	Account Titles	Debit	Credit

EXERCISE 11-5A or 11-5B

a.

	General Journal		
Event	Account Titles	Debit	Credit
1.			
2.			
3.			

b.

Stockholders' Equity:	

EXERCISE 11-6A or 11-6B

a.

Event	Assets	=	Stockholders' Equity			Rev	–	Exp.	=	Net Inc.	Stmt. of Cash Flow
	Cash	=	Pref. Stock	+ No-Par C. Stock	+ PIC in Excess						
1.											
2.											

b.

General Journal			
Event	Account Titles	Debit	Credit
1.			
2.			

EXERCISE 11-7A or 11-7B

a.

b.

Event	Balance Sheet						Income Statement			Stmt. of Cash Flows
	Assets	=	Stockholders' Equity			Rev.	–	Exp.	= Net Inc.	
	Cash	+	=	C. Stk.	+	PIC Exc.				
1.										
2.										

c.

General Journal

Date	Account Titles	Debit	Credit
1.			
2.			

EXERCISE 11-8A or 11-8B

a.

	General Journal		
Date	Account Titles	Debit	Credit
1.			
2.			

b.

Treasury Stock

EXERCISE 11-9A or 11-9B

a. & b.

Common Stock	Issued	Outstanding
Beginning Number of Shares		
Issued This Period		
Repurchased as Treasury Stock		
Resold Treasury Stock		
Ending Number of Shares		

c.

General Journal

Date	Account Titles	Debit	Credit
1.			
2.			
3.			

Cash

Common Stock

PIC in Exc. of Par, CS

Treasury Stock

PIC in Exc. of Cost, TS

11-13

d.

Stockholders' Equity		

EXERCISE 11-10A or 11-10B

a.

Date	Balance Sheet								Income Statement					Stmt. of
	Assets	=	Liab.	+	C. Stk.	+	Ret. Ear.		Rev	−	Exp.	=	Net Inc.	Cash Flows

b.

General Journal

Date	Account Titles	Debit	Credit

EXERCISE 11-11A or 11-11B

Computation of Preferred Dividends:							
Par	x	Dividend %	=	Dividend Per Share	x	Number of shares outstanding	=	Total Preferred Dividends for Year

a. Dividend arrearage as of January 1, 2014

b.

	Amount	Dist. to Shareholders	
		Preferred	Common
Total Dividend Declared			
2013 Arrearage			
2014 Preferred Dividends			
Total Preferred Dividends			
Available for Common Shs.			
Distributed to Common			
Total Distribution			

EXERCISE 11-12A or 11-12B

a.

Computation of Dividends to Be Paid:		
Preferred Stock		
Common Stock		
Total Dividend		

b.

Date	Account Titles	Debit	Credit

EXERCISE 11-13A or 11-13B

a. Distribution of Dividend:

	Total	Distributed to Shareholders	
		Preferred	Common
Total Dividend Declared			
Preferred Arrearage*			
Current Preferred Dividend			
Total Preferred Dividends			
Available for Common			
Distributed to Common			
Total			

b.

General Journal for 2013

Date	Account Titles	Debit	Credit

EXERCISE 11-14A or 11-14B

a.

b.

Balance Sheet						Income Statement			Stmt. of
Assets	= Liab	+	Stockholders' Equity			Rev.	− Exp.	= Net Inc.	Cash Flows
			C. Stock	+ PIC. Ex.	+ Ret. Ear.				

c.

General Journal		
Account Title	Debit	Credit

EXERCISE 11-15A or 11-15B

a.

b.

c.

EXERCISE 11-16A or 11-16B

EXERCISE 11-17A or 11-17B

Computation of Price Earnings Ratio:

1. **Compute Earnings per Share:**
   Net Income ÷ Number of Common Shares Outstanding

2. **Compute Price Earnings Ratio:**
   Selling Price per Share ÷ Earnings per Share

a. Company:

Earnings per Share (EPS):				
Net Income	÷	Common Shs. Outst.	=	EPS
	÷		=	
Price/Earnings Ratio:				
Selling Price/Share	÷	Earnings per Share	=	P/E Ratio
	÷		=	

Company:

Earnings Per Share (EPS):				
Net Income	÷	Common Shs. Outst.	=	EPS
	÷		=	
Price/Earnings Ratio:				
Selling Price/Share	÷	Earnings per Share	=	P/E Ratio
	÷		=	

b.

EXERCISE 11-18A or 11-18B

PROBLEM 11-19A or 11-19B

Transactions

Cash Acquired from Owner	
Revenues	
Expenses	
Withdrawals	

a. Sole Proprietorship

Financial Statements For the Year Ended December 31, 2013		
Income Statement		
Revenues		
Expenses		
Net Income		
Capital Statement		
Beginning Capital Balance		
Plus: Capital Acquired from Owner		
Plus: Net Income		
Less: Withdrawal by Owner		
Ending Capital Balance		

Financial Statements		
Balance Sheet **As of December 31, 2013**		
Statement of Cash Flows **For the Year Ended December 31, 2013**		
Cash Flows From Operating Activities:		
Cash Flows From Investing Activities		
Cash Flows From Financing Activities:		
Net Change in Cash		
Plus: Beginning Cash Balance		
Ending Cash Balance		

PROBLEM 11-19A or 11-19B (cont.)

b. Partnership

Financial Statements For the Year Ended December 31, 2013		
Income Statement		
Revenues		
Expenses		
Net Income		
Capital Statement		
Beginning Capital Balance		
Plus: Capital Acquired from Owners		
Plus: Net Income		
Less: Withdrawals by Owners		
Ending Capital Balance		

Analysis of capital accounts is not required.

Analysis of Capital Accounts:			Total
Beginning Capital Balance	$ -0-	$ -0-	$ -0-
Investments			
Net Income*			
Withdrawals			
Ending Capital Balances			

	Financial Statements		
	Balance Sheet		
	As of December 31, 2013		
	Statement of Cash Flows		
	For the Year Ended December 31, 2013		

PROBLEM 11-19A or 11-19B (cont.)

c. Corporation

Financial Statements
For the Year Ended December 31, 2013

Income Statement		
Revenues		
Expenses		
Net Income		

Statement of Changes in Stockholders' Equity		
Beginning Common Stock		
Plus: Issuance of Common Stock		
Ending Common Stock		
Beginning Retained Earnings		
Plus: Net Income		
Less: Dividend Distributions		
Ending Retained Earnings		
Total Stockholders' Equity		

PROBLEM 11-19A or 11-19B c. (cont.)

Financial Statements		
Balance Sheet **As of December 31, 2013**		
Statement of Cash Flows **For the Year Ended December 31, 2013**		

PROBLEM 11-20A

PROBLEM 11-20B

PROBLEM 11-20B (cont.)

The schedule below illustrates the after-tax cash flows under each form:

	Partnership	Corporation
Income before taxes		
Tax at entity level		
Net Income distributed to owners		
Less: Individual income tax (35%)		
After-tax cash flow		
After-tax cash flow available to each investor		
Effective tax rate		

PROBLEM 11-21A

a.

Date	Account Titles	Debit	Credit
1.			
2.			
3.			
4.			

b.

Stockholders' Equity		
Common Stock,		

PROBLEM 11-21B

a.

b.

c.

d.

	Outstanding Shares
Prior to Event 2	200,000

PROBLEM 11-22A or 11-22B

a.

Statements Model For 2013

| Event | Balance Sheet | | | | | | Income Statement | | | Statement of |
| | Assets | = | Stockholders' Equity | | | | Rev. | − Exp. | = Net Inc. | Cash Flows |
			P. Stock +	C. Stock +	PIC CS +	Ret. Ear.				
1.										
2.										
3.										
4.										
5.										
6a.										
6b.										
Totals										

b.

	General Journal		
Date	Account Titles	Debit	Credit

PROBLEM 11-22A or 11-22B b. (cont.)

T-Accounts for 2013

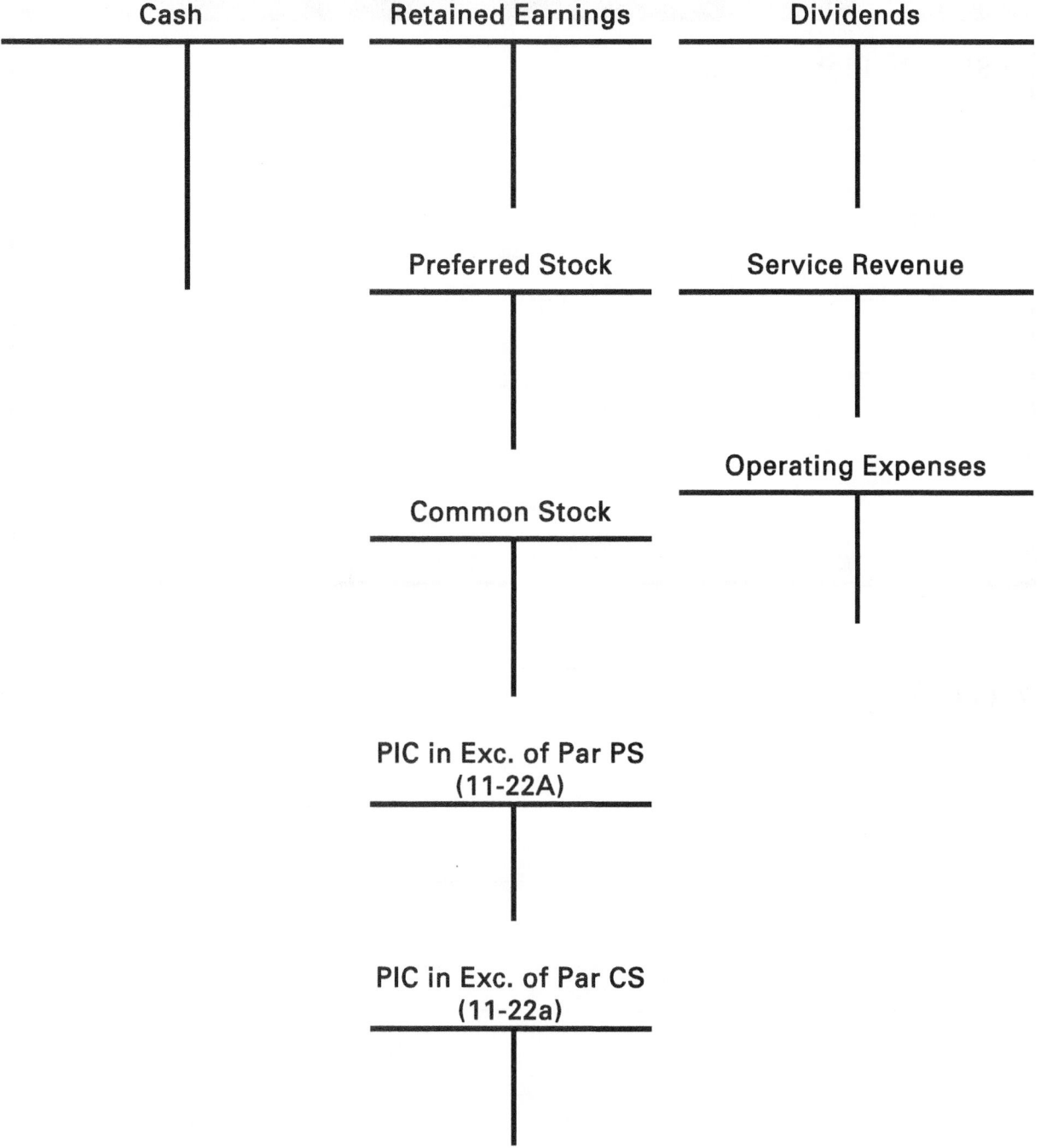

c.

Stockholders' Equity		

d. (11-22B)

PROBLEM 11-23A or 11-23B

a.

	General Journal		
Date	Account Titles	Debit	Credit

PROBLEM 11-23A or 11-23B a. (cont.)

	General Journal		
Date	Account Titles	Debit	Credit

PROBLEM 11-23A or 11-23B a. (cont.)

T-Accounts for 20__

Cash	Dividends Payable	Retained Earnings

Preferred Stock

Common Stock

PIC in Exc. of Par Pref. Stk.

PIC in Exc. of Par Com. Stk.

Dividends

Service Revenue

Operating Expenses

PROBLEM 11-23A or 11-23B a. (cont.)

T-Accounts for 20___

Cash

Dividends Payable

Retained Earnings

Preferred Stock

Common Stock

PIC in Exc. of Par Pref. Stk.

PIC in Exc. of Par Com. Stk.

Dividends

Service Revenue

Operating Expenses

b.
2013

Stockholders' Equity		
Total Stockholders' Equity		

b.

Western Corporation Balance Sheet As of December 31, 2013		
Assets		
Liabilities		
Stockholders' Equity		
Preferred Stock,		
Common Stock,		
Total Liabilities and Stockholders' Equity		

Western Corporation Balance Sheet As of December 31, 2014		
Assets		
Liabilities		
Total Liabilities		
Stockholders' Equity		
Preferred Stock,		
Common Stock,		
Total Liabilities and Stockholders' Equity		

c.

Schedule of Number of Shares of Common Stock		
Dates	Shares Issued	Shares Outstanding

c.

Malard Corporation Balance Sheet As of December 31, 2014				

PROBLEM 11-24A or 11-24B

a.

General Journal			
Date	Account Titles	Debit	Credit

PROBLEM 11-24A or 11-24B a. (cont.)

	General Journal		
Date	Account Titles	Debit	Credit

PROBLEM 11-24A or 11-24B a. (cont.)

T-Accounts for 2013

Cash	Dividends Payable	Retained Earnings

Appropriated Retained Earn.

Preferred Stock

Common Stock

PIC in Exc. of Cost TS.

PIC in Exc. Of SV Pref. Stk.

Treasury Stock

Dividends

PROBLEM 11-24A or 11-24B a. (cont.)

Service Revenue
```
        |
_____|_____
        |
        |
```

Operating Expenses
```
        |
_____|_____
        |
        |
```

PROBLEM 11-24A

b.

Stockholders' Equity			

PROBLEM 11-24B (cont.)

b.

	Balance Sheet As of December 31, 2013		
Assets			
Total Assets			
Liabilities			
Stockholders' Equity			

PROBLEM 11-25A or 11-25B

a.

b.

c.

d.

e.

f. (11-25A)

PROBLEM 11-26A or 11-26B

Statements Model

Event	Balance Sheet						Income Statement						Statement of Cash Flows
	Assets	=	Liab.	+	S. Equity		Rev.	−	Exp.	=	Net Inc.		
1.													
2.													
3.													
4.													
5.													
6.													
7.													
8.													
9.													
10.													

ATC 11-1

a.

b.

c.

d.

ATC 11-2

b. Wendy's stated value per share:

   Coca Cola par value per share:

   Harley Davidson par value per share:

c. Wendy's average issue price of common stock:
   2010:
   2009:

   Coca Cola's average issue price of common stock:
   2010:
   2009:

   Harley Davidson's average issue price of common stock:
   2010   :
   2009:

d. Wendy's stock outstanding at end of year:
   2010:
   2009:

   Coca Cola's stock outstanding at end of year:
   2010:
   2009:

   Harley Davidson's stock outstanding at end of year:
   2010:
   2009:

ATC 11-2 (cont.)

d. Wendy's average cost per share of treasury stock:
2010:

Coca Cola's average cost per share of treasury stock:
2010:

Harley Davidson's average cost per share of treasury stock:
2010:

f.

g.

h.

Wendy's (in thousands)		
Stockholders' Equity	2010	2009
Common Stock		
Capital in Excess of Stated Value		
Total Paid-in Capital		
Retained Earnings		
Other Adjustments		
Treasury Stock		
Total Stockholders' Equity		

Cola Cola (in millions)		
Stockholders' Equity	**2010**	**2009**
Common Stock		
Capital Surplus		
Total Paid-in Capital		
Retained Earnings		
Other Adjustments		
Treasury Stock		
Total Stockholders' Equity		

Harley Davidson (in thousands)		
Stockholders' Equity	**2010**	**2009**
Common Stock		
Additional Paid-in Capital		
Total Paid-in Capital		
Retained Earnings		
Other Adjustments		
Treasury Stock		
Unearned Comp./Other Adj.		
Total Stockholders' Equity		

ATC 11-3

a.

Company	Net Earnings		Shares Outstanding		EPS
Briston-Myers		÷		=	
eBay		÷		=	
Ford		÷		=	
Garmin		÷		=	
Starbucks		÷		=	
Brinks		÷		=	

b. and c.

Rank	Company	Market-Price per Share		EPS		P/E Ratio
1			÷		=	
2			÷		=	
3			÷		=	
4			÷		=	
5			÷		=	
6.			÷		=	

d.

Company	Stockholders' Equity		Shares Outstanding		Book-Value per Share
Briston-Myers		÷		=	
eBay		÷		=	
Ford		÷		=	
Garmin		÷		=	
Starbucks		÷		=	
Brinks		÷		=	

ATC 11-3 (cont.)

e.

Rank	Company	Market-Price per Share		Book-Value per Share		Ratio of Market Value to Book Value
1			÷		=	
2			÷		=	
3			÷		=	
4			÷		=	
5			÷		=	
6			÷		=	

ATC 11-4

ATC 11-5

Computation of Price Earnings Ratio:

1. Compute Price Earnings Ratio:
   Selling Price per Share ÷ Earnings per Share

a.
Google:

Price/Earnings Ratio:					
Selling Price/Share	÷	Earnings per Share	=	P/E Ratio
	÷		=	

IBM:

Price/Earnings Ratio:					
Selling Price/Share	÷	Earnings per Share	=	P/E Ratio
	÷		=	

b.

c.

ATC 11-6

ATC 11-7 (cont.)

a.

Event	Account title	Debit	Credit
Pacilio Security Services, Inc. **General Journal, 2021**			
1.			
2.			
3a.			
3b.			
4.			
5.			
6.			
7a.			
7b.			

Cost of Goods Sold:

	Pacilio Security Services, Inc. General Journal, 2021		
Event	Account Titles	Debit	Credit
8.			
9.			
10.			
11.			
12.			
13.			
14.			

Dividend on Preferred Stock:

COMPREHENSIVE PROBLEM – CHAPTER 11 a. (cont.)

	Pacilio Security Services, Inc. General Journal, 2021		
Event			
15.			
16.			
17.			
18.			
19.			
20.			
21.			
22.			
23.			

Event	Account Titles	Debit	Credit
Pacilio Security Services, Inc. **General Journal, 2021**			
24.			
25.			
26.			
27.			
28.			

Compute Uncollectible Account Expense:

Depreciation expense:

b.

Pacilio Security Services, Inc. T-Accounts for 2021

Assets	=	Liabilities	+	Stockholders' Equity

Assets

Cash

Bal.   113,718

Petty Cash

Bal.   100

Accounts Receivable

Bal.   39,390

Accounts Rec. Credit Cards

Allow. for Doubt. Accounts

Bal.   4,662

= Liabilities

Accounts Payable

Dividends Payable

Employee Inc. Tax Pay.

Bal.   1,000

FICA - S. S. Tax Pay

Bal.   840

FICA - Med. Tax. Pay

Bal.   210

Sales Tax Payable

Bal.   390

Warranty Payable

Bal.   918

+ Stockholders' Equity

Retained Earnings

Bal.   124,816

Preferred Stock

Common Stock

Bal   50,000

PIC in Excess CS

PIC in Excess PS

Dividends

Alarm Sales

Monitoring Service Rev.

Cost of Goods Sold

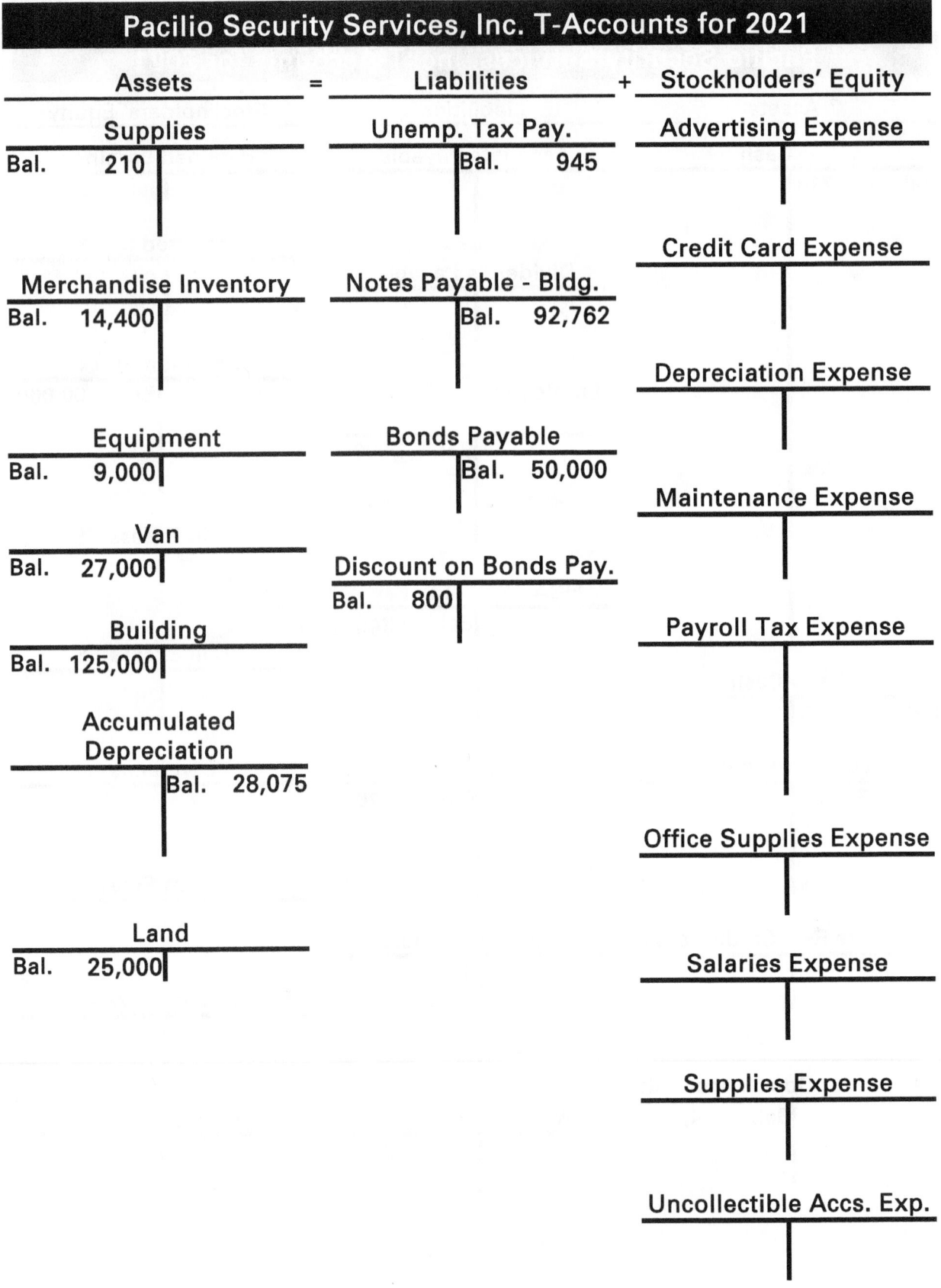

Pacilio Security Services, Inc. T-Accounts for 2021

Assets	=	Liabilities	+	Stockholders' Equity

Supplies
Bal. 210

Unemp. Tax Pay.
Bal. 945

Advertising Expense

Credit Card Expense

Merchandise Inventory
Bal. 14,400

Notes Payable - Bldg.
Bal. 92,762

Depreciation Expense

Equipment
Bal. 9,000

Bonds Payable
Bal. 50,000

Maintenance Expense

Van
Bal. 27,000

Discount on Bonds Pay.
Bal. 800

Building
Bal. 125,000

Payroll Tax Expense

Accumulated Depreciation
Bal. 28,075

Office Supplies Expense

Land
Bal. 25,000

Salaries Expense

Supplies Expense

Uncollectible Accs. Exp.

Pacilio Security Services, Inc. T-Accounts for 2021

Assets	=	Liabilities	+	Stockholders' Equity

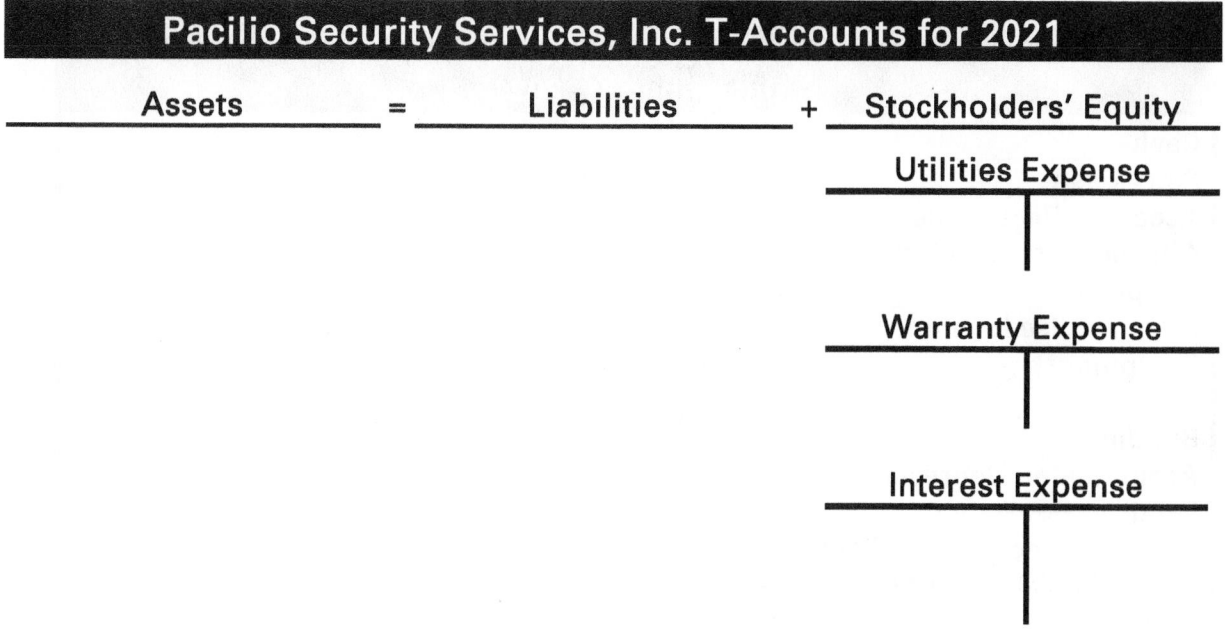

Utilities Expense

Warranty Expense

Interest Expense

c.

Pacilio Security Services, Inc. Trial Balance December 31, 2021		
Cash		
Petty Cash		
Accounts Receivable		
Allowance for Doubtful Accounts		
Supplies		
Merchandise Inventory		
Equipment		
Van		
Building		
Accumulated Depreciation		
Land		
Employee Income Tax Payable		
FICA – Social Security Tax Payable		
FICA – Medicare Tax Payable		
Sales Tax Payable		
Warranty Payable		
Unemployment Tax Payable		
Notes Payable		
Bonds Payable		
Discount on Bonds		
Preferred Stock		
Common Stock		
PIC in Excess of Stated Value Preferred Stock		
PIC in Excess of Par Common Stock		
Retained Earnings		
Dividends		
Alarms Sales		
Monitoring Service Revenue		
Cost of Goods Sold		
Advertising Expense		
Credit Card Expense		
Depreciation Expense		
Maintenance Expense		
Payroll Tax Expense		
Office Supplies Expense		
Salaries Expense		
Supplies Expense		
Uncollectible Accounts Expense		
Utilities Expense		
Warranty Expense		
Interest Expense		
Totals		

d.

Pacilio Security Services, Inc. Income Statement For the Year Ended December 31, 2021		

Pacilio Security Services, Inc. Balance Sheet As of December 31, 2021		
Assets		
Total Assets		
Liabilities		
Total Liabilities		
Stockholders' Equity		
Total Paid-in Capital		
Retained Earnings		
Total Stockholders' Equity		
Total Liabilities and Stockholders' Equity		

Pacilio Security Services, Inc.		
Statement of Cash Flows		
For the Year Ended December 31, 2021		

e.

Date	Account Titles	Debit	Credit
	Closing Entries		

Pacilio Security Services T-Accounts for 2021
T-Accounts with Closing Entries

| Assets | = | Liabilities | + | Stockholders' Equity |

Cash
Bal.

Employee Inc. Tax Pay
Bal.

Retained Earnings
Bal.

Petty Cash
Bal.

FICA – SS Tax Pay.
Bal.

Preferred Stock
Bal.

Accounts Receivable
Bal.

FICA – Med. Tax Pay.
Bal.

Common Stock
Bal.

Allow. for Doubt. Accts.
Bal.

Sales Tax Payable
Bal.

PIC in Excess of SV PS
Bal.

Supplies
Bal.

Unempl Tax Payable
Bal.

PIC in Excess of Par CS
Bal.

Merchandise Inventory
Bal.

Warranty Payable
Bal.

Dividends
Bal.

Equipment
Bal.

Notes Payable
Bal.

Alarm Sales Revenue
Bal.

Van
Bal.

Bonds Payable
Bal.

Monit. Service Revenue
Bal.

Building
Bal.

Disc. on Bonds Pay.
Bal.

Cost of Goods Sold
Bal.

Accumulated Depr.
Bal.

Pacilio Security Services T-Accounts for 2021
T-Accounts with Closing Entries

Assets	=	Liabilities	+	Stockholders' Equity

Land

Bal. |

Advertising Expense

Bal. |

Credit Card Expense

Bal. |

Depreciation Expense

Bal. |

Maintenance Expense

Bal. |

Office Supplies Expense

Bal. |

Payroll Tax Expense

Bal. |

Salaries Expense

Bal. |

Supplies Expense

Bal. |

Uncoll. Accts. Expense

Bal. |

Utilities Expense

Bal. |

Pacilio Security Services T-Accounts for 2021
T-Accounts with Closing Entries

Assets	=	Liabilities	+	Stockholders' Equity

Warranty Expense

Bal.

Interest Expense

Bal.

Pacilio Security Services, Inc. Post-Closing Trial Balance December 31, 2021		
Account Titles	Debit	Credit
Totals		

EXERCISE 12-1A or 12B

1.	
2.	
3.	
4.	
5.	
6.	
7.	
8.	
9.	
10.	
11.	

EXERCISE 12-2A or 12-2B

a.

Cash Flows From Operating Activities	

b.

c.

EXERCISE 12-3A or 12-3B

Net Cash Flow From Operating Activities	
Net Income	
Add:	
Deduct:	
Net Cash Inflow from Operating Activities	

EXERCISE 12-4A or 12-4B

Reconciliation of Unearned Revenue		
Beginning balance		
Increase due to collecting cash in advance		
Decrease due to recognizing revenue		
Ending balance		

Reconciliation of Prepaid Rent		
Beginning balance		
Increase due to the cash purchase of rent		
Decrease due to recognizing rent expense		
Ending balance		

Cash Flow from Operating Activities	
Inflow from customers	
Outflow for rent expense	
Total	

EXERCISE 12-5A or 12-5B

a.

Reconciliation of Accounts Receivable		
Beginning balance		
Increase due to revenue recognized on account		
Decrease due to cash collections from customers		
Ending balance		

Reconciliation of Interest Receivable	
Beginning balance	
Increase due to interest revenue recognized on acct.	
Decrease due to cash collections of interest rec.	
Ending balance	

Cash Inflow from Operating Activities	
Collections from customers	
Collections of interest receivable	
Total	

b.

Reconciliation of Other Operating Expenses Payable		
Beginning balance		
Increase		
Decrease		
Ending balance		

Reconciliation of Salaries Payable		
Beginning balance		
Increase		
Decrease		
Ending balance		

Cash Outflow from Operating Activities	
Cash paid for other operating expenses	
Cash paid for salaries	
Total	

EXERCISE 12-6A or 12-6B

a.

Operating Activities – Direct Method	
Cash receipts from customers	
Cash payments for expenses	
Net cash inflow from operating activities	

b.

Operating Activities – Indirect Method	
Net income	
Add: Increase in accounts payable	
Subtract: Increase in accounts receivable	
Net cash inflow from operating activities	

EXERCISE 12-7A or 12-7B

a. Direct Method

Reconciliation of Accounts Receivable		
Beginning balance		
Increase due to revenue recognized on account		
Decrease due to cash collections from customers		
Ending balance		

Reconciliation of Prepaid Rent		
Beginning balance		
Increase due to the cash purchase of rent		
Decrease due to recognizing rent expense		
Ending balance		

Reconciliation of Utilities Payable		
Beginning balance		
Increase due to recognizing utilities exp. on acct.		
Decrease due to cash settlements of utilities pay.		
Ending balance		

Reconciliation of Other Operating Expenses Payable		
Beginning balance		
Increase due to recognizing other oper. exp. on acct.		
Decrease due to cash settlements of other operating expenses payable		
Ending balance		

EXERCISE 12-7A or 12-7B a. (cont.)

Cash Flow From Operating Activities	
Inflow from customers	
Outflow for rent	
Outflow for utilities	
Outflow for operating expense	
Net cash inflow from operating activities	

b. Indirect Method:

Begin by determining the amount of change in the balances in the noncash current asset and current liability accounts.

	2014	2013	Change
Accounts receivable			
Prepaid rent			
Utilities payable			
Other operating expenses payable			

Cash Flow From Operating Activities	
Net income:	
Add:	
Deduct:	
Net cash inflow from operating activities	

EXERCISE 12-8A or 12-8B

a.

Reconciliation of Land Account		
Beginning balance		
Increase due to purchasing land		
Decrease due to selling land		
Ending balance		

b.

Cash Flow from Investing Activities	
Inflow from the sale of land	
Outflow for the purchase of land	
Net cash inflow from investing activities	

EXERCISE 12-9A or 12-9B

a.

Reconciliation of Delivery/Office Equipment Account		
Beginning balance		
Increase		
Decrease		
Ending balance		

b.

EXERCISE 12-10A or 12-10B

a.

Reconciliation of Investment securities Account		
Beginning balance		
Increase		
Decrease		
Ending balance		

b. and c.

Reconciliation of Machinery Account		
Beginning balance		
Increase due to purchasing machinery		
Decrease due to selling machinery		
Ending balance		

EXERCISE 12-10A or 12-10B (cont.)

d.

Reconciliation of Land Account		
Beginning balance		
Increase due to purchasing land		
Ending balance		

e.

Statement of Cash Flows		
For the Year Ended December 31, 2014		
Cash flows from investing activities:		
Net cash outflow from investing activities		

a.

Reconciliation of Bonds Payable Account		
Beginning balance		
Increase due to issuing bonds payable		
Decrease due to repayment of bonds payable		
Ending balance		

b.

Cash Flows from Financing Activities	
Inflow from the issue of bonds payable	
Outflow for repayment of bonds payable	
Net cash outflow from financing activities	

EXERCISE 12-12A or 12-12B

a.

Reconciliation of Common Stock Account		
Beginning balance		
Increase due to issuing common stock		
Ending balance		

b.

Cash Flows from Financing Activities	
Inflow from the issue of common stock	
Outflow for the purchase of treasury stock	
Net cash inflow from financing activities	

EXERCISE 12-13A or 12-13B

a.

Reconciliation of Bonds Payable Account		
Beginning balance		
Increase/Decrease		
Ending balance		

b.

Reconciliation of Common Stock Account		
Beginning balance		
Increase due to issue of common stock		
Ending balance		

c.

Statement of Cash Flows For the Year Ended December 31, 2014		
Cash flows from financing activities:		
Net cash flow from financing activities		

PROBLEM 12-14A or 12-14B

a. Direct Method

Reconciliation of Accounts Receivable		
Beginning balance		
Ending balance		

Reconciliation of Inventory		
Beginning balance		
Ending balance		

Reconciliation of Accounts Payable		
Beginning balance		
Ending balance		

PROBLEM 12-14A or 12-14B a. (cont.)

Reconciliation of Prepaid Insurance

Beginning balance		
Ending balance		

Reconciliation of Salaries Payable

Beginning balance		
Ending balance		

Reconciliation of Unearned Revenue

Beginning balance		
Ending balance		

Statement of Cash Flows
For the Year Ended December 31, 2014

Cash flows from operating activities:	
Net cash inflow from operating activities	

b. Begin by determining the amount of change in the balances in the current asset and liability accounts.

Account Title	2014	2013	Change
Accounts receivable			
Merchandise inventory			
Prepaid insurance			
Accounts payable			
Salaries payable			
Unearned revenue			

Statement of Cash Flows **For the Year Ended December 31, 2014**	
Cash Flows from Operating Activities:	
Net income	
Add:	
Deduct:	
Add/Deduct Noncash Expenses	
Net Cash Inflow from operating activities	

a.

Reconciliation of Investment securities Account		
Beginning balance		
Increase due to purchase of investment sec.		
Decrease due to sale of investment sec.		
Ending balance		

b.

c.

Reconciliation of Equipment Account		
Beginning balance		
Increase due to purchasing equipment		
Decrease due to selling equipment		
Ending balance		

d.

PROBLEM 12-15A or 12-15B (cont.)

e.

Reconciliation of Buildings Account		
Beginning balance		
Increase due to purchasing buildings		
Decrease due to building demolition		
Ending balance		

f.

Reconciliation of Land Account		
Beginning balance		
Increase due to purchasing land		
Decrease due to selling land		
Ending balance		

g.

Statement of Cash Flows For the Year Ended December 31, 2014		
Cash Flows from Investing Activities:		
Net cash outflow from investing activities		

PROBLEM 12-16A or 12-16B

a.

Reconciliation of Bonds Payable Account		
Beginning balance		
Increase due to issuing bonds payable		
Decrease due to cash settlements of bonds pay.		
Ending balance		

b.

Reconciliation of Common Stock Account		
Beginning balance		
Increase due to issuing common stock		
Ending balance		

c.

Reconciliation of Treasury Stock Account		
Beginning balance		
Increase due to purchasing treasury stock		
Ending balance		

PROBLEM 12-16A or 12-16B (cont.)

d.

Reconciliation of Retained Earnings Account		
Beginning balance		
Increase due to recognizing net income		
Decrease due to paying dividends		
Ending balance		

e.

Cash Flows from Financing Activities		
Net cash outflow from financing activities		

PROBLEM 12-17A or 12-17B

No.	Type of Activity	Add or Subtract
a.		
b.		
c.		
d.		
e.		
f.		
g.		
h.		
i.		
j.		
k.		
l.		
m.		
n.		

PROBLEM 12-18A or 12-18B

Statement of Cash Flows		
For the Year Ended December 31, 2014		
Cash flows from operating activities:		
Net income		
Less: Increases in current assets and		
Decreases in current liabilities:		
Plus: Noncash charges		
Plus: Loss on disposal of land		
Less: Gain on sale of equipment		
Net cash flow from operating activities		
Cash flows from investing activities:		
Net cash flow from investing activities		
Cash flows from financing activities:		
Net cash flow from financing activities		
Net increase in cash		
Plus: Beginning cash balance		
Ending cash balance		
Schedule of noncash invest. and financ. act.:		
Issued common stock for land		

Statement of Cash Flows
For the Year Ended December 31, 2014

Cash Flows From Operating Activities:		
Net Income		
Plus: Decreases in Current Assets and Increases in Current Liabilities:		
Less: Increases in Current Assets and Decreases in current Liabilities		
Plus: Noncash Charges		
Net Cash Flow from Operating Activities		
Cash Flows from Investing Activities:		
Net Cash Flow from Investing Activities		
Cash Flows from Financing Activities: Inflow from Stock Issue		
Net Cash Flow from Financing Activities		
Net Increase in Cash		
Plus: Beginning Cash Balance		
Ending Cash Balance		

PROBLEM 12-20A or 12-20B

a.

(1)

Reconciliation of Accounts Receivable Account		
Beginning balance		
Increase		
Decrease		
Ending balance		

(2)

Reconciliation of Salaries Payable Account		
Beginning balance		
Increase.		
Decrease		
Ending balance		

(3)

Reconciliation of Other Operating Expenses Payable		
Beginning balance		
Increase due.		
Decrease		
Ending balance		

PROBLEM 12-20A or 12-20B a. (cont.)

(4)

(5)

Reconciliation of Equipment Account		
Beginning balance		
Increase		
Decrease		
Ending balance		

(6)

Reconciliation of Notes Payable Account		
Beginning balance		
Increase		
Decrease		
Ending balance		

(7)

Reconciliation of Interest Payable Account		
Beginning balance		
Increase		
Decrease		
Ending balance		

(8)

Reconciliation of Inventory		
Beginning balance		
Increase		
Decrease		
Ending balance		

Reconciliation of Accounts Payable		
Beginning balance		
Increase		
Decrease		
Ending balance		

(9)

Reconciliation of Notes Receivable		
Beginning balance		
Increase		
Decrease		
Ending balance		

(10)

Reconciliation of Common Stock Account		
Beginning balance		
Increase		
Ending balance		

(11)

Reconciliation of Land Account		
Beginning Balance		
Increase		
Decrease		
Ending Balance		

PROBLEM 12-20A or 12-20B a. (cont.)

(12)

Reconciliation of Taxes Payable Account		
Beginning balance		
Increase		
Decrease		
Ending balance		

(13)

Reconciliation of Investments Account		
Beginning balance		
Increase		
Decrease		
Ending balance		

b.

Statement of Cash Flows For the Year Ended December 31, 20__		
Cash Flows From Operating Activities:		
Cash Receipts from:		
Sales		
Total Cash Inflows		
Cash Payments for:		
Total Cash Outflows		
Net Cash Flow from Operating Activities		
Cash Flows from Investing Activities:		
Net Cash Flow from Investing Activities		
Cash Flows from Financing Activities:		
Net Cash Flow from Financing Activities		
Net Increase/Decrease in Cash		
Plus: Beginning Cash Balance		
Ending Cash Balance		

PROBLEM 12-21A or 12-21B

(1) Reconciliation of Accounts Receivable

Beginning balance		
Increase		
Decrease		
Ending balance		

(2) Reconciliation of Inventory

Beginning balance		
Ending balance		

(2) Continued: Reconciliation of Accounts Payable

Beginning balance		
Ending balance		

(3) Reconciliation of Salaries Payable

Beginning balance		
Ending balance		

(4) Reconciliation of Utilities Payable

Beginning balance		
Ending balance		

(5) Reconciliation of Interest Payable

Beginning balance		
Ending balance		

(6)

(7) Reconciliation of Notes Receivable

Beginning balance		
Ending balance		

(8) Reconciliation of Land Account

Beginning Balance		
Ending balance		

(9) Reconciliation of Notes Payable Account

Beginning balance		
Ending balance		

(10) Reconciliation of Common Stock Account

Beginning balance		
Ending balance		

(11)

	Statement of Cash Flows For the Year Ended December 31, 2014		
Cash Flows from Operating Activities:			
Cash Receipts from Customers			
Cash Payments for:			
Total Cash Outflows			
Net Cash Flow from Operating Activities			
Cash Flows from Investing Activities:			
Net Cash Flow from Investing Activities			
Cash Flows from Financing Activities:			
Net Cash Flow from Financing Activities			
Net Increase in Cash			
Plus: Beginning Cash Balance			
Ending Cash Balance			

ATC 12-1

a.

b.

c.

ATC 12-2

ATC 12-3

	Transactions		Effect on Cash Flow
	Cash Received from Sales:		
		=	
	Merchandise Paid:		
		=	
	Other Operating Expenses Paid	=	
	Interest Paid	=	
1.	Sold Land	=	
2.	Sold Equipment	=	
3.	Purchased Equipment	=	
4.	Sold Marketable Securities	=	
5.	Purchased Marketable Securities	=	
6.	Paid Loan	=	
7.	Paid off Bond Issue	=	
	Issue New Bonds	=	
8.	Sold Treasury Stock	=	
9.	Issued Common Stock	=	
10.	Issued Preferred Stock	=	
11.	Paid Dividends	=	
	Change in Cash	=	

ATC 12-3 (cont.)

a.

	Statement of Cash Flows For the Year Ended December 31, 20__		
Cash Flows From Operating Activities:			
Net Cash Flow from Operating Activities			
Cash Flows From Investing Activities:			
Net Cash Flow from Investing Activities			
Cash Flows From Financing Activities:			
Net Cash Flow from Financing Activities			
Net Increase in Cash			
Plus: Beginning Cash Balance			
Ending Cash Balance			

ATC 12-3 (cont.)

a.

b.

c.

ATC 12-4

ATC 12-5

ATC 12-6

a.

Statement of Cash Flows		
For the Year Ended December 31, 2013		
Cash Flows From Operating Activities:		
Net Cash Flow from Operating Activities		
Cash Flows From Investing Activities:		
Net Cash Flow from Investing Activities		
Cash Flows From Financing Activities:		
Net Cash Flow from Financing Activities		
Net Increase in Cash		
Plus: Beginning Cash Balance		
Ending Cash Balance		

ATC 12-6 (cont.)

b.

c.

ATC 12-7

EXERCISE 13-1A

EXERCISE 13-2A

EXERCISE 13-3A

_____

_____

_____

_____

_____

EXERCISE 13-4A

a. Working capital before the transaction:

   Working capital after the transaction:

b. Current ratio before the transaction:

   Current ratio after the transaction:

EXERCISE 13-5A

a. Working capital before the transaction:

   Working capital after the transaction:

b. Current ratio before the transaction:

   Current ratio after the transaction:

EXERCISE 13-6A

a.

Pettit Corporation Income Statements			
	2011	2010	% Change
Sales	$1,300,000	$1,000,000	
Cost of Goods Sold	800,000	600,000	
Gross Margin on Sales	500,000	400,000	
Operating Expenses	300,000	200,000	
Income before Taxes	200,000	200,000	
Income Taxes	61,000	53,000	
Net Income	$ 139,000	$ 147,000	

b.

_____

_____

_____

_____

_____

EXERCISE 13-7A

	2011	% of Sales	2012	% of Sales
Conroe Company				
Vertical Analysis of Income Statements				
Sales	$1,000,000		$1,080,000	
Cost of Goods Sold	550,000		600,000	
Gross Margin on Sales	450,000		480,000	
Operating Expenses	130,000		150,000	
Income before Taxes	320,000		330,000	
Income Taxes	80,000		82,000	
Net Income	$ 240,000		$ 248,000	

EXERCISE 13-8A

All computations are rounded to the nearest single decimal point.

Working capital   =

Current ratio =

Liabilities to total assets =

Stockholders' equity ratio:

Debt to equity ratio

EXERCISE 13-9A

a. Earnings per Share:

b. Book value per share of common stock:

c. Price-earnings ratio:

d. Dividend yield:

EXERCISE 13-10A

1.	7.
2.	8.
3.	9.
4.	10.
5.	11.
6.	12.

EXERCISE 13-11A

a. Horizontal Analysis

Thompson Company Horizontal Analysis of Income Statements			
	2012	2011	% Change over 2002
Sales	$ 200,000	$180,000	
Cost of Goods Sold	142,000	120,000	
Selling Expenses	20,000	18,000	
Administrative Expenses	12,000	14,000	
Interest Expense	3,000	5,000	
Total Expenses	177,000	157,000	
Income before Taxes	23,000	23,000	
Income Taxes Expense	5,000	3,000	
Net Income	$ 18,000	$ 20,000	

b. Vertical Analysis

Thompson Company Vertical Analysis of Income Statements				
	2012	% of Sales	2011	% of Sales
Sales	$200,000		$180,000	
Cost of Goods Sold	142,000		120,000	
Selling Expenses	20,000		18,000	
Administrative Expenses	12,000		14,000	
Interest Expense	3,000		5,000	
Total Expenses	177,000		157,000	
Income before Taxes	23,000		23,000	
Income Taxes Expense	5,000		3,000	
Net Income	$ 18,000		$ 20,000	

EXERCISE 13-12A

a. Current ratio:

b. Earnings per share:

c. Quick (acid-test) ratio:

d. Return on investment:

e. Return on equity:

f. Debt/equity ratio:

EXERCISE 13-13A

	Current Ratio	Working Capital	Stockholders' Equity	Book Value	Retained Earnings
a.					
b.					
c.					
d.					
e.					
f.					
g.					
h.					
i.					

EXERCISE 13-14A

a. Net credit sales ÷ Average net receivables =

b. Cost of goods sold ÷ Average inventories =

c. Net income ÷ Total sales =

EXERCISE 13-15A

a.

b.

c.

PROBLEM 13-16A

Lowther Company Income Statements		
	2012	2011
Sales	$600,000	$500,000
Cost of Goods Sold		
Gross Margin		
Selling and Administrative Expenses		
Interest Expense		
Total Expenses		
Income before Taxes		
Income Taxes		
Net Income		

PROBLEM 13-17A

a. Number of times bond interest earned

b. 2010: Earnings per share =

   2011:   Earnings per share =

c. Price-earning ratio

   2010:

   2011:

d. 2010:

   2011:

e. Net margin:

   2010:

   2011:

PROBLEM 13-18A

	Current Ratio	Working Capital
a.		
b.		
c.		
d.		
e.		
f.		
g.		
h.		
i.		
j.		
k.		
l.		

PROBLEM 13-19A

a. Earnings per share:

Price-earnings ratio:

Return on equity:

b.

_____

_____

_____

_____

PROBLEM 13-20A

A.

B.

C.

D.

E.

F.

G.

H.

I.

J.

PROBLEM 13-21A

		2012	2011
a.	Net margin	———— =	———— =
b.	Return on investment	———— =	———— =
c.	Return on equity	———— =	———— =
d.	Earnings per share	———— =	———— =
e.	Price earnings ratio	———— =	———— =
f.	Book value per share of common stock	———— =	———— =
g.	Times interest earned	———— =	———— =
h.	Working capital	———— =	———— =
i.	Current ratio	———— =	———— =
j.	Quick ratio	———— =	———— =
k.	Accounts receivable turnover	———— =	———— =
l.	Inventory turnover	———— =	———— =
m.	Debt to equity ratio	———— =	———— =
n.	Debt to assets ratio	———— =	———— =

PROBLEM 13-22A

Bernard Company Horizontal Analysis of Balance Sheets			
	2012	2011	% Change
Assets			
Cash	$ 16,000	$ 12,000	
Marketable Securities	20,000	6,000	
Accounts Receivable (net)	54,000	46,000	
Inventories	135,000	143,000	
Prepaid Items	25,000	10,000	
Total Current Assets	250,000	217,000	
Investments	27,000	20,000	
Plant (net)	270,000	255,000	
Land	29,000	24,000	
Total Long-Term Assets	326,000	299,000	
Total Assets	$576,000	$516,000	
Liabilities			
Notes Payable	$ 17,000	$ 6,000	
Accounts Payable	113,800	100,000	
Salaries Payable	21,000	15,000	
Total Current Liabilities	151,800	121,000	
Bonds Payable	100,000	100,000	
Other	32,000	27,000	
Total Noncurrent Liabilities	132,000	127,000	
Total Liabilities	283,800	248,000	
Stockholders' Equity			
Preferred Stock	70,000	70,000	
Common Stock	50,000	50,000	
Paid-in Capital in Excess - Preferred	10,000	10,000	
Paid-in Capital in Excess - Common	30,000	30,000	
Retained Earnings	132,200	108,000	
Total Stockholders' Equity	292,200	268,000	
Total Liabilities & Stockholders' Equity	$576,000	$516,000	

Bernard Company Horizontal Analysis of Income Statements			
	2012	2011	% Change
Revenues			
Sales (net)	$230,000	$210,000	
Other	8,000	5,000	
Total Revenues	238,000	215,000	
Expenses			
Cost of Goods Sold	120,000	103,000	
Selling, Gen., and Admin. Expenses	55,000	50,000	
Interest Expense	8,000	7,200	
Income Tax Expense	23,000	22,000	
Total Expenses	206,000	182,200	
Net Income	$ 32,000	$ 32,800	

PROBLEM 13-23A

Because of space limitation, $ signs are omitted in these computations.

	2012	2011
a. Working capital		
b. Current ratio		
c. Quick ratio		
d. Receivables turnover		
e. Average days to collect accounts receivable		
f. Inventory turnover		
g. Number of days to sell inventory		
h. Debt to assets ratio		
i. Debt to equity ratio		
j. Number of times interest was earned		
k. Plant assets to long-term debt		
l. Net margin		
m. Turnover of assets		
n. Return on investment		
o. Return on equity		
p. Earnings per share		
q. Books value per share of common stock		
r. Price earnings ratio		
s. Dividend yield on common stock		

PROBLEM 13-24A

Bernard Company Vertical Analysis of Balance Sheets				
	2012		2011	
Assets	Amount	% of Total	Amount	% of Total
Cash	$ 16,000		$ 12,000	
Marketable Securities	20,000		6,000	
Accounts Receivable (net)	54,000		46,000	
Inventories	135,000		143,000	
Prepaid Items	25,000		10,000	
Total Current Assets	250,000		217,000	
Investments	27,000		20,000	
Plant (net)	270,000		255,000	
Land	29,000		24,000	
Total Long-Term Assets	326,000		299,000	
Total Assets	$576,000		$516,000	
Liabilities				
Notes Payable	$ 17,000		$ 6,000	
Accounts Payable	113,800		100,000	
Salaries Payable	21,000		15,000	
Total Current Liabilities	151,800		121,000	
Bonds Payable	100,000		100,000	
Other	32,000		27,000	
Total Noncurrent Liabilities	132,000		127,000	
Total Liabilities	283,800		248,000	
Stockholders' Equity				
Preferred Stock	70,000		70,000	
Common Stock	50,000		50,000	
Paid-in Capital in Excess - Preferred	10,000		10,000	
Paid-in Capital in Excess - Common	30,000		30,000	
Retained Earnings	132,200		108,000	
Total Stockholders' Equity	292,200		268,000	
Total Equities	$576,000		$516,000	

PROBLEM 13-24A (cont.)

Bernard Company Vertical Analysis of Income Statements				
	2012		2011	
Revenues	Amount	% of Total	Amount	% of Total
Sales (net)	$230,000		$210,000	
Other	8,000		5,000	
Total Revenues	238,000		215,000	
Expenses				
Cost of Goods Sold	120,000		103,000	
Selling, Gen., and Admin. Exp.	55,000		50,000	
Interest Expense	8,000		7,200	
Income Tax Expense	23,000		22,000	
Total Expenses	206,000		182,200	
Net Income	$ 32,000		$ 32,800	

EXERCISE 13-1B

EXERCISE 13-2B

EXERCISE 13-3B

_____

_____

_____

_____

_____

_____

EXERCISE 13-4B

a. Working capital before the securities purchase:

Working capital after the securities purchase:

Current ratio before the securities purchase:

Current ratio after the securities purchase:

EXERCISE 13-5B

a. Working capital before the equipment purchase:

   Working capital after the equipment purchase:

b. Current ratio before the equipment purchase:

   Current ratio after the equipment purchase:

EXERCISE 13-6B

a.

Everett Corporation Income Statements			
	2012	2011	% Change
Sales	$440,000	$400,000	
Cost of Goods Sold	264,000	254,000	
Gross Margin	176,000	146,000	
Operating Expenses	75,000	65,000	
Income before Taxes	101,000	81,000	
Income Taxes	45,000	31,600	
Net Income	$ 56,000	$ 49,400	

b.

_____

_____

_____

_____

EXERCISE 13-7B

Wallace Company Vertical Analysis of Income Statements				
	2011	% of Sales	2012	% of Sales
Sales	$100,000		$128,000	
Cost of Goods Sold	64,000		81,600	
Gross Margin	36,000		46,400	
Operating Expenses	19,000		23,000	
Income before Taxes	17,000		23,400	
Income Taxes	5,400		6,200	
Net Income	$ 11,600		$ 17,200	

EXERCISE 13-8B

Working capital =

Current ratio =

Liabilities to total Assets =

Stockholders' equity ratio =

Debt to equity ratio =

EXERCISE 13-9B

a. Earnings per share:

b. Book value per share of common stock:

c. Price-earnings ratio:

d. Dividend yield:

EXERCISE 13-10B

1.
2.
3.
4.
5.
6.

7.
8.
9.
10.
11.
12.

EXERCISE 13-11B

a. Horizontal Analysis

McAllen Company Horizontal Analysis of Income Statements			
	2012	2011	% Change over 2005
Sales	$480,000	$420,000	
Cost of Goods Sold	246,000	225,000	
Selling Expenses	28,000	24,000	
Administrative Expenses	52,000	49,000	
Interest Expense	8,000	10,000	
Total Expenses	334,000	308,000	
Income before Taxes	146,000	112,000	
Income Taxes Expense	25,000	21,000	
Net Income	$121,000	$ 91,000	

b. Vertical Analysis

McAllen Company Vertical Analysis of Income Statements				
	2012	% of Sales	2011	% of Sales
Sales	$480,000		$420,000	
Cost of Goods Sold	246,000		225,000	
Selling Expenses	28,000		24,000	
Administrative Expenses	52,000		49,000	
Interest Expense	8,000		10,000	
Total Expenses	334,000		308,000	
Income before Taxes	146,000		112,000	
Income Taxes Expense	25,000		21,000	
Net Income	$121,000		$ 91,000	

EXERCISE 13-12B

a. Current ratio:

b. Earnings per share:

c. Quick (acid-test) ratio:

d. Return on investment:

e. Return on equity:

f. Debt/equity ratio:

EXERCISE 13-13B

	Quick Ratio	Working Capital	Stockholders' Equity	Debt/Equity Ratio	Retained Earnings
a.					
b.					
c.					
d.					
e.					
f.					
g.					
h.					
i.					

EXERCISE 13-14B

a. Net credit sales ÷ Average net receivables =

b. Cost of goods sold ÷ Average inventories =

c. Net income ÷ Total sales =

EXERCISE 13-15B

a.

b.

c.

d.

PROBLEM 13-16B

Willrick Corporation Income Statements For the Years Ended December 31,		
	2012	2011
Sales	$750,000	$500,000
Cost of Goods Sold		
Gross Margin		
Selling and Administrative Expenses		
Interest Expense		
Total Expenses		
Income before Taxes		
Income Taxes		
Net Income		

PROBLEM 13-17B

a. Number of times bond interest earned

   2011:

   2010:

b. 2011:   earnings per share =

   2016:   earnings per share =

c. Price-earnings ratio

   2011:

   2010:

d. 2011:

   2010:

e. Net margin:

   2011:

   2010:

PROBLEM 13-18B

	Current Ratio	Working Capital
a.		
b.		
c.		
d.		
e.		
f.		
g.		
h.		
i.		
j.		
k.		
l.		

PROBLEM 13-19B

a. Earnings per share:

Price-earnings ratio:

Return on equity:

b.

_____

_____

_____

_____

PROBLEM 13-20B

A.   F.

B.   G.

C.   H.

D.   I.

E.   J.

PROBLEM 13-21B

a.

b.

c.

d.

e.

f.

g.

h.

i.

j.

k.

l.

m.

n.

o.

p.

q.

r.

s.

PROBLEM 13-22B

a.

b.

c.

d.

e.

f.

g.

h.

i.

j.

PROBLEM 13-23B

Addison Company Horizontal Analysis (In thousands)			
	2012	2011	% Change
Assets			
Cash	$ 3,000	$ 2,000	
Marketable Securities	5,000	4,000	
Accounts Receivable (net)	47,000	44,000	
Inventories	50,000	60,000	
Prepaid Expenses	2,000	1,000	
Total Current Assets	107,000	111,000	
Property, Plant, & Equipment	100,000	105,000	
Investments	1,000	1,000	
Long-Term Receivables	3,000	2,000	
Goodwill and Patents	2,000	4,000	
Other Assets	2,000	3,000	
Total Assets	$215,000	$226,000	
Liabilities			
Notes Payable	$ 3,000	$ 5,000	
Accounts Payable	12,000	16,000	
Accrued Expenses	9,000	11,000	
Income Taxes Payable	1,000	1,000	
Payments Due Within One Year	3,000	2,000	
Total Current Liabilities	28,000	35,000	
Long-Term Debt	50,000	60,000	
Deferred Income Taxes	30,000	27,000	
Other Liabilities	5,000	4,000	
Total Liabilities	113,000	126,000	
Stockholders' Equity			
Common Stock	5,000	5,000	
Preferred Stock	20,000	20,000	
Additional Paid-in Capital - Common	35,000	35,000	
Retained Earnings	42,000	40,000	
Total Stockholders' Equity	102,000	100,000	
Total Liabilities & Stockholders' Equity	$215,000	$226,000	

PROBLEM 13-23B (cont.)

Addison Company Horizontal Analysis (In thousands)			
	2012	2011	% Change
Net Sales	$180,000	$150,000	
Expenses			
Cost of Goods Sold	147,000	120,000	
Selling, Gen., and Admin. Expenses	20,000	18,000	
Other	2,000	2,000	
Total Expenses	169,000	140,000	
Income before Income Taxes	11,000	10,000	
Income Taxes	5,000	4,000	
Net Income	$ 6,000	$ 6,000	

PROBLEM 13-24B

Addison Company Vertical Analysis (In thousands)				
	2012		2011	
	Amount	% of Total	Amount	% of Total
Net Sales	$180,000		$150,000	
Expenses				
Cost of Goods Sold	147,000		120,000	
Selling, Gen., and Admin. Expenses	20,000		18,000	
Other	2,000		2,000	
Total Expenses	169,000		140,000	
Income before Income Taxes	11,000		10,000	
Income Taxes	5,000		4,000	
Net Income	$ 6,000		$ 6,000	

Problem 13-24B (cont.)

	Addison Company Vertical Analysis (In thousands)			
	2012		**2011**	
	Amount	% of Total	Amount	% of Total
Assets				
Cash	$ 3,000		$ 2,000	
Marketable Securities	5,000		4,000	
Accounts Receivable (net)	47,000		44,000	
Inventories	50,000		60,000	
Prepaid Expenses	2,000		1,000	
Total Current Assets	107,000		111,000	
Property, Plant, & Equipment	100,000		105,000	
Investments	1,000		1,000	
Long-Term Receivables	3,000		2,000	
Goodwill and Patents	2,000		4,000	
Other Assets	2,000		3,000	
Total Assets	$215,000		$226,000	
Liabilities				
Notes Payable	$ 3,000		$ 5,000	
Accounts Payable	12,000		16,000	
Accrued Expenses	9,000		11,000	
Income Taxes Payable	1,000		1,000	
Payments Due Within One Year	3,000		2,000	
Total Current Liabilities	28,000		35,000	
Long-Term Debt	50,000		60,000	
Deferred Income Taxes	30,000		27,000	
Other Liabilities	5,000		4,000	
Total Liabilities	113,000		126,000	
Stockholders' Equity				
Common Stock	5,000		5,000	
Preferred Stock	20,000		20,000	
Additional Paid-in Capital - Common	35,000		35,000	
Retained Earnings	42,000		40,000	
Total Stockholders' Equity	102,000		100,000	
Total Liabilities & Stockholders' Equity	$215,000		$226,000	